KINGDOMS

What You Believe –

Creates The World You Live In

By Paul Tubach, Jr.

KINGDOMS

"KINGDOMS" by Paul B. Tubach, Jr. is licensed under a Creative Commons Attribution-NonCommercial-NoDerivatives 4.0 International License

You are free to copy, share and redistribute the material in any medium, format or language as long as the text and content is not altered or misconstrued. Freely it was received... freely it is given. The licensor cannot revoke these freedoms as long as you follow these license terms:

- **Attribution** — You must give appropriate credit, provide a link to the website, and indicate if any changes were made. You may do so in any reasonable manner, but not in any way that suggests the author endorses you or your use. "Attribute this work" as: Paul Tubach, Jr., www.newearthministries.org.
- **NonCommercial** — You may not use the material for commercial purposes, i.e. not for any private, corporate, nonprofit or otherwise financial gain.
- **NoDerivatives** — If you remix, transform or build upon the material, you may not distribute the modified material. The creation or development of any derivatives, secondary workbooks or manuals from this book is reserved solely by the author.
- **No additional restrictions** — You may not apply legal terms or technological measures that legally restrict others from doing anything the license permits.

Paperback ISBN 978-1-949892-40-6
Library of Congress Control Number - pending
Produced in the United States of America
New Earth Ministries

Scriptures taken from the New King James Version.
Copyright © 1982 by Thomas Nelson. Used by permission. All rights reserved.

Cover Design by Lucy Henry Studio

Books and other materials are available online through
www.newearthministries.org.

April 2019

Table of Contents

Introduction	xv
Kingdom of What	1
Three Kingdoms	11
The Kingdom of Self	19
Gateways of Meekness	23
Kingdoms – In The Beginning	27
Why Are You Here	29
Beginning – Yet Again	33
Darkness Exposed	42
Battle Waged On Earth	44
What Is Darkness?	46
Redemption	56
Kingdoms In General	67
Kingdoms In Conflict	73
The Kingdom of God	84
Kingdom of Paradox	97
Parable Take-a-ways	100
PARA – Is A Four Letter Word	103
Kingdom of The Spirit	111
Mind of The Spirit	122
Father Of Us	126
Two Kingdoms – Two Spirits	130
Created As Worshippers	134
God Is Spirit	138
The Father With/In Us	140
The Spirit With/In Us	144
Operate According To Faith – & Glory	147
The Kingdom of Glory	150
Where Does Glory Originate	154
The Father's Dominion	162

Honor The King	165
Our Sojourn to Comprehend – God	169
Kingdom of Christ	182
In Christ	185
Christ In You	187
Kingdom of Mercy	195
An Hour With God	199
Through Christ	200
Kingdom of Grace and Truth	204
Noah Found Grace	205
Moses Found Grace	205
Greater Grace Found You	206
Grace – In Christ	212
Final Salutation on Grace	214
Kingdom of Truth	215
Truth Is Not An Opinion	215
Kingdom of Love	221
Gateways of Love	226
Kingdom of Joy	241
Types of Supernatural Joy	251
Joy and Biblical Suffering	261
Kingdom of Rest	281
Mone and Meno	290
Shekinah Glory	300
Kingdom of Oneness	308
The One Thing	315
The Inner Witness	317
Communion	318
Marriage – The Covenant of	324
Prayer With Thanksgiving	325
Worship With Sacrifice	327
Kingdom Built With Tithe	334
Tithing On Purpose	339

Kingdom of The Heavens 343
Grant Them Dominion 346
Kingdom of Heaven People 347
Heaven-hearted and Heaven-minded 352
Heaven On Earth 354
Angel Army On Earth 361

Kingdom of Heaven Messages 373
Heaven Come Down 379
Closure 380

The Image Bearer Series

The Image Bearer Series is based upon Genesis 1:26-28: "Let us make man in Our image, according to Our likeness... and grant them dominion."

1. Regenesis – A Sojourn To Remember Who We Are
2. Listen – How To Hear God's Voice – better
3. Image – The Revelation Of God Himself
4. Dominion – Our Heavenly Mandate To Occupy Earth
5. Understand – What Jesus Wants You To Know – and Why
6. Commission – Created On Purpose For A Purpose
7. Gateways – Manifesting Heaven In The Midst Of Chaos
8. Here – The Kingdom Of Heaven Is
9. Kingdoms – What You Believe – Creates The World You Live In

"Regenesis" helps us discover man's true identity: we are spiritual beings that are having a human experience, who were created good and upright by God "in His Own image according to His likeness" (Gen. 1:26-27), whereby we've been blessed with many wonderful grace attributes by the Lord to accomplish all that He purposed for man... since the beginning.

"Kingdoms" – is one of two chapters the Lord told me to take out of Regenesis in 2014.

About the books: "Image" explains 'who' the Lord of Heaven and Earth is, "Understand" explains 'why' we are here, "Commission" explains 'what' man is and 'how' we were created by the Lord, "Dominion" explains 'what' we are supposed to be doing, "Gateways" explains 'how' we are to accomplish our earthly mission, and "Here" explains our eternal destination is actually – Earth. "Kingdoms" puts all these books into context to explain why things happen on earth, what our purpose is and how we accomplish the Lord's agenda to manifest heaven on earth.

Many tools were given to mankind by God that enables us to accomplish our mission objective – to have dominion over the kingdom of darkness – and we need to comprehend this truth: earth is our 'Here' – and our 'when' is now! How God created us – and why – is directly related to our sanctification and accomplishing our multifaceted mission for being on earth.

Why are you here – and what's your purpose in life? These books will answer those questions.

Yet for most of us, we've forgotten who we are… and we've forgotten what we're supposed to be doing. The Image Bearer series reminds us what we are supposed to be doing – and more importantly – "why" we are doing it: to bear His image, imitate Jesus in every respect according to His earthly example – and operate as His heavenly ambassadors for earth.

The heavenly pattern for mankind is: imitate Jesus.
The earthly pattern for this world is: become like heaven.

The numeric order in which the Spirit directed these books: 1,2,8,3,5,4,6,7,10,11,9 was not linear in the least. Let the Spirit guide you in the order He wants you to read them; however, learning how to "Hear God's Voice" (#2) is always mission critical to get started on His path for anyone.

Jesus said: "My sheep hear My voice, I know them and they follow Me" (John 10:27). This is the litmus test for goats and sheep: the Lord's sheep must be able to hear His voice.

On October 24, 2015, the Lord told me to put these books on the internet for free. This was unexpected, and then the Lord whispered to me, "Can you make money on My words? Freely you have received… freely give."

Free PDF's are available for all books.

When the Lord tells you what to do, He will also give you His authority, with power and provision, to do all that He commands.

We need to embrace this perspective regarding our life on earth in order to understand and comprehend who we are and what we are supposed to be doing. There is much joy and peace living in this manner, and yet… we all make this choice daily to live according to His purpose for His glory – or to live according to our best laid plans. If I can do it – so can you.

Jesus did it, and therefore – "As He is, so are we in this world" (1 John 4:17). I hope you enjoy the Image Bearer series. Grace and peace be yours in abundance.

It's all about Jesus – and God gets the glory!

Glossary of Terms and Definitions

These are some keys to help navigate and understand the scriptures.

Heaven – God's throne, God's home and the permanent place where God's glory dwells

heaven – the spiritual reality of God's kingdom and Christ's presence upon earth

Glory – the fullness of God's presence; '*doxa*-1391-glory' means: a good opinion (toward God)

Shekinah Glory – the manifest presence of God as you rest in His presence

Christ – the manifest expression of God in Jesus, and regenerate (born anew) men

Jesus – the manifested Living God; Lord of heaven and earth; Lord of Glory; Lord of Hosts

Host – army (a very important term omitted in the NIV and some other versions)

Host of heaven – angels; sons of God and our heavenly brethren (Rev. 19:10)

Host of earth – sons of men, becoming sons of God in the regeneration

Man – the generic term for male and female that conveys mankind, humanity, etc.

Earth – the planet; one of three permanent places within the kingdom of God

Hell – the absence of God; one of three permanent places within the kingdom of God; the pit

World – temporary realm on earth under the dominion and operational control of Satan

Satan – Prince of "this world" (formerly known as Lucifer before he rebelled and fell to earth)

Sin – the operating system of this world in opposition to God's sovereignty; separation from God; things done that cause separation

Spirit – the operating system on earth under the Lord's dominion; the Holy Spirit; God's Spirit
Grace – attributes of God's character that are freely given to man
Light – a metaphor implying God's truth
Darkness – a metaphor implying evil – and sinful lies of "this world"
Wickedness – taking credit for what God has done
Evil – using God's glory and power to accomplish your personal agenda
Paradigm – the operating systems of sin or "by the Spirit" on earth
Paradise – the earthly realm in oneness with God apart from sin
Dwelling – a temporary place to live (*meno*)
Abode – a permanent place to live (of existence; *mone*)
Rest – the permanent state of being where God's presence abides (in your heart and in heaven)
Kingdom of God – all places under the authority of Jesus
Kingdom of heaven – a term used exclusively in the gospel of Matthew to describe the kingdom of God as it pertains to earth under the Lordship of Jesus Christ

- Life – the source from which all creation exists, and is made alive, as coming from God through Christ Jesus, who is "the Life" and the "author and finisher" of faith (John 14:6; Heb. 12:2)
- Living – those persons spiritually alive with life, who no longer operate in the shadow of Death while sojourning in earthen vessels that will eventually perish for lack of life
- Alive – the spiritual state of being in existence from God's perspective, even apart from the body, and abiding eternally in communion with God's Presence and Spirit
- Dead – the spiritual state of being in existence from God's perspective, but temporarily separated from Him; the eventual disposition of the earthen body without life
- Death – the spiritual state of being permanently and eternally separated from God; the temporary holding place of unregenerate dead that wait there until the judgment

Introduction

Perceptions shape perspectives.

Perspectives produce paradigms.

Thoughts and opinions are perspectives – which we use to create the belief system (paradigm of thought) that governs the world we choose to live in.

It is mission critical to comprehend this very short introduction. There are two kingdoms on earth and they are at war with one another: the kingdom of God vs. the kingdom of darkness. God gave the sons of men a commission – with authority and power – to have dominion over the earth (Gen. 1:26) and this is why we were sent into the kingdom of darkness: to come against it, take back what the enemy stole from God, redeem it, deliver it back to God, and rescue other souls taken captive to sin by lies – with the message of truth.

The battle being waged in the minds of men is between good and evil and the result is either life or death. These kingdoms have different operating systems: grace vs. sin. Two princes govern them: the Prince of Peace (Jesus) and the prince of the power of the air (Satan). And two competing spirits – the Spirit of Christ and the spirit of antichrist – influence and guide the minds of men to believe one prince or the other to serve one kingdom or the other.

This is the big picture that explains why things happen the way they happen on earth. For some mysterious reason, though, mankind keeps forgetting his true reason for being here. The earth was created for man – and man was created for the earth – and they belong together. We need to remember the purpose God intended for us and get back to doing what we were sent to accomplish: preach the kingdom of God – and have dominion over the earth!

We were sent to usher in a regime change from darkness to light!

Our reason for being here is the same reason that Jesus came:

> "For this cause I was born, and for this cause I have come into the world, that I should bear witness to the truth" (John 18:37).

But the #1 problem with mankind is: we've forgotten the truth and believed a great many lies.

> Jesus said: "Repent. The kingdom of heaven is at hand."

What these kingdoms are and what mankind must do to achieve victory over darkness is what this book is about. If you've ever wondered what your purpose in life is, then keep reading.

Two-thousand years later… the Lord's message remains the same and the battle wages on, but time is running out. The darkness knows this… and this is why the battle will get more intense as the end draws near. Two world wars were allowed by God as the means to prepare us for the great tribulation. A third global conflict is on the horizon.

> "For nation will rise against nation, and kingdom against kingdom. And there will be earthquakes in various places, and there will be famines and troubles. These are the beginnings of sorrows" (Mark 13:8)

We are standing at the precipice! We are in transition. The church age is over – the kingdom age has begun. One kingdom, one God, one King, and one Lord – Jesus Christ!

> "Therefore wait for Me," says the Lord, "Until the day I rise up for plunder; **My determination is to gather the nations to My assembly of kingdoms**, to pour on them My indignation, all My fierce anger; all the earth shall be devoured with the fire of My

jealousy" (Zeph. 3:8).

What an intriguing message from the Lord. He will gather the nations (Gr. *ethnos*; people groups) to the assembly of kingdoms! Where and when does this occur? This event – the Day of Judgment – happens after the great and final conflict following the millennium. This is the day when the Lord repays everyone according to their work.

- "For the Lord is the God of recompense, He will surely repay" (Jer. 51:56)
- "Repay them, O Lord, according to the work of their hands" (Lam. 3:64)

On the Day of Judgment, everyone will be assembled according to groups, all will be judged, and all will be recompensed – some to the resurrection of life – but others to the resurrection of condemnation.

> "All the nations will be gathered before Him, and He will separate them one from another, as a shepherd divides his sheep from the goats. [33] And He will set the sheep on His right hand, but the goats on the left. [34] Then the King will say to those on His right hand, 'Come, you blessed of My Father, inherit the kingdom prepared for you from the foundation of the world" (Matt. 25:32-34).

Following the judgment and resurrection, the Lord will repay His faithful ones with a kingdom on the New Earth. This message is true, and this is what this book is about: kingdoms!

> "... but you ***go and preach the kingdom of God***" (Luke 9:60).

Jesus said: "Do not fear, little flock, for it is your Father's good pleasure to give you the kingdom" (Luke 12:32).

"And I bestow upon you a kingdom, just as My Father bestowed one upon Me" (Luke 22:29).

Two kingdoms are on earth right now… which kingdom are you faithful to?

Kingdom of What – In The Land of "Why"

Life on earth is complex. There are aspects of life and death that are reliable and predictable, yet the spectrum of various realities and seasons we experience throughout life rarely seems to make sense. This is curious. Poets, philosophers and theologians have been trying to reconcile the meaning of life for 6,000 years... with mixed results.

The second wisest man on earth, King Solomon, sought out this elusive means to understand why things happen on earth: he determined (in a negative sense) – all is vanity. Solomon said everything on earth is fleeting... a chasing after wind. Generations come and go; nations rise and fall; rich people perish in their wealth without finding joy and poor people are defrauded without benefit of justice, yet both die in the end; kingdoms are established and then overthrown – and yet – the means to understand why these things happen eludes even the wisest of men. This is very curious, indeed!

The issue Solomon confronted is the same issue everyone on earth must confront: what is the meaning of life? What is man's purpose under heaven? And why do bad things happen? Read Ecclesiastes, but you will not find the answer because – Solomon never asked the Holy Spirit to help him understand the reason why things happen. Job struggled to know the reason why calamitous things were happening to him, but Job was asking the wrong question. Instead of asking "Why do bad things happen to me?" Job should have been asking: "Who will help me through it?" In both accounts, the Holy Spirit is the answer!

Solomon's questions and Job's predicament have the same solution: let the Holy Spirit guide you and let God help you through it!

If you want to understand why things happen on earth, then ask the Holy Spirit... and in the meantime read: The Image Bearer series!

What is the meaning of life… and what can we say about life in general? I offer these thoughts:

- The true meaning of life is to live the true meaning of love
- Your soul is eternal both pre and post humanity (Ps. 49:8,9)
- Everything we experience on earth is a test – in preparation for eternity
- You reap what you sow. The kingdom you establish in your heart is your future self – as an angel or a devil. Who you will be is a continuation of who you are now
- You must be born anew from above by the Spirit of God (John 3:3-8) to understand any of this!!!

I offer these additional thoughts:

- The answer to every question and every problem is: ask Jesus. Keep asking!!! Seek Jesus and know Him. What matters most is: if Jesus knows you (Matt. 17:21-23)
- Without the Holy Spirit, you will never understand how the kingdom of God operates
- Let the Holy Spirit guide you… dwell in you… and change your thought process
- Stuff is meaningless. Everything on God's planet belongs to Him, so seek Him first
- Everything about life on earth is either a test or training in righteousness. There will be pain, suffering and tribulation, so learn to deal with it properly and trust Jesus through it
- The next time you have an impossible situation, ask Jesus – what are "we" going to do
- Know the truth and the truth shall make you free (John 8:32)
- Truth is not a good opinion; Truth is a Person (John 14:6)

The single greatest thing I could ever possibly (and properly) communicate to as many people as are willing to listen would be… to lower your defensive guard long enough to wait in silence to hear God's voice. As long as it takes, keep waiting and seek Jesus until you hear His voice! There are multitudes of people who claim to know the truth, yet when they open their mouth and spout on about their opinions, it becomes instantly clear: they believe their opinions are correct – but they are in error. How can I definitively say this? Because you cannot know the truth without having a personal relationship with "The Truth"!

> Jesus said: "I am the way, the truth, and the life" (John 14:6).

Truth is not an opinion; Truth is a Person! Your truth may be valid in your self-made kingdom, as well as those who agree with you (temporarily) until another good opinion captures their attention, but allow me to let you in on a little secret: your good opinions (and mine) are hooey horse hockey! In God's kingdom, His truth is the means whereby His people walk in wisdom and understanding ... wherein all things operate according to His purposes and plans! And, by the way, the entire universe is under His command... and that includes even you.

God has given everyone free will to believe whatever they want, do whatever they want, produce whatever they want and become whatever they want, as well as influence other peoples and nations to agree with their ideas and opinions, but in the end... unless our agenda is aligned with God's agenda, all our best laid plans will result in futility – a chasing after wind. God gave us dominion to implement His purpose and plan for earth and men, not the other way around.

The only things that will withstand the test of time – are those things which are eternal. Many things seem to last forever, but that is an illusion. Only those things that are aligned with God's kingdom will remain – both now and forevermore.

- One generation goes, another comes
- Nations rise, nations fall
- Kingdoms come, kingdoms go

Is there any reason for the numerous things which appear permanent yet are temporary? Yes! The whole point of life is to cling to that which is eternal in the kingdom of God. Everything else is temporary and fleeting… and I mean everything.

It is well for us to ponder the reason why billions have died on this planet from wars alone, not including plagues, natural catastrophes, earthquakes, and a multitude of illnesses and diseases. Some may ask: if God really loves us, then why does He allow all this death to occur? The answer is simple: your body is temporary…. but your soul is eternal. Contrary to the accusatory sentiment within the question above – God loves all of us! God is Love! God loves you just as you are right now, but not so much to let you stay that way. God is more interested in the salvation of your soul and becoming who He intended you to be more than anything else happening to you on earth; however, you must be willing to be changed by the Spirit of God to come into alignment with His kingdom.

This life – is a test – in preparation for life eternal in Paradise.

> "But seek first the kingdom of God and His righteousness, and all these things shall be added to you" (Matt. 6:33).

Everything you are going through is in preparation for eternity. If you have sensed that life on earth is one giant test, then you are absolutely correct! You were sent here on probation for the testing and proofing of your soul for this reason: for "you" to decide your eternal fate. Please understand and don't misconstrue what I've written: you are deciding your ultimate fate and final disposition in eternity by your own words and actions – in this life. Jesus will judge you (and everyone else) on judgment day based upon what you did or didn't do on earth – based upon God's standards, not yours. If you think being good is the litmus test for entry into Paradise, well, it isn't… because you will never be good enough. Being good or doing good is a works-based program… and you will never be good enough! God's standard is perfection. The kingdom of God is about walking in righteousness and goodness –

from a faith perspective.

The Lord is testing us… but the proofing of our soul to determine our steadfast devotion and allegiance to Jesus – is done by you. "You" will bear witness either for or against yourself on the Day of Judgment. "Did you do all that Jesus told (commanded) you to do?"

> "… for the kingdom of God is not eating and drinking, but righteousness and peace and joy in the Holy Spirit" (Rom. 14:17).

The first question placed before you is this: if you want to live in eternity with God, then you must be aligned with His kingdom and adopt His way of living. If you are sad about billions having perished, well so am I, but the body is actually irrelevant because your body belongs to God (1 Cor. 6:20). If you gain entrance into God's kingdom, ***then your soul gets another body***… a glorified body… and it will be infinitely better than the one you have now.

The second question is: "what" are you willing to exchange in this life in order for your soul to be saved (Matt. 16:26) and experience bliss in Paradise with the Lord? Are you willing to be changed by the Holy Spirit to become the person He originally intended? If you are unwilling to be changed by Him, then you remain the king within your own earthen tabernacle… the one that ends up in the trash heap and is thrown into the fire.

God gave us free will to choose His way – or any other way. There are millions of choices we make during this life, but only one leads to life eternal. The correct choice only has one option: faith in Jesus Christ as Lord of your life by declaring full obedience in allegiance with Him and walking in His way.

> Jesus said to him, "I am the way, the truth, and the life. ***No one comes to the Father except through Me***" (John 14:6).

Somehow, the church started preaching a watered-down gospel that says all you have to do is believe in Jesus and you will be saved. Yes, that phrase appears in the bible, so let me ask you: are demons in hell saved since they believe like you do?

> "You believe that there is one God. You do well. Even the demons believe—and tremble!" (James 2:19)

Demons believe Jesus is Lord God, but they're in hell because their belief does not rise to the level of faith. Do you believe… or do you have faith? Believing Jesus is God gets you into the baseball stadium called grace on the first base line, but in order to get onto first base called – faith – you must make a firm declaration that Jesus is Lord of your life and you have exalted Him upon the throne of your heart – as Lord over you. This declaration of faith enables you to stand on first base, but you cannot advance home plate from first base. You must continue by faith toward second base (called sanctification) whereby you are being changed to become the likeness of Jesus He intended for you – and continue toward third base (called discipleship) so you think like Jesus and act like Him. The path from third base toward home is called: patient endurance. Our salvation in Christ is not a once-and-done altar call… it is a lifelong commitment to stay on course, endure, and be changed to become like Jesus. Everyone has been invited to live this way, but many reject it because God's way is difficult.

> Jesus said: "Because narrow is the gate and difficult is the way which leads to life, and there are few who find it" (Matt. 7:14).

We've all been predestined for faith, but not all get started nor stay the course.

"The spiritual state of the soul is normal for the believer, but to this state all do not attain, nor when it is attained is it always maintained."[1]

People come and people go. Nations rise and nations fall. God has a reason for it all.

For example, take a map from the year 1900 and examine the nations – and you will see many nations have changed their boundaries and names within three generations. What caused these shifts among nations… is "what" this book is about. No, it isn't a book about wars and rumors of wars… it's a book about kingdoms. Nations are temporal; kingdoms are eternal.

God is always looking and seeking a remnant – a very small group of faithful followers who are willing to come into alignment with His kingdom. As you will see in the following pages… it's not a numbers game. This world cries out, "Numbers, O Lord, many will perish unless you save them." Yes, the Lord Jesus is our Savior; however, "you" must enter into His salvation. The kingdoms you are building now cannot come with you into eternity. Those who build the kingdom of heaven on earth – now – will enjoy that kingdom in eternity.

Now do you see it: you are building your future habitation and inheritance for the New Earth.

The glorified body you will receive when you get to the other side will enable you to "continue to live eternally" (Psa. 49:9) and continue doing what you are doing right now. Death of this mortal body is merely an intermission between ages, yet your soul continues in the direction you are going now. You are deciding your future place in the kingdom as well as the type of '*oiketerion*' habitation-body you will get in the regeneration. So I say: choose wisely!

Throughout human history, human leaders have wielded great authority with power to create and subdue empires, such as

---

[1] Strong's Concordance, notes on *pneumatikos*-4152.

Assyrians, Persians, Egyptians, Babylonians, Turks, Medes, Greeks, Romans, English, Spanish, French, German, Portuguese… not to mention numerous dynasties in Asia and Africa – and democracy in America. This authority was given by God to all men in order to have dominion over earth… but it seems some men have greater administrative and organizational skills than most of us… yet nearly all relied on human effort (rather than God's Spirit) to accomplish their agenda.

God is seeking those who rely on His Spirit to accomplish His dominion mandate!

> "'Not by might nor by power, but by My Spirit,'
> says the Lord of hosts" (Zech. 4:6).

Some men are king-makers and others are kingdom-builders, yet the Lord governs them all.

Why are you here? What are you supposed to be doing? How did you get here? What is the meaning of life? This book is radically different in its method and application. You are a world changer! You have a purpose for being here… and it isn't to get saved and receive the guarantee of heaven. You were sent here on a mission – which includes remembering what you are and why you were sent here – in order to establish the kingdom of heaven on earth by coming against this ever present darkness that destroys men's souls.

You are a member of the host of earth that was sent to disperse the kingdom of darkness with the light God formed within you (Zech. 12:1). You were sent into enemy territory to recover and redeem that which was taken captive from God by Satan (the earth), but the first man sent to initiate this earthly recovery was tempted and deceived to surrender his dominion and authority to Satan. We've all become like him and we've all succumbed to sin's temptation; however, before anyone can get back on track, we need to be saved by a Savior, Jesus our Lord, before we can have dominion and get back to doing what we were sent here to do.

Now let me ask you: have you ever sensed some greater force operating behind the scenes that affects life on earth to establish nations and kingdoms? You, my friend, are not alone. Some may perceive the hand of an invisible entity working in relative obscurity is altering the affairs of man on earth for some unknown reason... and you would be correct! This is not the ranting of a conspiracy theorist trying to expose illuminati, mafia, or anything like that. Those specific entities may exist, but I am not concerned whether they do or don't exist because... if they can be seen.... then they are merely a physical manifestation of something much larger which operates in total obscurity. Once again... I'm talking about kingdoms. Keep reading.

Three Kingdoms

The first thing we must clarify as this book begins – is to define the word: kingdom.[2]

- *Mamlakah* (Hebrew-4467) or '*malkuw*-4437' both from the root of '*malak*-4427' meaning: to reign.
- *Basileia* (Greek-932) meaning: a realm. It can be an abstract noun denoting sovereignty, royal power, dominion; or a concrete noun denoting the territory or people over whom a king rules.

Kingdoms are the realm of a king who reins over people in a territory (within either a physical or spiritual realm). This definition should be consistent with our preconceived meaning. In its most basic sense, a kingdom is when a monarch, ruler or king reins over a people group as a nation within a territory.

On planet earth, there are three major classifications of kingdoms:

1. God's kingdom and His dominion (Dan. 7:14; Rev 11:15)
2. Man's dominion and earthly kingdoms (Gen. 1:27; Matt. 4:8; 24:7; Luke 22:28-30).
3. Satan's dominion and worldly kingdoms (Matt. 12:26; Rev. 16:10)

There is an interesting detail about these three kingdoms: only one is visible. A good friend of mine had a vision in which he saw a person standing between two tall buildings; however, my friend was unable to see the buildings. This is a perfect illustration to explain man's position between two kingdoms – we are able to see man and everything man does, but the other two kingdoms are invisible to man's natural senses; they must be spiritually perceived and discerned.

---

[2] Definitions taken from Strong's Concordance.

The second point we need to grasp is a difference in names associated with these two invisible kingdoms. This planet has two designations: the "Earth" as a permanent realm in the kingdom of God (as is Heaven) – and "this world" which refers to "the kingdom of darkness."

"The earth is the Lord's and the fullness thereof", "The earth abides forever" and "Holy, holy, holy *is* the LORD of hosts; the whole earth is full of His glory" (Psa. 24:1; Eccl. 1:4; Isa. 6:3)."

Jesus is Lord of Heaven and Earth, but when Jesus was questioned by Pilate prior to His illegal crucifixion, Jesus said:

> "My kingdom is not of ***this world***. If My kingdom were of ***this world***, My servants would fight, so that I should not be delivered to the Jews; but now My kingdom is not from here" (John 18:36).

To be certain, Christ's kingdom is on earth, but it was not a kingdom the Jews were willing to defend on account of Jesus – their Messiah! "This world" refers to any group of people hostile to Jesus that is under the demonic influence of Satan. Understanding this terminology will enable you to unlock many mysteries within the scriptures… as well as understand why many evil and terrible things are happening to mankind on earth that God never intended![3]

> "The earth is the Lord's, and all its fullness, the world and those who dwell therein" (Psa. 24:1).

Two kingdoms are represented in this scripture! To which kingdom do ***you*** belong?

The third point we need to understand is: heavenly places are on the earth. Within those three kingdoms mentioned above, there are at least fourteen specific places recorded in the scriptures.

---

[3] The author found only two instances when this terminology was used inconsistently, both times in Peter's gospels.

Heavenly places represent the earthly interface between either the kingdom of Heaven or the kingdom of Hell – with Earth sandwiched in the midst of both. Spiritual forces from both kingdoms are advancing their kingdom through the host of earth (i.e. mankind).

When the Lord asks: "What is man that You are mindful of him, and the son of man that You visit him?" (Psa. 8:4), our presence on earth to do His will is monumental to say the least! Epic is closer to the point! So you ask: why are we here to begin with? A: Keep reading and find out.

> "One generation passes away, and another generation comes; but the earth abides forever" (Eccl. 1:4).

Some doctrines teach the earth will be destroyed by fire, but the scriptures say otherwise: the earth abides forever! The earth, more specifically, the "new earth" is the eternal home of the saints after the second resurrection and regeneration. Even those saints who were martyred for their faith who wait in a temporary holding place under an altar in Heaven are coming back "Here" in the first resurrection to rule to reign with Christ for a millennium.

> "Then I saw the souls of those who had been beheaded for their witness to Jesus and for the word of God, who had not worshiped the beast or his image, and had not received his mark on their foreheads or on their hands. And they lived and reigned with Christ for a thousand years. [5] But the rest of the dead did not live again until the thousand years were finished. ***This is the first resurrection***" (Rev. 20:4, 5).

There are two resurrections. Why – do you curiously suppose – this may be inconsistent with your doctrines? Well, it's probably because we've all been taught a "heaven-only" doctrine for 1,600 years whereby the faithful really think they go to heaven when they die. This is a false heaven doctrine – the proof of which is found by reading "Here: The Kingdom Of Heaven Is" (book #8 in the Image Bearer series). Study it carefully before your preconceived opinions based upon manmade doctrines attempt to deny the infallibility of scripture. This comes as a warning: study like a Berean before judging. Study… and show yourself approved!

Jesus never promised us heaven, the apostles never preached it and our creeds don't teach it. Jesus promised us life eternal… in a (*topos*-topographic) *place* He went to prepare for us.

> "Come, you blessed of My Father, inherit the kingdom prepared for you from the foundation of the world" (Matt. 25:34).

After the judgment and resurrection, saints will inherit the kingdom… on earth.

Angels in Heaven are "the host of Heaven" and the sons of men are "the host of Earth" (Gen. 2:1). Earth is not only your eternal home… earth is your birthplace and the birthplace of your children. You are the host of earth! You were born here, grew up here, raised children here, were born again here, served Jesus here, will die here, will wait for the judgment and resurrection HERE, and you will rule and reign with Christ Jesus for all eternity in a brand new glory suit that comes down to you '*ex*' – "from out of" Heaven (2 Cor. 5:2) in the regeneration. Your HERE – is Earth! However, heaven – as man's eternal destination – was created by the spirit of religion to get your eyes off our homeland to keep this planet captive in Satan's kingdom of darkness and sin. We were all bamboozled! We were sent as light-bearers to come against the kingdom of darkness, but it seems demons and devils are more aware of our true identity than we are.

You get your identity and commission from Jesus; "who you are" is based upon "what you are." You are a spiritual being having a human experience! What you do is based upon what you are. Ponder that! If you are a soldier, painter, writer (like me), builder, architect, administrator, farmer, teacher, engineer, mother, whatever... these are commissions by which you serve Him. What you do (in service to Christ) is based upon your identity "in Christ" and whatever the Lord Jesus has commissioned you as one member of the host of earth. Accept this responsibility as your commission and faithfully accomplish all the Lord Jesus commands of you.

> "Heaven is My throne, and earth is My footstool.
> What house will you build for Me? says the Lord,
> or what is the place of My rest?" (Acts 7:49).

God is asking a very serious question: what place are you building for God to dwell? Throughout most of human history, we've been constructing buildings "for God to dwell" but the house which God wants us to build is a *'mone'* heart-house in our soul (John 14:2, 23). By doing what God asks of us... to establish a permanent home for Him to abide in our heart (Eph. 3:17), it doesn't matter where we go or when we die or what happens to us when we die – because God is dwelling within us the entire time through faith in Jesus Christ. Even in our pain and suffering, God suffers with us! You've never been alone! God is caring for both habitation and inhabitant (house/body and soul); He is taking care of both house and inhabitant (your *oiketerion* i.e. the soul of your inner being within your body... which is your true self).

'*Oiketerion*-3613' is a very interesting word; it is a combination of two words (*oiketer*- "an inhabitant" + *oikos*- "a dwelling") which means more than just a habitation, residence or house... it implies the inhabitant and the habitation are – one and the same. The person and the dwelling "co-habit" the same space and place... in oneness.

You don't have a soul, per se... you are a soul. Your body was superimposed upon your soul as one type of habitation, which means... you are a spiritual being having a human experience in an earth suit named (state your name). And (by the way) you get a new '*oiketerion*' house/body for your soul in the resurrection of life![4] The current body of flesh you have counts for nothing in eternity! Jesus said:

> "It is the Spirit who gives life; the flesh profits nothing. The words that I speak to you are spirit, and they are life" (John 6:63).

Did Jesus ever promise the resurrection of the body? A: Never! Did the apostles? No! Jesus promised us the resurrection of the dead; your current body is immaterial to your eternal mission.

Think about this: Jesus said of Himself: "I am the resurrection and the life" (John 11:25). If Jesus abides in you according to faith, then the resurrection is already within you… it just hasn't happened yet! (John 5:29) You are already – not yet! This is really Good News! Which means: you are already living eternally – now. We need to thoroughly understand this truth! Whether you die in two minutes or twenty years, through faith, Jesus promised you life eternal – if – you abide in Him!

So I ask: why wait for eternity when you can go all in and live for Jesus now?

GO ALL IN – NOW!!!

Today is the first day of the rest of your life – beginning now and continuing into eternity.

In the regeneration, the Father is pleased "to give you a kingdom" along with a new glorified body to accompany your soul with life eternal in the New Earth. How incredibly awesome is this truth to fully comprehend! And this promise gets better because our eternal reward is incentive based! Whatever you did for the Lord – in His name – that brings glory to Him – will be recompensed as true riches.

---

[4] In the resurrection of condemnation (John 5:29), souls will receive a body to match the condition of their heart.

KINGDOMS

We must open our mind to see the big picture of God's plan for Earth and mankind. We must! The impending revival and third great awakening is dependent upon it! God is about to show Himself strong – which the darkness will attack! We are seeing the evidence of this even now with chaos, confusion and anarchy rising up in many nations creating violence and mayhem to destroy one thing: God's truth revealed through Christ Jesus.

You are one member of a spiritual people group known as "the host of earth." The earth was created for you and you were created for the earth. In the New Earth, the Father will give you a kingdom HERE according to your faithfulness to Jesus in obedience to Him as your Lord, Savior, Eternal King and Everlasting Father. Is that last statement scriptural? Absolutely!

> "For unto us ***a Child is born, unto us a Son is given***; and the government will be upon His shoulder. And ***His name will be called*** Wonderful, Counselor, Mighty God, ***Everlasting Father***, Prince of Peace" (Isa 9:6).

If the above scripture is somewhat confusing to you, then read "Image" (book #3 in the Image Bearer series) to see Jesus from His perspective as Everlasting Father…and not from manmade doctrines!

Heaven is God's throne… and it is perfect! The heavens on earth, however, need regeneration.

Earth is the place where "the kingdom of the heavens" (Matt. 4:17) is being wrought, fought and brought into reality by saints of God in faithful service to Jesus – the Lord of Heaven and Earth. Jesus started it... and you were sent here to finish what He started! Now, let's finish the job!

When the Lord says He will make new heavens and a new earth, new heavens pertains to the kingdoms God promised to give His saints in the regeneration. Disobedient twigs, however, are hypocrites who are thrown into outer darkness, and rebellious twigs are cast into the fire.

Which kingdom are you establishing on earth? The kingdom of God is the only one that matters because it's the one "which shall never be destroyed" (Dan. 2:44). It's time to realign your priorities to establish the kingdom of heaven on earth wherein you shall dwell eternally.

> "Therefore wait for Me," says the Lord, "Until the day I rise up for plunder; My determination is to gather the nations to My assembly of kingdoms, to pour on them My indignation, all My fierce anger; all the earth shall be devoured with the fire of My jealousy" (Zeph. 3:8).

The Father has a kingdom to award faithful saints in the regeneration. You may have never heard about God's incentive plan for having dominion on earth and being given territory in His kingdom as a reward for faithful service and patient endurance in service to your Lord – King Jesus, so keep reading – and perhaps a paradigm shift will happen – which will compel you to live radically in love with Jesus and obediently do all that He commands!

Jesus is everything!!! How could He not be enough for thee!

If you think this book is going in an entirely new direction contrary to scripture, then you would be mistaken. Every book the Lord commissions me to write has between 300-500 scripture verses from the New King James version (not message versions or whatnots). This book is not going in a new direction... it's going in the original direction the apostles preached before the spirit of religion put its claws in Christianity and institutionalized it with manmade doctrines.

Institutional Christianity has been taking believers and turning them into members – but these books were commissioned to turn believers into disciples of Jesus – Lord God Almighty!

It's all about Jesus – and God gets the glory!

The Kingdom of Self

There are three primary kingdoms: God's, man's and Satan's. The kingdoms of man have been categorized throughout history as epochs shaping humanity... and the planet itself. But there is another type of kingdom – a subset of the kingdom of man – a kingdom in which most of us are very familiar with: the kingdom of self.

What can I say about the kingdom of self? What a giant waste of time! The kingdom of self will pass away. Why spend time building the kingdom of self which will not withstand the test of time which is part of the kingdom that will be destroyed. Arrogant hubris exemplified. The kingdom of self is built by pride – upon the mountain of selfish, self-centered arrogance, self interest and self promotion. The mountains of "me" "my" and "mine" are puny hills that will melt like wax in the presence of the Lord. Build anything apart from Jesus... and it will melt.

If the kingdom of self is futility and a chasing after wind, then why are so many of us doing it? Perhaps it's some type of spiritual blindness or neurosis. Perhaps it's a cousin of doubt and unbelief born from fear. More likely, it's something that has been passed down to us from one generation to the next which began in the Garden of Eden. We've been deceived to build anything in human effort to glorify self and gain name recognition (myself included) as some measure to validate our existence through meaningful expression. We can build anything – and so we do – without counting the cost. Getting ahead to get the most out of life without any regard for life eternal devoid of true riches suddenly has a hollow ring... doesn't it!

"The best laid schemes of mice and men / often go awry" (John Steinbeck).[5]

Creating a legacy to leave for others to follow and build upon – is what Jesus did!!! When we build a personal legacy for our self, our family, future generations, future leaders – but we do not build it upon the mountain of God that exalts Jesus as King of kings, then our tiny little molehills will melt in the ensuing judgment fire.

Any time we build a church or ministry or denomination that causes people to seek "a man thing" rather than Jesus is – is an utterly worthless endeavor. If it doesn't give glory to Jesus – and Jesus only – then it is a vain endeavor. It is chaff that will be burned in the judgment fire. So I say this again and again – Jesus only!!! Anything added to or detracted from Jesus results in futility! So I ask: why do it?

My grandfather was highly regarded in Dushore, Pennsylvania serving as Mayor for 37 years and a day was named in honor of him, yet he died penniless in a nursing home from Alzheimer's. My father is still alive at the time of this message and yet… this highly intelligent and successful US Marine Corps Lt. Col., GE manager and father of four may leave little behind. Hundreds of thousands of dollars spent on collectibles, antiques, homes, magazine subscriptions and whatnots with closets filled to capacity – all non-eternal stuff – must be left behind. What are you doing that is any different than all generations past and present? Has any generation in your family bestowed wealth that lasted beyond the fourth or fifth generation? Do you even know anything about your family heritage beyond two generations past or present? What, then, is the purpose of a legacy with your name attached to it if… no one remembers who you were?

These words I write under the inspiration of the Holy Spirit will outlast anything my family has done generations past or present

---

[5] "But Mouse, you are not alone, in proving foresight may be vain: The best laid schemes of mice and men go often askew, And leave us nothing but grief and pain" (Scott Burns, 1785, Kilmarnock volume; Wikipedia).

because all glory goes to Jesus – and yet – I type these words in a minivan parked in a parking lot at 9:30pm with barely a shred of evidence to prove I existed. Better to glorify Jesus in relative obscurity than to glorify self... and suffer eternal ruin.

Time, is seems, in concord with the Holy Spirit... is the final arbiter of man's existence. Death is our common enemy and also our great equalizer! Who I am is irrelevant... unless I do all things to the glory of God. Amen.

Man's worldly kingdoms... are in opposition to "Father, in Heaven, Thy will be done."

The kingdom of self is agenda-driven and purpose driven; in contrast, the kingdom of God is Spirit directed, Spirit guided, Divinely empowered and governed by grace to operate in love.

> "Love suffers long *and* is kind; love does not envy; love does not parade itself, is not puffed up; [5] does not behave rudely, does not seek its own, is not provoked, thinks no evil; [6] does not rejoice in iniquity, but rejoices in the truth; [7] bears all things, believes all things, hopes all things, endures all things" (1 Cor. 13: 4-7).

The kingdom of love believes all things according to God's goodness and doing good. Consider all the phrases in scripture that teach us to avoid certain types of conduct and you will discover they are antagonistic to the kingdom of love, grace, goodness, righteousness, holiness and truth.

The kingdom of self is arrogant, uncharitable, conceited, proud, boastful, rude, disrespectful, offensive and uncouth, unkind, impatient in suffering, unwilling to endure pain, cruel toward strangers, entitled, disregards others needs, uncaring, unsympathetic, bad mannered, impolite; is vulgar, verbally abusive, promotes gossip, speaks lies, defends hearsay; is unwilling to ask forgiveness, and incapable of forgiving others, harbors small offenses, exaggerates unintended offenses, promotes speculation, ridicules honesty, denigrates sincerity; refuses to provide assistance when asked; is incapable of blessing others that promotes others; refuses to show honor and respect to authority including parents, pastors, teachers, employers, law enforcement, military, elected officials, heads of state, and neighbors.

This list could fill many pages! The kingdom of self is unloving, uncaring, unforgiving, merciless, angry, hateful, wicked, vengeful, violent, vitriolic, evil-minded, manipulative, shameless, controlling, dishonest, corrupt, sensual, void of all understanding regarding spiritual matters, and is hostile toward Jesus and the ways of God. The kingdom of self is rooted in unbelief; it distorts truth and promotes lies; it does not trust God and therefore cannot abide in peace. The kingdom of self is temporary and futile.

The kingdom of self is rooted in demonic darkness and is divisive, belligerent, rebellious, hostile and antagonistic toward the kingdom of God and God's truth.

The kingdom of self cannot abide in faith, hope and love because its core is based upon a worldly system with worldly principles that are contrary to the truth of God.

In a word: the kingdom of self is – ungodly! Since God is thoughtful toward us all the time with good thoughts, the kingdom of self in two words is: thoughtless and careless.

Do all to the glory of God – and forsake not His benefits!

The kingdom of self is diametrically opposed to the spirit of meekness wherein God is preeminent (first in all) and all others are considered ahead of self. The ones who walk in meekness will inhabit the New Earth.

Gateways of Meekness[6]

> Jesus said: "Blessed are the meek, for they shall inherit the earth" (Matt. 5:5; Psa. 37:11).

Of all the character qualities that God esteems highly – meekness is supreme. Meekness was exhibited by Jesus Himself, as our example according to how we are intentionally to live:

> Jesus said: "Take My yoke upon you and learn from Me, for I am gentle [meek] and lowly in heart, and you will find rest for your souls" (Matt. 11:29).

Consider, now, the response by first century believers to the Gospel of Jesus, to live according to kingdom principles, who gathered together in '*koinonia*' fellowship to "share all things" in common. They exemplified the true essence of meekness toward other believers, which is: exalting God as preeminent, and esteeming others ahead of self.

The two great commandments Jesus spoke on – help us to model this truth in action:

> "So he answered and said, " 'You shall love the Lord your God with all your heart, with all your soul, with all your strength, and with all your mind,' and 'your neighbor as yourself.'" (Luke 10:27).

This is the imagery of the cross with both vertical and horizontal alignment of our soul in relationship to others: loving God and exalting Him (vertical) and loving others (horizontal).

"Love is the power that enables us to live according to humility and meekness that exalts God as preeminent in our life and considers the needs of others ahead of self."[7]

---

[6] Excerpt from "Gateways" section titled "Gateways of Meekness."
[7] Excerpt from "Commission" section titled "Love!!!"

"The will of God for mankind is to love the Lord and love one another, and thus, we are here to help one another as we get through this probationary phase of eternity. Our interest to help others ahead of our own self-interest – is one aspect of meekness… and the other is (most importantly) establishing the preeminence of God in our life as our number one priority. The good deposit within us is how God designed us to live in uprightness, but when we use this goodness to better our "self" at the exclusion and detriment of others is what the Law warned us about, yet could never teach us apart from the tutoring of the Spirit in divine wisdom *with* understanding… and with mercy!"[8]

> "Let nothing be done through selfish ambition or conceit, but in lowliness of mind [meekness] let each esteem others better than [ahead of] himself" (Phil. 2:3).

"Jesus sacrificed His life for yours, so that "through faith" you sacrifice your life for His. The gift of salvation is born out of a covenant relationship between two people (God and any person) that agree to enter into this covenant willingly whereby both parties bring "gifts" to offer one another and pledge unto one another: "What's mine is yours, and what's yours is mine. My enemies are your enemies and my family is your family." The bond of covenant between two persons abandons the concept of self-interest and adopts the concepts of fellowship and meekness to look out for one another's common (*koinos, koinonia*) interests."[9]

So I ask: which kingdom are you perpetuating? Are you advancing the kingdom of self (me, my, mine) or the kingdom of love (others ahead of self)? Let me challenge you in this: consider the prayers you recently prayed and ask yourself… were more prayers asking God for things to help your agenda or were these prayers offered as petitions to help others?

Whatever we focus upon… gets bigger. Thus, by esteeming others

---

[8] Excerpt from "Commission" section titled "Created Upright – In Rightness."
[9] Excerpt from "Commission" section titled "The Free Gift."

ahead of your personal self-interest, you will operate as a gateway of meekness that glorifies God and magnifies Him in the earth. The operating system of this world would have you believe otherwise... by adopting the "Dead Sea" mentality (with water flowing in but nothing flowing out) to glorify self at the expense of others... even while your salvation in Christ hangs in the balance.

What is the meaning of life?

A: Love Jesus. Love others. Do justly. Love mercy. Walk humbly with your God. (Micah 6:8).

A: Exalt Jesus and give glory to Him in all you think, say and do.

A: Focus on Jesus and love others... even your enemies. Everything else – is futility!!!

Kingdoms – In The Beginning

What happened in Heaven which caused all this chaos and confusion on earth? This chapter will try to explain what happened, what is happening now… and what we can do about it.

Two spiritual kingdoms are at war on earth for global supremacy. Man stands in the midst of this cosmic battle. This is the big picture regarding many things happening which few are able to perceive – yet we all experience daily. Man must make a decision either to align his soul with Jesus, the King of Heaven – or remain in rebellion against God. Man is guided either by the Spirit of Christ… or the spirit of antichrist… to declare allegiance to one kingdom or the other.

In order to make sense of the scriptures and this book about kingdoms, it is important to know about various places within the kingdom of God and some terminology describing them:

- Heaven – is the manifest presence of God – and eternal place where God's glory dwells. "Heaven is My throne." Heaven has numerous places and some interesting creatures as well, including a throne where spiritual beings offer praise and worship to glorify the greatness and goodness of God whose glory fills the heavens – and earth as well
- Earth – is the celestial planet orbiting the cosmos within the kingdom of God, and is the eternal residence for the host of earth (sons of men; i.e. you and me; Gen. 2:1)
- This world – is the same celestial planet currently under the rule and domination of Satan that operates according to sin and rebellion resulting in spiritual death
- The kingdom of God – represents every place God created… which is every place including Heaven, Hell, Earth, Hades and Death
- Hell – is the absence of God's presence
- Hades and Death – are two of three temporary holding places for all dead awaiting judgment; Hades holds those

who professed faith in God, yet Death restrains persons apart from faith in rebellion against God (Rev. 1:18)

Heaven is God's throne, yet it is "different" than the kingdom of heaven. In fact, there are many heavens within the "kingdom of heaven." Jesus said in Matt. 4:17: – ἡ βασιλεία τῶν οὐρανῶν (Greek) is literally: "the kingdom of the *heavens*" (*ouranos*-3772) *heaven* is plural. There are different places in the heavens and God Himself is higher than the heavens.

> "Indeed heaven and the highest heavens belong to the Lord your God, *also* the earth with all that *is* in it" (Deut. 10:14).

Heaven is God's throne, but the kingdom of heaven is wherever Jesus extends His kingdom and His influence through His ambassadors, governors, magistrates and subordinates – which He accomplishes through you and me.

Wherever King Jesus goes, He establishes His kingdom. Wherever the King of Heaven goes, He establishes the kingdom of heaven. And if Jesus abides in you, then the kingdom of heaven is within you as well, and wherever you go on planet earth, you are extending the kingdom of the heavens just as Jesus did.

> "The kingdom of God is within you" (Luke 17:21).

Jesus told us the kingdom of God is within you… and yet you are also in the kingdom of God. And through faith, Christ dwells in your heart and likewise heaven also. The King of heaven and heaven itself… are a package deal. You cannot have one without the other. When this reality becomes clearer and fully known by you, it will in fact revolutionize your thought process to say and do the same things Jesus did and said. When Jesus began preaching, He made a simple declaration that you and I are obligated to declare:

> "Repent, for the kingdom of heaven[s] is at hand" (Matt. 4:17).

We are His ambassadors and heaven-sent evangelists to proclaim the good news, come against the kingdom of darkness with the light of truth – and – rescue sinners trapped in sin and darkness. Sadly, sinners have been blinded from perceiving this truth and thus they remain in rebellion against God. Sinners in rebellion… are destined for eternal damnation.

Therefore, you've been commanded to know the truth… and the truth will set you free from demonic thought patterns that you and all captives and prisoners have been brainwashed to believe which are inherently hostile to God's truth.

Our efforts may seem like we're draining a swamp with just a teacup, but keep doing what Jesus tells you to do because there are many others armed with teacups like yours. Regardless of what you are going through or what happens to you – endure all things through patient endurance until the end and you will receive your great reward in the New Earth.

> "Nevertheless we, according to His promise, look for new heavens and a new earth in which righteousness dwells" (2 Pet. 3:13).

Why Are You Here

Two questions have always caused man to re-think the meaning of life regarding man's purpose on earth: 1) who am I, and 2) what's my purpose. This section will explain "what" you are, as well as your reason for being on earth, before we discuss your heavenly purpose in God's plan.

For nearly 2,000 years, we've been taught salvation with the hope of attaining heaven is our primary objective of being saved through faith. Well, Jesus never promised us heaven, the apostles never preached it and our creeds don't teach it. Jesus promised us life eternal! So why do some preachers keep teaching heaven? Because it's a simplistic way to teach unintelligent, stubborn and hard-hearted sheep about the afterlife instead of provoking them to pursue righteousness and search the scriptures to find out for themselves what the New Earth is going to be like. The answers are all in the Bible. Read it! Oh, how misguided we've been all these years with a false-heaven doctrine.

In Genesis 2:1, God said: "Thus the heavens and the earth, and all the host of them, were finished." This is important, as "all the host of them" represents two groups of people in God's kingdom – the host of heaven (angels) and host of earth (men)… thus ending the creation narrative with "the history of the heavens and the earth" (Gen. 2:4). At this point, all spiritual beings are in a state of existence, and the first soul destined for earth is about to be sent and formed upon the earth to initiate God's plan of renewal and Regenesis – on the Eighth Day. This may be difficult to comprehend, so let me introduce this thought: you don't need a body in order to be in a state of existence; however, on earth during this season of eternity… you need one. Again I say: your soul does not need a body in order to be in a state of existence. When your body dies, it leaves your soul, and your spirit returns to God who gave it (Eccl. 12:7; Psa. 146:4), yet your soul continues in a state of existence where it waits for the resurrection. Your soul is eternal (Psa. 49:9) and you existed "in Christ before the foundation of this world" (Eph. 1:4).

We are currently living on earth during one season of eternity and then our body returns to the earth (where it came from) and our spirit returns to God (where it came from)… yet the soul remains here – on earth – waiting for judgment, resurrection, redemption and regeneration.

Suffice to say, there are a great many things we are presently unable to comprehend regarding the spiritual person (soul with spirit) within us.

"We were created good and upright, a little lower than angels, crowned with glory and honor (Psa. 8:5), called *elohim* by God (i.e. lacking little of God; John 10:34-36) and have been given a divine nature (2 Pet. 1:4). We **existed** (*thought by God into a state of existence*) in God's presence before we were inserted into the fabric of time (by the Holy Spirit); we were in Christ before the foundation of the world (Eph. 1:4), God knew us before we were born (Psa. 139:13; Jer. 1:5) and we are on earth to accomplish His will for the earth, by grace through faith. I have no idea what we were like before we came to earth, but I do know the soul is eternal, God placed eternity in our heart (Eccl. 3:11), and we (our souls) are currently being tested, proofed and sanctified so that we may "continue to live eternally" (Psa. 49:9; John 3:15). This means you (your soul) is eternal (both pre and post humanity): we existed in God's presence before we were inserted into the fabric of time (Gen. 1:26 - 2:1), then we were formed of the earth (Gen. 2:7) and we will continue to live eternally in one of several places after the judgment based upon what we did (or didn't do) on earth."[10]

If this is the first time you've ever read this much truth about your soul's existence, then this may be a good stopping point in the book for you to ponder your true spiritual reality – apart from the earth suit that was formed upon you. You are a spiritual being having a human experience.

> "...who has saved us and called us with a holy calling, not according to our works, but according to His own purpose and grace *which was given to us in Christ Jesus before time began*" (2 Tim. 1:9).

God knew us "in Christ" and sent us as His representatives – as the host of earth – in His image according to His likeness – to come against the kingdom of darkness on earth with the light of truth to establish the kingdom of heaven – HERE. Just as Jesus was sent here by the Father, likewise... so were you! And you got here the same way Jesus did – by the overshadowing of the Spirit. And we are having a wilderness experience just like Jesus, so I encourage you to study the life of Jesus and imitate His example whereby you will eventually comprehend your reason for being here – and your commission as well.

---

[10] Excerpt from "Commission" section titled "We Are Spiritual Beings."

> "As He [Jesus] is, so are we in this world" (1 John 4:17).

We were all sent to earth – and everyone sent here was given a commission to come against the darkness. Earth has always been our eternal home whereby God sent us here to redeem the land that was taken captive when Satan was cast here… and have dominion over the darkness as well. We are fighting to recover the Promised Land that God gave us – before Satan took earth captive and set up the kingdom of darkness. We are fighting to recover our homeland… and the scriptures have numerous examples whereby we see a recurring pattern: called, sent out, occupy, defend, advance, call out to save other souls captive in darkness, repeat.

We are all being saved and transformed and sent out to save other souls and take heart territory.

Consider the history of Israel as a large scale event for one nation that happens to every one of us during our lifetime! We are established in a place, we raise families and expand our territory, but then lose touch with God's presence, we forget our destiny and purpose, and then we go our own way to build our own kingdom and construct tall towers into heaven (Babel) only to be dispersed and later taken captive as slaves in bondage to various things in darkness. Then we have a God-encounter whereby God manifests Himself to deliver us (Exodus) and invites us to enter into a covenant with Him by hearing His voice to live in faithful obedience to Him. Land is promised to us, and we operate for a season like this but eventually fall back into our original way of thinking to become enslaved – yet again – to sinful thought patterns.

This process can be repeated ad infinitum in a person's life… and for nations as well.

The Lord promised much land to the Israelites so they might dwell in peace and commune in oneness with God as His own special people, yet here now is the big picture: the New Earth is the Promised Land for the saints of God… those who are called according to His purpose!

What is the single greatest truth we can discern from this? Stay in God's presence, remember the testimony, listen to hear His voice, do what He tells you, and patiently endure until the end.

God's plan according to goodness which He purposed for man – is to have dominion over earth, but darkness had other plans. What they meant for evil, God intended for good. Once we've dedicated our allegiance to Jesus to accomplish the plan of God, our soul will be tested and perfected through various trials and tribulations (sanctification) to reward us according to faithful obedience (or punish some for faithlessness)

It seems we make much ado about raising money for missionaries and we even get excited to send some out, but church… this has always been the Fathers will… to form us, call us and send us into the darkness to establish His presence with the light of His truth. Sometimes, the mission field is across the street to help your neighbor.

Our dominion mandate from God is: called, send out, occupy, defend, advance, call more souls out of darkness, give God glory, and repeat. Our service unto God in doing His will is: receive it, bless it, break it, multiply it, share it, and give God glory in it.

It's all about Jesus – and God gets the glory!

Beginning – Yet Again[11]

In the beginning (Gen. 1:1) describes a new beginning point in earth history from an earlier state of existence. The word "beginning" wasn't the beginning of earth; it was a new moment in the history and timeline of earth – as a period intended for earth's salvation and redemption – in preparation for the regeneration.

---

[11] Excerpt from "Regenesis" section titled: "Creation Happens, Time Begins."

"The first five words of the bible tell a story. "In the beginning, God created" is a brief recap of an earlier creation event of the heavens and the earth by God (prior to Gen. 1:1). This is mentioned to help man understand his place within the context of time within eternity. The verb "created" is singular and means "to fashion anew."[12] Literally, creation is being fashioned anew from a previous version that was new. John, a New Testament apostle, describes this era that predated creation (John 1:1).

"The earth was without form, and void; and darkness *was* on the face of the deep" (Gen. 1:2). The italicized word '*was*' is not found in the original Hebrew, and was added by scholars to help us understand the message. It would also be helpful if scholars added another italicized word at the beginning of this verse to read, "*Now* – the earth was without form, and void"… for it speaks of a new moment in creation history.

The earth is described as void and formless. Several Hebrew words[13] are used here:

- **Darkness** (*choshek*-2882) means: darkness, misery, destruction, death, ignorance, sorrow, wickedness; obscurity; from (*chashak*-2821) meaning: to be dark (as withholding light)
- **Formless** (*tohuw*-8414) means: to lie waste; desolation, i.e. a desert; fig. a worthless thing; is translated as: vain (4x), confusion (3x), without form (2x) wilderness (2x)
- **Void** (*bohuw*-922) means: to be empty; a vacuity; an undistinguishable ruin; emptiness

"When we combine these words together, as the scripture has done, we get a very clear graphic representation what the surface of earth was like: it was utterly destroyed.

"Darkness is everywhere on the earth – and it is in ruins! The Hebrew word for darkness implies chaos and disorder. The literal

---

[12] NKJV Study Bible, notes on Gen. 1:1, Thomas Nelson Publishers.
[13] All terms and definitions taken from Strong's Concordance.

meaning is: "there was disorder." The earth was without form, void, chaotic and disorderly, and this is the condition of the earth in which man was formed.

"The Holy Spirit is commissioned to hover over the earth to restrain darkness (chaos, evil) (Gen. 1:2), and the Holy Spirit is still hovering over the earth – and also hovers over us. When we profess faith in Christ, then the Holy Spirit comes to dwell in us. When we walk according to grace, the sanctifying work of the Holy Spirit is accomplished in us and through us by the indwelling Spirit. When we walk in the Spirit, the Spirit enables us (through His power) to do the will of the Father upon earth, to avoid sin and to be faithful followers of Christ.

"'Then God said' and thus, the Genesis story of creation begins in Genesis 1:3 and then culminates with "this is the history of creation" in Genesis 2:4. These initial 35 verses constitute *the history of creation*, and then – *the history of man* upon the earth begins in Gen. 2:7. Please note: there are *two* time periods in creation history as recorded in the scriptures and they appear to operate under different time parameters. There are six days of creation, the days of old, but these are different than the years of man since Adam, known as the years of many generations. As Moses said,"[14]

> "Remember the days of old, consider the years of the many generations" (Deut. 32:7).

As mentioned earlier, a cataclysmic event happened in heaven. We may not understand what happened or when it happened (which we will get to), but it happened – and earth became shrouded in darkness. The beginning described in Genesis 1 with "darkness on the face of the deep" describes (at this point moving forward in history) the condition of earth after Lucifer was cast out of Heaven and landed on earth whereby his demonic presence

---

[14] End of excerpt copied from "Regenesis" section titled: "Creation Happens, Time Begins."

rendered earth chaotic and disorderly. Search these scriptures to get a better sense of what happened:

- Lucifer was "the anointed cherub that covers" (Ezekiel 28:11-19), but he initiated a rebellion against God whereby he was incinerated by God as he fell to earth (v.18)
- Jesus witnessed this event: "I saw Satan fall like lightning from heaven" (Luke 10:18)
- This rebellion by Lucifer swept away one third of heaven (Rev. 12:4), including many angels, who were cast from heaven onto earth (Isa. 14:12-16; Rev. 21:7-9)
- "Darkness on the face of the deep" represents both the complete absence of God's presence on earth and the utter destruction by Satan's impact on God's creation
- Earth was obliterated...
- And then there was light!

When it happened and how long the earth remained in this darkened condition is speculative, but it is important to know... *it happened before time began*. Earth had a prior state of existence that was good, Satan fell from heaven and destroyed the earth, God developed a plan of salvation for the earth including a plan of regeneration to restore it to its' former glory wherein the saints will rule and reign with Him for eternity, then God established order in the midst of chaos, then God created time to mark the seasons, and thus...

... man is living in one season of eternity called – the redemption – whereby man is being tested and proofed (sanctified) to determine his eternal position and place on the New Earth.

That is the big picture that explains why you and I are here on earth. The mystery of man on earth is: sanctification – we are here for the proofing of our soul.

Calamity happened, the Spirit hovered, and then God created time to help man understand this period in earth history – which has a beginning and an end.

> "Then God said, "Let there be light"... so the evening and the morning were the first day" (Gen. 1:3-5 abbreviated).

It is very important to perceive what happened in Heaven because it explains what continues to happen to us, but in order for us to fully comprehend what happened, we need to insert – between Genesis verse 1:1 and verse 1:2 – the cataclysm in Heaven (the war between God and His angels fighting a spiritual battle against Satan and his angels; Ezekiel 28:11-19; Isa. 14:12-16; Rev. 21:7-9). All teachers of truth understand the enormous responsibility of not adding to scripture or taking any away, so I am merely inserting prophetic text into chronological order to help us comprehend what happened... and what continues to happen to us as a result.

God created earth, Satan initiated a rebellion, then Satan was cast to earth and Satan's presence rendered earth chaotic and disorderly, and then God initiated His plan of regeneration (Regenesis):

> "And the Spirit of God hovered" (Gen. 1:2).

Satan set up his counterfeit kingdom in rebellion against God which the scriptures refer to as "the kingdom of darkness" which operates according to sin. It was through one man, Satan, that sin entered "the world":

> "The man who made the earth tremble, who shook kingdoms, [17] who made the world as a wilderness and destroyed its cities..." (Isa. 14:16, 17).

Ok, so let's put this in some sort of chronological order:

A. Eden is called the holy mountain of God, and also the garden of God – which is "earth" in her pre-captive Paradise glory (Ezek. 28:12-19)

B. Satan's attempt to take God's glory captive and ascend above heaven (higher than God) instigated a war against God in heaven which resulted in him being cast from heaven onto earth, and the appearance of this angelic star's departure from heaven looked much like lightening, according to Jesus (Luke 10:18)
C. God cast Satan and his rebellious angels out of Eden (Heaven) to earth – along with one third of heaven's angels (also called stars or fiery stones), but not all these angels were part of the rebellion (as some were taken captive in the rebellion)
D. Satan was utterly destroyed and turned to ash, yet being full of great wrath, he searches to and fro over the earth to torment men, but he cannot take human life (see Job 1:12; 2:6)

When Satan set up his counterfeit kingdom on earth, the operating system of this rebellious kingdom was based upon: sin. However, the church's doctrine of sin teaches us things which are inconsistent with scripture like "through one man, Adam" sin entered into the world, but as you can see – sin and darkness were already in the world as a result of Satan being cast here. Sin was here… and sin was presented to Eve in the form of Satan's temptation in the Garden. Sin's desire has always been to tempt mankind and corrupt our thought process so we act independently of God, sin against God and enter into rebellion against God which results in spiritual death. Read below where sin originates:

> "So the LORD said to Cain, "Why are you angry? And why has your countenance fallen? [7] If you do well, will you not be accepted? ***And if you do not do well, sin lies at the door. And its desire is for you,*** but you should rule over it" (Gen. 4:6,7)

Sin (it's a thing) lies at the door (as the threshold of a doorway), and "it" desires to have you… and it desires to keep you in bondage to "it."

But you must rule over "it"!

This imagery is absolutely incredible. Where is this door located? In your heart! Jesus called Himself the Door (John 10:7-9) and Jesus is the only way to get to the Father... which is through the Door. However, there is a "thing" that lies at the Door (the threshold of offence) that prevents many from entering through the door of their salvation. This "thing" varies from person to person, yet everyone must step over "it" (i.e. rebellion against God) in order to be saved.

Your current life is temporary. Your salvation, however, is dependent upon repentance from this rebellion and entering into faithful obedience to Jesus – who is Lord of heaven and earth.

Adam and Eve did not pass along sin to their children – as church's doctrine of sin teaches! What an evil, presumptuous, and preposterous thought! Sin is what we do on an individual basis to turn away from God's plan of redemption to stay in rebellion. We are sojourners walking through the valley of the shadow of death in a swamp of sin wherein we are being tempted to sin against God every day – and stay in bondage to "it." Sin is not part of man's true nature; we are spiritual beings (souls) with a divine nature (our spirit; 2 Pet. 1:4). Having a sinful nature (as the NIV erringly implies) contradicts God's plan and purpose for man on Earth.

Avoid evil, but do not fear evil. Fear the Lord! Walk in the light!

> "And to man He said, 'Behold, the fear of the Lord, that is wisdom, and to depart from evil is understanding' " (Job. 28:28).

> "The fear of the Lord *is* the beginning of wisdom; a good understanding have all those who do *His commandments*. His praise endures forever" (Psa. 111:10)

Darkness may be likened to a sea of evil and sin covering the entire planet... and this world in which man lives became an unregenerate wilderness in need of salvation (Luke 4:1). Even the earth needs a Savior to "take away the sin of this world" (John 1:29), and this is why "creation groans" waiting for the sons of God to be revealed (Rom. 8:22). This is why the scripture indicates we were all born in sin (Psa. 51:5), not because original sin was passed down to us through our parents as Catholic doctrines erringly teach, but because we were born into a place swamped in sin called: "this world." Sin is the operating system of this world – and we were all born into it – but One Person was born into sin… but never sinned: Jesus Christ – our Redeemer!

Sin is any willful disobedience and rebellion against God. Babies, however, are born in a state of grace and little children remain in that state until they are able to understand right from wrong – yet at some point everyone willingly enters into sinful disobedience of our own free will.

> ***"The earth is the Lord's, and all its fullness,***
> ***the world and those who dwell therein" (Psa. 24:1).***

"The earth is the Lord's" yet was rendered "void and formless" by sin's evil presence. Sin has the same effect upon man as it had on the earth; it renders us lost, void and "utterly destroyed."

A very important distinction must be clarified at this point: the terms "earth" and "world" represent two kingdoms on this celestial planet. Jesus is Lord of Heaven and Earth, yet when questioned by Pontius Pilate, Jesus said: "My kingdom is not of *this world*" (John 18:36). The earth is under the operational control of Jesus; He is Lord of Heaven and Earth. This world, however, is under the temporary operational control of Satan as the dominion of sin. Satan set up a counterfeit kingdom governed by sin, lies, doubt and deception.

Jesus, however, came to testify to the truth. And Jesus said (concerning the sons of men):

> "You are not of the world, but I chose you out of the world, therefore the world hates you" (John 15:19)

This radically different view of two kingdoms in opposition to one another (and your identity within one or the other) will set revelation fires in your mind to seek the truth regarding your reason and purpose for being on earth. Your identity is found – in Christ!

"You are the light of the world. (Matt. 5:14) Jesus put the light of His truth in you (your spirit) for you to illuminate His truth into this world of darkness as His "manifested" agent of change. Your spirit is the "divine nature" God formed within you (2 Pet. 1:4; Zech. 12:1) to overcome this world of darkness with "truth." "The spirit of a man is the lamp of the Lord" (Prov. 20:27).

"You are the salt of the earth. (Matt. 5:13) You are the "new earth" seasoning that Jesus is using to flavor the earth with the character attributes of Christ in you. You are spiritual MSG (messenger of saving grace) that was sent to share the good news of Jesus and save other souls from pollution and condemnation.

"Your light is for "the world" yet your salt is for "the earth."
Your dominion over the earth that was granted to you by God is a two-fold commission: to take authority over the kingdom of darkness (with light) and to establish the kingdom of heaven on earth (as salt). Ask Him what He purposed and planned for you (your commission) since before the foundation of this world and I guarantee this: it will change the world! ***<u>That is your purpose… because that is His plan</u>***.

"You were sent here to come against and overthrow the kingdom of darkness. ***This is your primary purpose for being on earth – to occupy earth – have dominion*** – fight against Satan – and to fill the earth with glory."[15]

> "One generation passes away, and another generation comes; but the earth abides forever" (Eccl. 1:4).

---

[15] Excerpt from "The Renewed Mind" section titled: "Earth vs. This World."

Darkness Exposed

Within the definition of darkness is the inherent loss of hope of ever attaining light again. Thank you Father for providing your own Solution: Jesus Christ!

Darkness (which God called Night; Gen. 1:5) divides one day from another. Night was not included as part of the Day (which includes evening and morning), but was considered a "non day." The Hebrew day began in the morning (see Gen. 19:33-35; Judges 19:9; 1 Sam. 19:11). The idea of a calendar day that includes both light and darkness is a cultural phenomenon.

Nonetheless, Night is not an intrinsic component of Day for a very good reason: in the regeneration – Night (darkness) does not exist. When the Lord creates new heavens and a New Earth, there will no longer be any darkness to war against the saints of God; the Lamb of God will be our Light. Read this description of the New Jerusalem in the regeneration:

> "But I saw no temple in it, for the Lord God Almighty and the Lamb are its temple. [23] The city had no need of the sun or of the moon to shine in it, for the glory of God illuminated it. The Lamb *is* its light" (Rev.21:22, 23).

However, there will still be darkness. This may seem like a contradiction in terms, so consider where the Lord told us He will send all hypocrites, wicked servants, unprofitable stewards, and those persons judged unworthy of the resurrection of life; in the resurrection of condemnation they are cast into outer darkness where there is weeping and gnashing of teeth (Matt. 7:22, 23; 8:12; 22:11-13; 24:50, 51; 25:12, 30; Jude 13). Read them all!!! In my opinion, these souls will know the light is near, but they are eternally unable to have it again. They know they should have sought the Lord more and dedicated their whole life (heart, mind and soul) to serving Him, but instead – they chose to build the kingdom of self rather than the kingdom of heaven on earth. And this is why they weep and gnash their teeth: because they refused to go all in! They could have done more, they could have prayed more, they could have cared for the least of these, they could have honored Him more with praise and thanksgiving, they could have worshipped more in spirit and in truth…but no!!! They could be enjoying the bliss of Paradise with Jesus, and they could have inherited the kingdom, but they chose mediocrity and complacency instead of being a disciple… and going all in! Yet outer darkness is preferable to the lake of fire.

> "But the cowardly, unbelieving, abominable, murderers, sexually immoral, sorcerers, idolaters, and all liars shall have their part in the lake which burns with fire and brimstone, which is the second death" (Rev. 21:8).

This should serve as a wake-up call to believers and make-believers in church: do not behave as the world does. Claiming faith in Jesus yet living a life that contradicts the truth Jesus taught – is worse than hypocrisy – it is treasonous rebellion!

How then shall we live? Walk as sons and daughters of light!

> "You are all sons of light and sons of the day. We are not of the night nor of darkness" (1 Thess. 5:5).

The battle you fight today – which sanctifies and transforms the character of your soul – must reject this world and live according to goodness, godliness, righteousness and truth (Eph. 5:9).

The soul you have right now (which is your mind and heart) – is the same soul you will "be" in eternity. You get a new body, but your soul does not get "upgrades." If you were to die right now – some of us would not even want to live as us or with us in that condition for eternity.

The battle you fight today and tomorrow – is for your future destiny in eternity.

Choose today who you will serve, but as for me and my house, we will love and serve the Lord!

Go all in! In Jesus' name, Amen.

Battle Waged On Earth

Every kingdom going to war will have a battle plan for success. Before we discuss this aspect, let's talk about what happened that caused this cosmic battle.

Lucifer was a marvelous angel, whose body was an instrument of worship and was adorned with every precious jewel. At some point, Lucifer received God's glory yet decided to keep it to himself. This was an act of treason, yet Lucifer did not stop there. He was able to deceive and convince one-third of Heaven to follow him whereby a great cataclysm in Heaven resulted.

> "You were in Eden, the garden of God; every precious stone *was* your covering: the sardius, topaz, and diamond, beryl, onyx, and jasper, sapphire, turquoise, and emerald with gold. The workmanship of your timbrels and pipes was prepared for you on the day you were created" (Ezek. 28:13).

Lucifer was in the Garden of God called: Eden. This point will be very important when we get toward the end of this book.

Lucifer's angels made war against the Lord's angels. How long this war lasted is unknown to man, but Lucifer was cast out of Heaven onto a planet called Earth whereby he established the kingdom of darkness. God's people responsible for managing the dominion of earth, who were as yet not formed, are about to be thrust into the middle of Satan's war of rebellion against the Lord's army (angels in Heaven) and the sons of men (saints of God) for dominion of Earth.

This next point is essential to comprehend: mankind has been under attack since the day we got here. There are many theories and explanations for how and when we got here, but the important point to know is this: ever since the beginning of this new era in earth history, mankind has been under attack by a demonic army that is in open rebellion against the Lord of Heaven and Earth – whereby it takes out its vitriolic hatred of Jesus against the sons of men (the host of earth).

If the outstretched hand of the Lord had not protected us, and the Spirit not hovered over us… our story would have ended in disaster long ago.

Here, now, is the Lord's battle plan to redeem creation:

1. Establish a new point of time for earth called: beginning anew (Gen. 1:1)
2. Initiate the plan of regeneration to make all things new again – on the Eighth Day
3. Create man as the host (army) of earth to have dominion over earth (Gen. 1:26; 2:7)
4. Create new things (Gen. 2:4-6)
5. Restore everything in newness – through truth, change and oneness
6. On the last day, resurrection happens followed by regeneration
7. "Make all things new [again]" (Rev. 21:5)

> "Behold, I create new heavens and a new earth; and the former shall not be remembered or come to mind" (Isa. 65:17).

In the regeneration, God is *not* going to make all new things … He is going to make all things *new again*. The Lord will "create new heavens" which seems to go against our doctrine of heaven which implies heaven is perfect and heaven is man's final destination (which it isn't – the New Earth is). This book explains Heaven (capital H – God's throne) is perfect and does not need regeneration, but there are other places in relation to the heavens (or heavenly places) that will be made new again in the regeneration.

So what is the regeneration anyway? This is one of the main subjects the Lord has called me to write about. The word regeneration *'palinegenesia*-3824' literally means: "genesis again." In a nutshell way of explaining things... we are going back to the beginning – to Paradise in Eden – in which righteousness dwells.

> "Nevertheless we, according to His promise, look for new heavens and a new earth in which righteousness dwells" (2 Pet. 3:13).

> "Now I saw a new heaven and a new earth, for the first heaven and the first earth had passed away. Also there was no more sea" (Rev. 21:1).

Sanctification is the renewal process whereby we are being transformed to become what we were to begin with: sons and daughters of God! Yield to the Spirit's sanctification of your mind and heart – and embrace the love of Christ.

What Is Darkness?

It's really important to understand this spiritual truth: everything in the universe had a state of existence before a physical or material state began... and this is true with the origin of man as well. This concept is very hard for man's mind to comprehend, so let me help you create a word picture in your mind: close your eyes and design something in your mind (either a garden, the layout of a room with furniture, a house, a bookcase, or even the menu for a dinner party with table settings). Everything you've just created exists as thoughts in your mind (in a spiritual state) that waits for you to take action before it materializes in physical form.

God created everything by the thought of His intellect, and then He spoke them into existence.

And so do you!

Many of us have been taught that darkness is the opposite of light, but it isn't. Darkness isn't the opposite of light – ***darkness is the absence of light***! Something happened on earth that resulted in the absence of light. The Spanish word for darkness is '*obscuridad*' – darkness obscured the glory of God's kingdom on earth behind a veil called: sin. This is a critical point in earth history which is illustrated by the presence of sin; darkness covered the earth. All of it! God didn't bring judgment. Satan brought destruction!

Mankind has read over the Genesis 1 verses so quickly without understanding the basic problem. Before moving forward onto verse three in Genesis (chapter one), earth history and creation was thought and conceived by God's intellect… and then He spoke it into existence… and it was very good! This spiritually enlightened perspective of creation culminates in…

> "This is the history of the heavens and the earth
> when they were created, in the day that the LORD
> God made the earth and the heavens…" (Gen. 2:4).

The first six days describe the history of earth… and then the history of God's plan begins to unfold in the next couple verses with the introduction of the first human. God made "everything" in Genesis 1 by the thought of His intellect and then God began creating and forming the things He made (Gen. 2:4-7).

> "… before any plant of the field was in the earth
> and before any herb of the field had grown. For the
> LORD God had not caused it to rain on the earth, and
> there was no man to till the ground; [6] but a mist
> went up from the earth and watered the whole face
> of the ground" (Gen. 2:5, 6).

The key to understanding this truth will continue to guide you in how the kingdom of God operates: God thinks things into a spiritual state of existence, and then God acts to manifest (create) those things He "made" by the thoughts of His mind. And man operates the same way!

We think things into being by the thought of our intellect. You "made" a bookshelf in your mind which enables you to "create" it. And God did the same thing in Genesis regarding the earth – and man. He "made" it, then He "created" it and then He "formed" it.

So, what's the purpose of knowing this detail regarding creation? A): to help you see how the kingdom of God operates because… you operate the same way God does. He created you "in His Own image according to His likeness" to think like Him, operate like Him, act like Him and accomplish His plan of regeneration for earth. When God speaks of things as though they are – yet are not, He does so with the authority and power to think it – and then manifest an expressed utterance (spoken word) into material form. Expression – and manifestation! This is how the kingdom of God operates! We think it – we speak it. We express it – we manifest it! Don't focus on formation. Form follows function! Formation is God's department. Function precedes formation! All of your words (and mine) are spirit – and power – and then the material utterance is made audible through our mouth. That's when God takes over. Our words are spirit (as being constructed by thoughts in our mind). However, what comes out of our mouth is capable of producing either life or death. Study these three verses carefully:

> Jesus said: "It is the Spirit who gives life; the flesh profits nothing. ***The words that I speak to you are spirit, and they are life***" (John 6:63).
>
> "Death and life are in the power of the tongue" (Prov. 18:21).
>
> "Out of the same mouth proceed blessing and cursing. My brethren, these things ought not to be so" (James 3:10).

With our tongue, we bless and create life – or we curse and destroy life.

What possible reason does this have to do with the Genesis account of earth and man? Because darkness is the manifestation of thoughts conceived and uttered by Satan that are hostile toward God. Every thought has an origin. Darkness is the absence of light because it rejected the light because - it did not comprehend the light – or the love of God.

Jesus is Love Incarnate! Jesus is the Light (John 8:12; 9:5)!

> "And the light shines in the darkness, and the darkness did not comprehend it" (John 1:5).

Darkness hates Light!!! And darkness hates you – and love – and the kingdom of light as well!

The problem we have in church today is this: sons of light don't comprehend darkness! In fact, church members play with it! They watch zombie shows and violent criminal programs that desensitize them to manifestations of darkness. We should be waging war against chaos, but we entertain our mind with it. We are clueless about the methods of darkness and remain woefully unaware of its influence around us. Study very carefully these next couple paragraphs.

Consider what happened after King Jesus made a covenant with Abram (Gen. 15:1-11)… Abram went to sleep – and darkness attacked him (verse 12). If King Jesus is there with Abram, then why was darkness allowed to manifest itself against Abram? The correct understanding of this event was reveled to me recently after I experienced the same thing. Our church had just finished a conference to initiate revival wherein great power and fire was released for three days. On the morning of the third day, I was awake at 5:12 AM to hear a voice say to me: "Get ready to go on a long trip." So I asked the Lord for more details, and then a tremendous weightiness came upon me which I initially thought was the '*kabod*' (H3519) of God's presence, so I called out to Him – but heard no reply. Then the weightiness got darker and heavier as I felt my body being physically pushed into the bed. This weighty darkness upon me has happened at least six times in seven years, but this time – something different happened – I felt this dark entity insert hands under me and begin to lift my spirit out of me – even as it pushed my body down. This – wasn't – God! So I called on the name Jesus three times and the heaviness left. I prayed in tongues until daybreak.

What was the lesson of Abram (and mine) trying to teach us? A: ***darkness is ever-present and it seeks to destroy the destiny and testimony of everyone walking with the Lord***.

Consider the first time the Lord appeared to Abraham (Gen. 12:7)… when he got to his destination… darkness created a famine in the land. When the Lord spoke with Abraham (Gen. 15:1-12) darkness and great terror seized him (v.12). Consider what happened when Jesus told the disciples to go to the other side of the lake (Mark 6:48): a storm arose against them. Does Satan really have power over natural forces? Yes, he does! A similar event happened previously with Jesus in the boat, but this time Jesus rebuked the wind and waves (Luke 8:22-25). At that moment, Jesus was teaching His disciples – faith must arise – in order to rebuke demonic forces whenever things rise up and work against your Godly commission and mission (which in this case... was for disciples to get to the other side).

Famines do not happen instantly, which is why some may deny the ability of darkness to affect weather, but Abram's journey to cover about 680 miles likely took many years – with clearly enough time for demonic forces to create a famine in the land of Abram's destination.

Some may doubt the ability of dark demonic forces to affect weather, but it can and it does!!! Did the outstretched hand of Moses part the Red Sea? Yes! Did Ezekiel prophetically speak to dry bones and breath came back into regenerated beings (Ezek. 37:1-10)? Yes! Don't our doctrines teach some sicknesses are the result of sin and disobedience (1 Cor. 11:30)? Yes! It seems our own doctrines teach us we can effect changes in our human anatomy, so why do we doubt demonic influenced weather and climate changes within their own demonic kingdom on earth? Now... here is the real eye opener: what do you suppose is the real cause behind global warming? Yes – darkness! And what is the solution these global warming alarmists propose? More control through a one-world antichrist government called – the United Nations!

Wake up, church!!! Darkness is cunning, fear-based, deceitful – and diabolical. Abortion began in the 1970's as a global effort to control population explosion. Global warming is no different!

One of the most important take-a-ways from this book is: understanding the global impacts of darkness upon the earth and its negative impacts upon man and God's plan of redemption.

Perhaps the most interesting scripture in need of divine wisdom to comprehend it this:

> "I form the light and create darkness, I make peace and create *calamity*; I, the Lord, do all these things" (Isa. 45:7; the KJV says: I make peace and create *evil*).

So I ask: who created the darkness? The Lord did. Who is the Lord? Jesus. Why in the world would the Lord do this, you might ask, since Jesus is Lord of Heaven and Earth? If darkness is considered evil and contradictory to light and goodness – and is opposed to God's kingdom – then why would the Lord create it in the first place? Ponder deep mysteries – and you will receive deep revelation! The reason is woven into the most beautiful mystery found within God's crowning jewel of creation:

Free will!

In order for anyone to know what something is, there needs to be something to compare it to: i.e. a corresponding opposite. For example: heat cannot be known unless cold is also present. There are degrees of hot and cold by the presence of one and/or the absence of the other. The same is true with love/hate, obedience/rebellion, order/lawlessness, good/evil, light/darkness. Perceiving one – enables us to perceive the other.

Why did God create darkness and evil? A: to give us choices when acting upon free will. If there was only one choice, then it would not be a choice – and we would be automatons and puppets.

All this blather seems like a long way around the mountain, but it goes to the core and substance of why you and I are here in the first place. Darkness covered the earth… but God didn't put the darkness there. Someone spoke it into existence – and his name is Lucifer. Darkness represents the spiritual reality where God's presence is not manifested. Darkness can be manifested by persons, families, communities, towns, cities, nations, organizations, cultures, and ideologies to form a particular way of thinking which acts – in dark ways – according to darkness. All darkness is evil… yet acting on evil is a choice. We see this in the news every day when a person takes another human life in a vile or merciless manner… or they speak deceitful lies.

Lucifer was cast out of Heaven and landed on Earth, whereby he spoke darkness into existence. Renamed Satan, and the Devil, and the prince of the power of the air, he created the kingdom of darkness whereby even planet earth became a captive prisoner to his domination. The entire earth has been under his control since that moment; however, the Lord created a plan to take back and recover what Satan stole from God:

"And the Spirit of God hovered" (Gen. 1:2)!!!

This new plan must be seen for what it is: God's battle plan to redeem earth from the prince of darkness (Eph. 2:2). This battle plan is what we read about in Genesis, so read it again with this perspective in mind:

- In the beginning, God created (by the thoughts of His intellect) the heavens and the earth, whereby God envisions what this restored kingdom on earth will look like

- Now… darkness covered the earth. God's presence was not manifested on earth. How long the earth was in this state of darkness is important yet likewise – irrelevant
- The Spirit of God hovers over the face of the waters (Gen. 1:2) – like "a mothering stork over her brood" is oftentimes the analogy used in this word picture, but we need to see this as the restraining hand of God that contains darkness and keeps it restrained for a purpose (which we'll get to)

God's battle plan to redeem the earth continues by envisioning things as they will be – but as yet are not. This is how God operates: He speaks of things as though they are, though not yet being. God manifested creation in this manner, and man is able to manifest many things in this same manner. God created us this way, not only to represent Him – but also to act like Him!

God envisioned something absolutely remarkable… a creature called man… created in His Own Image… and gave him the spiritual ability to operate according to His likeness (just like Him!).

> "Let Us make man in our image according to our likeness…" (Gen. 1:26).

This story of a new beginning in earth history is about to get very interesting! Man is going to be given a purpose... a divine commission by God to operate on earth under His authority… and operate like Him… with power, and have dominion over the darkness. "Whatever you loose on earth is loosed in heaven."

> Jesus told His disciples: "And I will give you the keys of the kingdom of heaven, and whatever you bind on earth will be bound in heaven, and whatever you loose on earth will be loosed in heaven" (Matt. 16:19).

Allow this truth to permeate every aspect of your consciousness because – it's why you're here!

You were activated for duty to be a soldier servant to take back, redeem, recover, hold onto, push forward and advance the kingdom of heaven – by pushing against darkness and taking back this planet stolen by Satan. Allow this truth to permeate every aspect of your consciousness!

"God created us good and upright as His representatives and His workmanship to produce good works! That is our reason and purpose for being on earth, but 'evil' represents the invisible, diabolic entity of Satan and his demonic army to produce chaos and disorder on earth in the kingdom of darkness – to tempt us to sin – in order to destroy us and prevent us from doing God's redemptive work on earth. This is the big, big picture that explains why things happen."[16]

Some astute students of scripture may have perceived a disconnect by now, such as – why didn't God just eliminate sin and toast everything on earth by destroying Satan and the kingdom darkness before ever introducing mankind? Well, I'm so glad you asked because this goes to the core and substance of what we are – and why we are here. Men (mankind) are co-redeemers[17] sent by God as "spirits" (Luke 9:55) to save souls taken captive by Satan in sin! When Satan was cast out of heaven along with many angels (now devils) and demonic minions, the scriptures record some "persons" were taken captive during this cataclysmic event in heaven (read below). For the sake of this remnant that was taken captive against their will, God would never destroy an entire planet (it's the message of Sodom and Gomorrah and the lesson of the Great Flood). For the sake of a remnant, sons of men were sent to earth and are going through this torturous process for the redemption of fallen angels taken captive and bound in prison in the kingdom of

---

[16] Excerpt from "Regenesis" section titled: "Truth, Faith and Sin In Perspective."

[17] Some denominations might bristle with this concept of men being co-redeemers by saying God is the only Redeemer! However, God created us to act like Him and Jesus said we are to imitate Him, so please read Ex. 21:8-30; Lev. 19:20; Lev. 25; Neh. 5:7-9 and especially the book Ruth.

darkness. This is what earthly soldiers of the Lord do: they win battles and set captives free.

> "The Spirit of the Lord GOD *is* upon Me, because the LORD has anointed Me to preach good tidings to the poor; He has sent Me to heal the brokenhearted, ***to proclaim liberty to the captives, and the opening of the prison to those who are bound***; ² to proclaim the acceptable year of the LORD, and the day of vengeance of our God; to comfort all who mourn, ³ ***to console those who mourn in Zion***, to give them beauty for ashes, the oil of joy for mourning, the garment of praise for the spirit of heaviness; that they may be called trees of righteousness, the planting of the LORD, that He may be glorified" (Isa. 61:1-3).

"To console those who mourn in Zion" represents a people group who are above the realm of this devastation who look down with dread in their eyes.

> "Therefore rejoice, O heavens, and you who dwell in them! Woe to the inhabitants of the earth and the sea! For the devil has come down to you, having great wrath, because he knows that he has a short time" (Rev. 12:12).

Consider what the Lord spoke to the prophet Isaiah regarding Satan:

> "Those who see you will gaze at you, and consider you, saying: '***Is this the man*** who made the earth tremble, who shook kingdoms, ¹⁷ who made the world as a wilderness and destroyed its cities, ***who did not open the house of his prisoners***?'" (Isa. 14:16, 17).

And again:

> "Thus says God the LORD, Who created the heavens and stretched them out, Who spread forth the earth and that which comes from it, Who gives breath to the people on it, and spirit to those who walk on it: ⁶ "I, the LORD, have called You in righteousness, and will hold Your hand; I will keep You and give You as a covenant to the people, as a light to the Gentiles, ⁷ **to open blind eyes, to bring out prisoners from the prison, those who sit in darkness from the prison house**" (Isa. 42:5-7).

This theme occurs within the New Testament as well. The apostles were put in prison by the High Priest and Sadducees...

> "But at night an angel of the Lord opened the prison doors and brought them out, and said, ²⁰ 'Go, stand in the temple and speak to the people all the words of this life' " (Acts 5:19, 20).

"The words of this life" which the apostles proclaimed... is the Word of Life, which is the testimony of Jesus Christ. Our primary mission on earth is to have dominion – and proclaim the same message Jesus proclaimed and set prisoners free:

> "Repent, for the kingdom of heaven is at hand" (Matt. 4:17).

Captivity is a theme throughout scripture... as is redemption. Liberty through repentance – are words of life for captives and prisoners sitting in darkness.

Redemption is made known to us through two related words: '*apolutrosis*' (629) and '*lutrosis*' (3085-a ransoming) are both translated "redemption in the sense of deliverance" as a "releasing for payment of a ransom" and indicates the act of freeing and releasing "prisoners" by paying a ransom price; it includes the act of buying back (family lands and members) by paying a ransom such that those persons and lands are "totally set free, never to be sold again."[18]

"If everything belongs to God, then why would He have to pay a ransom to redeem and buy it back? And more so, who had it and how did they get it? This was stolen from God by Satan and was being held captive by him. So, why didn't God just go and get it back? Well, that is exactly what He purposed to do, and the will of God determined the host of earth (aka the sons of men) should recover it and give God the glory in it."[19] God – sent – you!!!

The Lord is Sovereign over all creation including heaven and earth... and man. What we need to perceive at this point is the true reason why we are on earth and what has been happening since the beginning. Satan set up a counterfeit kingdom on earth that operates in rebellious opposition against the kingdom of God. Satan, who is a slave to sin, took earth captive and made it – and all dwelling in it – a slave to sin. Enter, stage left, is God's battle plan to redeem it and take it back:

> "... and let them have dominion over all the earth" (Gen 1:26-28; condensed).

Did you sense a shift in your soul when you read that? This is your reason for being here! You and I are part of God's battle plan as the host (army) of earth to retake earth from Satan – and set captives free – in the name of Jesus. The Apostle Paul said:

> "...this grace was given, that I should preach among the Gentiles the unsearchable riches of Christ, [9] and to make all see what *is* the fellowship of the mystery, which from the beginning of the ages has been hidden in God who created all things through Jesus Christ; [10] to the intent that **now the manifold wisdom of God might be made known by the**

---

[18] Strong's Concordance.
[19] Excerpt from "Image" section titled: "Once Upon A Cross."

church to the principalities and powers in the heavenly *places,* [11] according to the eternal purpose which He accomplished in Christ Jesus our Lord..." (Eph. 3:8-11).

You and I were created and sent here to effect a regime change in the name of Jesus Christ! You are I are members of "the Church" which is Christ's Body which is administered by the Holy Spirit for pulling down strongholds in heavenly places and setting captives free.

If the gospel message being preached in your church is not the message of liberty that sets captives free, then they didn't understand the Message of the Messenger.

We are here as members of the church militant to fight against principalities, powers and strongholds with the weapons of love, faith, hope, truth, righteousness and prayer. Our fight is not against flesh and blood (other people) because man is not the problem. Sin is! The kingdom of darkness is! Rebellion against God is! Antichrist is! Get your armor on and let's get going!

Dominion – is the delegated authority with power given to a subordinate to act on behalf of a king or sovereign. Both kingdoms have dominion, but only one kingdom lasts forever.

God gave us dominion over the earth which not only includes everything on the planet itself, but more to the point...also the kingdom of darkness that Satan established. Man was – and continues to be – inserted into the timeline of earth history to accomplish one primary task: have dominion. God's original intent for man was to have dominion over all things on earth under God's governance, but once we got here... the tables were turned on us by a diabolical demonic entity known as sin – and we became captive to darkness in sin which always results in spiritual death. And to make it worse – sin blinds us from perceiving our true identity in Christ.

Satan's curse over us needed to be broken. Christ our Redeemer came to break the curse and set all captives free. ***Liberty or death… is the New Earth battle cry of the redeemed to sinners who are blinded by sin and remain bound in sin.***

"Have dominion" is God's first command to man. We were given His authority with power to act, but so often is the case, man uses these God-given gifts to accomplish his own agenda, whereby the history of man on the earth has been a constant tug-of-war between dominion and domination. Unregenerate man seems chiefly concerned with his ability to promote himself, as well as peoples and nations upon the earth supporting his agenda. In contrast, the history of man's true nature, as a spiritual being residing upon the earth, has been a biblical history of God's commission to enlist the sons of men as agents of His redemption to usher in a regime change. These two dominions by two radically different people groups create two radically different kingdoms upon the earth, which has created a constant dynamic tension between true faith – and a counterfeit reality. One reality is based upon a lie, while the paradigm of Christ is based on truth: it's all about Jesus and Jesus is the Truth (John 14:6).

Sin – is an "it" that deceives us by questioning God's truth and rejects the good and upright attributes God put in us when He created us, and then rejects God's numerous, wonderful and good thoughts toward us all the time. Sin's desire is to master us as slaves in darkness – but you must exercise mastery of "it."

Are you getting a better sense of the big picture? You were made and created by God as the host of earth – and you had a spiritual state of existence in God's presence before you were sent to earth as an invading army to come against the kingdom of darkness with the light of truth. Most people would find conflict in that last statement – and indeed many must – because it conflicts with the understanding of man they were taught in church and Sunday school. How can I say we had a prior state of existence in God's presence? Pay careful attention to this verse:

> "The history of creation of heaven and earth was finished including the host of them" (Gen. 2:1).

This is the history of creation. The only problem is… nothing has been created yet. How can God say something is one way yet the evidence a few verses later contradicts it? Well, my friend, that's because you are thinking like a human again; you need to start thinking the way God thinks. When He thinks it, He then speaks it into existence… from a spiritual perspective.

And you are the same way. Take, for example, if you watch your child do something incredibly childish and you might say to them, "That was stupid." This child will begin to think – I am stupid. Our perspectives on anything (children, sports, jobs, social reform, politics, religion) project attitudes and opinions that are entirely yours (rightly or wrongly), but when you share them '*dialogos*' (dialogue) "through words," you are making an official determination about something, and thus… causing it to come into existence. I grew up stupid, as did many of you. For this, I am so heartbroken for you… because that is not who you are.

Think of your words like the umpire in a baseball game. The runner and the ball arrive at base at nearly the exact same moment, and in this moment, the umpire must make a call. Whatever comes out of his mouth will become reality regardless if his call is right or wrong. Do you see what I mean? We can think about making the call all day long, but until we utter something (or use a hand gesture) it's as if the play never happened.

God created everything (His battle plan), He said it was finished, He rested on the seventh day (not because He was tired but rather to show us, by example, that we need to enter into His rest), and then… BOOM! God began work again on the eighth day and we are still in this state of existence from God's perspective whereby we are all working on the second phase of creation called: God's plan of redemption and regeneration!

God put all the elements in place – and now – God is going to continue His work upon the earth with three secret weapons called:

KINGDOMS

man, resurrection and regeneration. God is even going to put a special covering upon man to hide his unique identity among all creation. Yes, that's right! Adam was a secret weapon... and so are you. The problem is, it seems, we've been prisoners behind enemy lines for so long we've forgotten about the mysterious 'thing' that was hidden within each of us. We've forgotten where we came from, and we've forgotten about our primary mission on earth: have dominion over the earth – including the kingdom of darkness!

In Genesis 2:1 (above), God finished creation – including the host of them. This is incredibly important for you to perceive: host means – army. Jesus is the Commander of the Army (singular) of the Lord, and there are two divisions in His army: a heavenly division (angels) and an earthly division (the sons of men). For example, the United States Marine Corps is divided into two divisions: artillery and infantry. In the Army of the Lord, we humans are the infantry; angels are the artillery. We fight the land battle and they fight the air campaign! Now do you understand why Satan is called the prince of the power of the air? And angels are a flame of fire? Beloved, I teach the truth: the day is coming when we will call upon our angelic brethren (Rev. 19:10) for air support just as Elijah did.

> "And you *He made alive,* who were dead in trespasses and sins, ^{2} in which you once walked according to the course of this world, ***according to the prince of the power of the air***, the spirit who now works in the sons of disobedience" (Eph. 2:1, 2; "this world" refers to the kingdom of darkness).

> "And of the angels He says: "Who makes His angels spirits and His ministers a flame of fire" (Heb. 1:7).

You are not just one person; you are one person within the host of earth (the army of earth) and your mission (dominion mandate) is to occupy earth. Your reason for being here is to occupy earth with the indwelling presence of God that was hidden within you (your spirit). Does everybody have this presence when they are born? Absolutely... but many are trained at an early age to reject God's presence in their life and adopt patterns that are sinful and demonic in nature. We were created in grace and we were sent here with grace, but most of us have been taught to reject grace, trip over the threshold of offence, and stumble freely into sin and open rebellion against God. All babies are born of grace and in grace – and have no knowledge or understanding of sin or darkness. Babies don't need salvation, but even when they become old enough to know and understand the difference between right and wrong, they may continue to walk in grace for many, many years until... "it" happens. Mary, the mother of Jesus, most likely walked in this state of grace when she conceived Jesus as a young teenage sinless virgin. Some kids are able to grow up this way, but they are few in number. In 2014, I spent three days in the presence of the Lord and did not sin. Grace! We are able to operate according to grace and live as little children without the knowledge of good and evil... but we need grace and truth in order to live this way. As the end of the age gets closer, the path for many will become very perilous even for children at a young age.

>"For the law was given through Moses, *but* grace
>and truth came through Jesus Christ" (John 1:17).

Since God's indwelling presence is within everyone, does that mean everyone goes to Heaven? No! Some religious sects teach this, which means they know probably more than some religions that God is everywhere and God is in everyone, but this indwelling is a temporary '*meno*' *place of staying*; however, God want us to establish a permanent '*mone*' *house* (dwelling place) in our heart for Him to abide eternally (John 14:23).

Every person that has ever existed on earth is an eternal soul that was created good and upright, and crowned with glory and honor. You do not have a soul, per se... you "are" a soul that is having a human experience on earth. You are not a human being in search of a spiritual experience... you are a spiritual being having a human experience! The enemy switched the terminology around and got us thinking backwards! In fact, much of what this world teaches us is upside-down, inside-out and backwards from the true spiritual reality that God created. Why? To keep you captive in sin and remain in disobedient rebellion against Him, just like Satan and his horde of devils and demons.

You had a prior state of existence in God's presence [20] before you were sent here with a commission to disperse the darkness with the spirit of life (divine nature; 2 Pet. 1:4) that God formed within you.

> "Thus says the LORD, who stretches out the heavens, lays the foundation of the earth, and *forms the spirit of man within him*" (Zech. 12:1).

What is our goal in life? To have dominion under the Lord's governance and take back, recover, redeem and set free everything Satan and the kingdom of darkness has taken captive. Yet this is more than just a rescue and recovery mission; we are here to advance the kingdom of heaven and establish it on enemy territory against a demonic army that is hell-bent on obliterating all presence of man upon earth. The enemy doesn't want your things, as some are inclined to think – the enemy wants you dead! Their goal is to obliterate you!

Look at all biblical and modern events from this perspective and you will see a continuous theme: forces are working against mankind to prevent him from staying close to God, doing well (spiritually) and living in peace. There have always been bad actors in this world under the influence of invisible elements that have compromised good people to do bad things in order to cause chaos and confusion. Read that sentence again and let it soak in.

This is the big picture concerning two kingdoms in conflict on

---

[20] You can discover more biblical examples by reading Psalms 8; 82:6, 7; 139:13-18; and esp. Prov. 8:22-31. Also Eph. 1:4. Even Sampson was known according to his life's work – before he was even conceived (Judges 13:2-8).

earth and why it seems man has been placed in the midst of a cosmic battle between good and evil. Well, now you know!

Man's initial establishment within the kingdom of darkness has much to teach us in this regard. A bad actor (Satan) tempted Eve and they forfeited much by acting upon it. They didn't just lose their place in Paradise, they surrendered their dominion authority – and glory – to Satan as well. Read carefully what Satan said to Jesus as he tempted Him in the wilderness:

> And the devil said to Him, "All this **authority** I will give You, **and their glory**; for this has been delivered to me, and I give it to whomever I wish" (Luke 4:6).

Where did Satan get his authority to have dominion on earth? He stole it from Adam and Eve… and whenever we enter into sin, we deliver our authority and glory to Satan as well. That's the bad news – and now here is the good news: Jesus recovered our authority after He was tempted by the Devil. Even though He was tempted just like every human on earth, Jesus did not "enter into" sin. Because the first man transgressed, another Man had to be sent that would nullify the transgression in order to restore our authority.

Dominion is often preached from man's perspective, but rarely understood from God's. The best way to put the dominion of earth into context is to follow this linear process:

- "And Jesus came and spoke to them, saying, "All authority has been given to Me in heaven and on earth" (Matt. 28:18).
- Dominion of heaven and earth in God's kingdom belongs to the Lord Jesus Christ; "For by Him all things were created that are in heaven and that are on earth, visible and invisible, whether thrones or **dominions** or principalities or powers. *All things were created through Him and for Him*" (Col. 1:16). "Then to Him was given dominion and glory and a kingdom, that all peoples, nations, and languages

should serve Him. His dominion is an everlasting dominion, which shall not pass away, *and His kingdom the one which shall not be destroyed*" (Dan. 7:14).
- The Lord God gave dominion of earth to the host of earth – mankind; "Then God said, "Let Us make man in Our image, according to Our likeness; ***let them have dominion*** over the fish of the sea, over the birds of the air, and over the cattle, ***over all the earth*** and over every creeping thing that creeps on the earth." (Gen. 1:26). "So God created man *in His own image*" (v.27) and our Creator's name is… Jesus Christ.
- Adam was put in the Garden of God with dominion in order to be a caretaker for the earth, but Adam delivered man's dominion to Satan when he successfully tempted Adam in getting him to rebel against God. This is the same dominion that Satan tempted Jesus with: "Then the devil, taking Him (Jesus) up on a high mountain, showed Him all the kingdoms of the world in a moment of time. [6] And the devil said to Him, "***All this authority*** I will give You, and their glory; for ***this has been delivered to me***, and I give it to whomever I wish. [7] Therefore, if You will worship before me, all will be Yours" (Luke 4:5-7).
- Jesus accomplished perfectly the will of the Father and got this dominion and all authority back. "At that time Jesus answered and said, "I thank You, *Father, Lord of heaven and earth*, that You have hidden these things from the wise and prudent and have revealed them to babes. [26] Even so, Father, for so it seemed good in Your sight. [27] *All things have been delivered to Me* by My Father, and no one knows the Son except the Father" (Matt. 11:25-27).
- And now Jesus has given it back to us; "Behold, I give you the authority to trample on serpents and scorpions, and over all the power of the enemy, and nothing shall by any means hurt you" (Luke 10:19).
- And furthermore, Jesus said: "And I will give you the keys of the kingdom of heaven, and whatever you bind on earth

will be bound in heaven, and whatever you loose on earth will be loosed in heaven" (Matt. 16:19).

This should help explain the complexity of man's purpose and reason for being on earth, as well as our positional relationship and subordinate dependence upon Jesus within a larger context. Our creeds and doctrines have correctly taught us "what" to believe, yet have difficulty explaining "why."

We were sent to earth to usher in a regime change – from darkness to light! We are world changers sent to manifest Christ's dominion – under His authority – with His power manifested through us.

Back on point: our initial parents sinned and forfeited much. Now let's scrutinize the first family. Two kids were born and then a time came for them to acknowledge something; one of them presented gifts to God that acknowledged Him as the source of all provision while the other took credit for what God did through him. Thus, Cain's offering was not acceptable to God and he became angry. We mess up and then get angry at God for it: situation normal… in this world.

Look carefully at what happens next: Cain is going to get advice from two persons: God and Satan. First in order, God will tell him the truth so Cain can do well…

"If you do well but sin lies at the door" and "it" desires to have you but you must rule over it.

Some may question the evidence of the other conversation since it isn't found in scripture, so let me show it to you from another perspective. Where did Cain get the idea to kill his brother? From Satan! No one had ever done such a thing before! God would never author such a thought because God is good all the time and God's *thoughts 'machashabah'* toward us are always good all the time, so it is impossible for Cain to have originated this idea to kill his brother. Our arch enemy: Satan – the destroyer – whispered it into Cain's mind. Satan cannot kill us, but he can deceive us to kill one another... and Abel became his first victim!

So I ask: who are you listening to?

Your soul has been in peril since the day you were born here, so who are you listening to? There are always three voices talking to you all the time: yours, God's and Satan's. You need to focus on One and silence the others. If you don't know how to do that, then read "Listen – How To Hear God's Voice – better" and start listening to the Voice that wants to save you and prevent calamity from happening to you.

Back to the point about your soul... there is one infinitely-important point you must also comprehend: your soul is eternal. Since your soul is eternal, it is eternal both pre- and post-humanity; it means you had a prior state of existence in God's presence which we've already discussed, you're having one now, and you will have another state of existence after the judgment. What you are doing now will decide where your soul will spend eternity. As I mentioned previously: the soul you have now is the soul you shall have in eternity.

We must be mindful and vigilant to properly tend to, nurture and protect our soul so we may continue to live eternally as we have dominion and accomplish others tasks on earth as well.

> "For the redemption of their souls *is* costly, and it shall cease forever— [9] that he should continue to live eternally, and not see the Pit" (Psa. 49:8, 9)

What good is life eternal... if you wind up in the wrong place?

Kingdoms In General

The kingdom of God is comprised of the kingdom of heaven and the place called hell. Since it exists, then a Creator created it... but the enemy does not have the power to create. Both kingdoms have armies. The army of heaven has two divisions: heaven and earth.

The army of earth operates in – "truth and righteousness." This is basic training, through faith, to determine our future place in the kingdom of heaven. The Commander of the Army of the Lord is Jesus Christ, and He is also Supreme Commander over the entire universe.

What, then, shall I tell you about God's kingdom on earth? How does it operate? Can you conjure a guess? It operates from faith. What shall I say to the person that does not operate from faith but rather from fear? Is such a person regarded as a faithful soldier? Can any person advance forward a column of soldiers against an enemy having fear or trepidation?

Fear is faith in reverse. The kingdom of God operates according to Faith and Love…

> "There is no fear in love; but perfect love casts out fear, because fear involves torment. But he who fears has not been made perfect in love" (1 John 4:12).

Fear enables Satan to act – yet faith allows God to act. When we operate from fear, we "enable" Satan to do something that he is permitted to do according the scriptures. Yes, that's true. God's word enables Satan to act (negatively) but only when we give him authority to act… which happens when we operate from fear. The converse is true as well. When we operate from faith, we are allowing God to act (positively) on our behalf. When we take this truth to either extreme, we see fear produces torment, yet faith produces love… and also greater works to establish God's kingdom in you and through you.

Faith can operate in two directions: stepping into faith (believing God to truth the action) and pressing into faith (going deeper in truth to imitate Jesus, become a disciple and claim His precious promises that He's made available for us – through faith). How many promises has God made? You may remember only a couple, but there are over 7,400 promises in the book of life, and since God promised them, then perhaps we should start operating from faith and start walking in them.

If you have prayed to the Lord to guide your steps and there seems to be conflicting messages, then perhaps the same message may be guiding you in two directions: walk toward the goal in faith or walk away by fear and confusion. Enter in – or walk away!

Like Abraham said to Lot (paraphrased): if you go left then I will turn and go right, or if you go right then I will turn and go left, but our very large herds cannot keep overgrazing this same pasture; we must separate. In one regard, the separation appears as a division of resources, but in reality, if they did not separate, then their resources would cease to multiply.

Receive, bless, divide, give. I heard a preacher's message about this spiritual principle regarding God's kingdom that always operates according to this principle: receive, bless, divide, give. This principle can be observed in the Lord's miracle of feeding five thousand, in the Last Supper, and in every biblical story where God's kingdom is being advanced.

Division creates an opportunity for multiplication on a kingdom scale. What may initially seem as a reduction, division or diminishment of your purpose or plans is actually working something out of you or from you in order to create multiplication in you and through you.

Divide some of your things, bless them, and give them away. Don't be like the Dead Sea where water flows in but nothing flows out. To hoard is a lack of faith and a lack of trust in the Lord to multiply what you have to advance the kingdom.

Your setbacks… may actually be setups by the Lord to increase your territory.

This is deep theology. We must become less in order to become more. This won't make sense to most because it contradicts the pattern of the worldly system we've been living in that has been engrained in us to think and act this way: get, have more, get more.

So I ask: which kingdom do you want to live in?

- In the creation narrative, God made man, blessed him, divided Eve from him and gave them a garden with a command: be fruitful and multiply
- In the earth narrative, everything belongs to God: He created man, blessed the earth, divided it into nations and kingdoms, and then He commissioned (let have; granted) it to rulers and kings
- In the tithe narrative, God owns everything. God gave it to us to steward properly and produce an increase (multiply), then we return the first portion (divide a tenth from it) as dedicated (holy means "set apart") unto the Lord, and this, then is given out to advance the kingdom of heaven on earth

Understanding how the kingdom of heaven operates on earth – is both a privilege and a responsibility given to born anew disciples to continue His works. Now that we know what to do – and why – it is incumbent upon every one of us to get busy!

> "But Jesus answered them, "My Father has been working until now, and I have been working" (John 5:17).

> Jesus said: "Do you not believe that I am in the Father, and the Father in Me? The words that I speak to you I do not speak on My own authority; but the Father who dwells in Me does the works" (John 14:10).

> "Most assuredly, I say to you, he who believes in Me, the works that I do he will do also; and greater works than these he will do, because I go to My Father" (John 14:12).

We were sent to have dominion over earth. We were given authority with power to implement a regime change. Greater works should always be at the forefront of church theology… but it isn't. For this reason the church age is over and the kingdom age has begun because…

> … it's time for a course correction!

"For this purpose the Son of God was manifested, that He might destroy the works of the devil" (1 John 3:8).

You are the Lord's representative! Go and do likewise!

Kingdoms In Conflict

Two kingdoms are fighting for dominion of earth. Sons of men were sent on behalf of the Lord as an army (the host of earth; Gen. 2:1) to come against the kingdom of darkness and chaos with the light of the spirit that God formed within them. Armed with the truth of the gospel and the testimony of Jesus, we are strengthened by grace through faith to operate our primary weapon i.e. truth... which is the sword of the Spirit.

> "For behold, the darkness shall cover the earth, and deep darkness the people; but the Lord will arise over you, and His glory will be seen upon you" (Isa. 60:2).

As mentioned earlier, it seems we have lost all understanding and comprehension regarding the kingdom of darkness upon the earth. Over the years, even some of my friends have regarded this word as merely a metaphor for sin and unbelief, which it is, and yet... darkness is also a veiled spiritual reality of evil that surrounds us – even now. The trick of the enemy is to deceive us and prevent us from perceiving the reality of evil and the existence of Satan whereby we remain unwitting slaves in bondage to sin and unbelief... thereby remaining unintelligent concerning spiritual matters and, thus, fail to establish the kingdom of heaven upon the earth.

Let's examine two passages of scripture to illuminate and illustrate two kingdoms in conflict: Genesis 1:1-2:4 and John 1:1-5.

> "In the beginning God created the heavens and the earth. [2] The earth was without form, and void; and darkness *was* on the face of the deep. And the Spirit of God was hovering ..." (Gen. 1:1, 2).

The earth is described as void and formless. Several Hebrew words[21] are used here:

- Darkness (*choshek*-2882) means: darkness, misery, destruction, death, ignorance, sorrow, wickedness; obscurity; from (*chashak*-2821) meaning: to be dark (as withholding light)
- Formless (*tohuw*-8414) means: to lie waste; desolation, i.e. a desert; fig. a worthless thing; is translated as: vain (4x), confusion (3x), without form (2x) wilderness (2x)
- Void (*bohuw*-922) means: to be empty; a vacuity; an undistinguishable ruin; emptiness

When we combine these words together, as the scripture has done, we get a very clear graphic representation what the surface of earth was like: it was utterly destroyed.

'Darkness' is best described as: chaotic. There was a prior condition of earth that was good and orderly, but something happened to make it chaotic (which was explained earlier "In The Beginning"). Earth was orderly when God created it, as is everything that God creates, yet something happened afterward (between the first and second sentence) that made it chaotic.

"The first five words of the bible tell a story. "In the beginning, God created" is a brief recap of an earlier creation event of the heavens and the earth by God (prior to Gen. 1:1). This is mentioned to help man understand his place within the context of time within eternity. The verb "created" is singular and means "to fashion anew."[22] Literally, creation is being fashioned anew from a previous version that was new. John, a New Testament apostle, describes this era that predated creation (John 1:1).

"'The earth was without form, and void; and darkness *was* on the face of the deep' (Gen. 1:2). The italicized word '*was*' is not found in the original Hebrew or Aramaic, and was added by

---

[21] All terms and definitions taken from Strong's Concordance.
[22] NKJV Study Bible, notes on Gen. 1:1, Thomas Nelson Publishers.

scholars to help us understand the message. It would also be helpful if scholars added another italicized word at the beginning of this verse to read, "*Now* – the earth was without form, and void"… for it speaks of a new moment in creation history."[23]

What the Lord is revealing to us becomes the basis for understanding why bad things happen to people on earth. Earth was orderly – then chaos happened. We are living in chaos! Yet we have a Way of escape. His name is Jesus, the Lord our God.

This next point is extremely important to comprehend: when Lucifer (Satan, the Devil) was cast to earth, he obliterated the earth and rendered it – chaotic! Earth became a wicked, vacuous, wilderness shrouded with darkness. And we are living within this sea of chaos and confusion surrounded by darkness.

> "So the great dragon was cast out, that serpent of old, called the Devil and Satan, who deceives the whole world; he was cast to the earth, and his angels were cast out with him" (Rev. 12:9).

> "How you are fallen from heaven, O Lucifer, son of the morning! *How* you are cut down to the ground, you who weakened the nations! [13] For you have said in your heart: 'I will ascend into heaven, I will exalt my throne above the stars of God; I will also sit on the mount of the congregation on the farthest sides of the north; [14] I will ascend above the heights of the clouds, I will be like the Most High.' [15] Yet you shall be brought down to Sheol, to the lowest depths of the Pit. [16] "Those who see you will gaze at you, and consider you, saying: 'Is this the man who made the earth tremble, who shook kingdoms, [17] Who made the world as a wilderness and destroyed its cities, who did not open the house of

---

[23] Excerpt taken from "Regenesis" Chapter 2: The Divine Plan, section titled "Creation Happened, Time Begins."

his prisoners?'" (Isa. 14:12-17; see also Ezek. 28:12-19).

We are living in a sea of chaotic darkness… yet we have this hope:

"And the Spirit of God hovered…"

God developed a plan to regenerate earth by making and creating many things including mankind. This next point is highly significant: bible scholars will teach us God is bringing order out of chaos, but this is untrue. Study the text carefully and you will see… God is bringing order "to" the chaos. It is impossible to bring order out of chaos because the only thing that chaos can produce… is more chaos. A similar idea would bring immortality out of corruption, life out of death… or love out of hate. Utterly impossible!

Our God is a God of order. God always brings order in the midst of chaos and confusion.

God came to earth (i.e. Jesus) to take away the chaos and confusion by giving us an opportunity to escape the darkness and enter into God's grace – through faith.

Thus, I illustrate two ways in which theologians have interpreted scripture: humanistic and God-centric. The humanistic approach tries to understand scripture apart from the Spirit to make sense of the darkness whereby the humanistic model of earth's formation as a molten glob of cosmic dust that took 6 billion years to cool before plants and animals could be introduced to make it good enough to support life is based upon the scientific model. The God-centric approach understands this, but darkness can only be explained from a spiritual perspective.

Darkness – obscures light! Darkness is the absence of light – and darkness also represents the loss of all hope of ever getting light again. Yet… we have hope! His name is Jesus!

> "The people who walked in darkness have seen a great light; those who dwelt in the land of the shadow of death, upon them a light has shined" (Isa. 9:2).
>
> Then Jesus spoke to them again, saying, "I am the light of the world. He who follows Me shall not walk in darkness, but have the light of life" (John 8:12).

Darkness, then, is the absence of God's presence (light) without ever hoping to have it again. Reread the Genesis account and try to image these events from God's perspective. God's plan of salvation (which includes the regeneration of the earth in newness) will be accomplished when Jesus takes away the sin of the world – and righteousness is restored.

> "The next day John saw Jesus coming toward him, and said, "Behold! The Lamb of God **who takes away the sin of the world**!" (John 1:29)

Darkness on the face of the deep – is the condition of earth wherein all men have been born. Plants and animals were reintroduced onto earth (Gen. 2:4-6), yet underneath the beauty within God's creation (version #2) looms a diabolic, cruel, chaotic, evil that continues to operate as the kingdom of darkness on earth with one sole purpose: to destroy life, man and creation. The Lord will regenerate creation in the New Earth (version #3) back to its original glorious luster and magnificent beauty wherein the saints of God will live eternally to govern the earth with Him.

> "<u>**Now**</u> **I saw a new heaven and a new earth**, for the first heaven and the first earth had passed away. Also there was no more sea. [2] Then I, John, saw the holy city, New Jerusalem, coming down out of heaven from God, prepared as a bride adorned for her husband. [3] And I heard a loud voice from heaven saying, "Behold, the tabernacle of God *is*

with men, and He will dwell with them, and they shall be His people. God Himself will be with them *and be* their God. ⁴ And God will wipe away every tear from their eyes; there shall be no more death, nor sorrow, nor crying. There shall be no more pain, for the former things have passed away. ⁵ Then He who sat on the throne said, "***Behold, I make all things new***." And He said to me, "Write, for these words are true and faithful" (Rev. 21:1-5).

Let me expound upon this point about darkness as much as possible. When God created light, He did not associate it as being part of the day (in the way we traditionally think of a day with nighttime). God divided the darkness from the light. They are separate entities. The darkness He called Night and the light He called Day. Night and Day represent two very different things. Day represents the presence of Light (Jesus is the Light of the world; John 8:12; Jesus is the Dayspring; Luke 1:78). In contrast, the purpose and intent of darkness (evil) is to obscure Light.

> "Then God said, "Let there be light"; and there was light. ⁴ And God saw the light, that *it was* good; ***and God divided the light from the darkness***. ⁵ God called the light Day, and the darkness He called Night. So the evening and the morning were the first day" (Gen. 1:3-5).

During the Exodus, when the Israelites were being led out of Egypt by the Lord (and Jesus is Lord), He went before them to guide them through the darkness.

> "And the LORD went before them by day in a pillar of cloud to lead the way, and by night in a pillar of fire to give them light, so as to go by day and night. ²² He did not take away the pillar of cloud by day or the pillar of fire by night *from* before the people" (Ex. 13:21, 22).

Please pay close attention: Jesus is leading them through the Night where there is no darkness. Did you grasp it? We are all living in a world of darkness and unless the Lord is your light ("In Him was life, and the life was the *light of men*"; John 1:4), then you are regrettably still walking in darkness. You are still dead... living and walking in the shadow of death. Our Hope and our Salvation (Jesus) has been calling out to all people to "come out of the darkness and into the light" so the Lord can lead us in righteousness and truth for His name's sake... and be made new again... and live!

> "The people who sat in darkness have seen a great light, and upon those who sat in the region and shadow of death *Light has dawned*" (Matt. 4:16).

> Jesus said: "Most assuredly, I say to you, he who hears My word and believes in Him who sent Me has everlasting life, and shall not come into judgment, but has passed from death into life" (John 5:24).

We must pass from death *into life*! We must leave darkness and come into the Light. Even the sons of Noah had enough sense to "come into the Ark" to escape judgment... and live (Gen. 7:1)

> Jesus said: "I have come *as* a light into the world, that whoever believes in Me should not abide in darkness" (John 12:46).

> "And this is the condemnation, that the light has come into the world, and men loved darkness rather than light, because their deeds were evil" (John 3:19).

> "Then Jesus spoke to them again, saying, "I am the light of the world. He who follows Me shall not walk in darkness, but have the light of life" (John 8:12).

Therefore, since we have been called out of darkness and have been washed (sanctified by the truth) and been made clean, we are admonished to have nothing in common with darkness.

> "Do not be unequally yoked together with unbelievers. For what fellowship has righteousness with lawlessness? And what communion has light with darkness?" (2 Cor. 6:14).

> "For you were once darkness, but now *you are* light in the Lord. Walk as children of light" (Eph. 5:8).

> "You are all sons of light and sons of the day. We are not of the night nor of darkness" (1 Thess. 5:5).

Early one morning, the Spirit began teaching me about God's plan – and darkness. Earth was orderly. Then Lucifer was cast to earth and darkness (chaos) ensued. God implemented a plan of regeneration to bring order to the chaos which included creating man and granting him authority with power to establish dominion over the earth – in His name. "This *is* the history of the heavens and the earth when they were created" (Gen. 2:4). God's plan was completed, and then God implemented His plan of regeneration on the eighth day (Gen. 2:5). God then formed man and placed him in a garden eastward of Eden (v. 2:7) to initiate His conquest of darkness through man, but Adam and Eve were tempted to operate independently (apart from) God and sin claimed its first two humans. What a dramatic turn of events! God created earth. Man was created to inhabit earth, yet darkness intervened to take earth captive, then man was sent to come against the darkness yet became captive to it. And it gets even more interesting! God has been calling out to as many who will listen to His voice – to come out of the darkness and into the light. Those who hear and obey His command are called '*ekklesia*-1577' – the called out ones – which is also the root word for "church." We are called for a purpose – to come out of darkness and to walk in the Light of Truth! Once you've accepted the Lord's invitation, you are being preserved for salvation by the Spirit by walking in God's truth. Remain in the Truth! This next point is so important: the Lord's plan will send you back into the darkness for two reasons: 1) to help redeem other souls taken captive to sin, and 2) to accomplish the purpose for which you were created: to come against the darkness with the light of truth. Walk in the Truth! BUT... do not become a captive again!

If you've been taught (as was I) that getting saved is all there is to life on earth, then you would be mistakenly deceived. There is much work to accomplish under the Lordship of Jesus Christ.

You are a world changer! Jesus called us "the light of the world" (Matt. 5:14) because His plan always intended us to come against the darkness with the light of truth He gave us.

> "... and to make all see what *is* the fellowship of the mystery, which from the beginning of the ages has been hidden in God who created all things through Jesus Christ; [10] ***to the intent that now the manifold wisdom of God might be made known <u>by the church</u> to the principalities and powers in the heavenly places,*** [11] according to the eternal purpose which He accomplished in Christ Jesus our Lord" (Eph. 3:9-11).

This world is demonic! God sent us here to come against the darkness and against those principalities and powers that operate in rebellion against God and His plan for earth. If you truly want to know what your purpose in life is... then you just read it! Now do it!

Let me ask you this: if God knew "darkness" was going to cause so much human pain and suffering, then why didn't God just obliterate darkness before proceeding with His plan of creation? That is an excellent question that I've pondered many years... and this is my response: Satan was cast from heaven to earth with about a third of the angels he took captive to sin. God is merciful and kind. God is redemptive. God would never totally destroy anything without first seeking a remnant, so there must have been a remnant from heaven that was taken captive (as we read in a previous scripture; Isa. 14:12-17). As for mankind, God's plan of salvation provided the means whereby we were sent to earth (on probation) to be tempted and proofed to determine our steadfast allegiance to Jesus, the Lord of Heaven and Earth – or remain as reprobate captives in sin to suffer the consequence of our disobedience and rebellion. Free will allows us to choose between life eternal or remain in death. God gave us free will and grace to choose between that which sets us free from sin and the power death has over us... or to remain in darkness to suffer eternal torment. Therefore, not even God's enemies can accuse Him of wrongdoing (Deut. 32:26, 27) because... we ultimately decide our own fate in the judgment. Earth is our second chance to get right with God. Hello everyone... welcome to planet earth!

Faith makes possible what Grace makes available.

> For "whoever calls on the name of the Lord shall be saved" (Rom. 10:13).

Darkness prevents the fullness of God's redemptive plan for earth... and God's plan for you as well. Jesus came and got the victory over darkness and even death itself whereby – through faith in Jesus Christ – we are saved to walk in newness of life.

> "And the light shines in the darkness, and the darkness did not comprehend it" (John 1:5).

> "But we speak the wisdom of God in a mystery, the hidden wisdom which God ordained before the ages for our glory, [8] which none of the rulers of this age knew; for had they known, they would not have crucified the Lord of glory" (1 Cor. 2:7, 8).

The Apostle John knew Jesus more intimately than perhaps anyone on earth, and thus, he is able to communicate deep theological truth regarding Jesus Christ and the kingdom of God. John did not write his four gospels until about sixty years after Christ's ascension, which allowed him much time for reflection and meditation regarding the "Word of Life" he beheld... and the truth which Jesus taught.

When I read 1 John, it is crystal clear to me that he is presenting the truth of God within a compare-and-contrast framework to convey many principles:

- Jesus established the kingdom of heaven to expose and come against Satan's kingdom of darkness which Jesus referred to as "this world"
- The kingdom of heaven is based upon truth; darkness is based upon a lie
- Believers in Jesus will abide in Him and live according to the Spirit in truth and in love, but doubters and scoffers of the truth will deny Jesus is Lord with unbelief in their heart
- Jesus is the Savior of the world; Satan is the destroyer and the accuser of the brethren
- The ruler of this world (Satan) is diametrically opposed to (anti) Christ
- Christ has His Spirit, and the Antichrist also has a spirit to deceive mankind

God has been calling out to as many as will hear His voice – and obey the message. Even for the sake of one, God is faithful to seek and save all who are lost in darkness. But this wake-up call to come out from the darkness to walk with Jesus must be enacted by us according to faith. Repentance means to turn away from one thing and turn towards another. Repentance requires – a change in our thought process!

> "What man of you, having a hundred sheep, if he loses one of them, does not leave the ninety-nine in the wilderness, and go after the one which is lost until he finds it?" (Luke 15:4)

God relentlessly pursues us to save us, but we must choose between remaining lost in the wilderness or following the

Shepherd. Jesus said that He came "to seek and save the lost" (Luke 19:10). The word "lost" does not mean a little lost or wayward in the wilderness; the word '*apollumi*-622) means: utterly destroyed.

The earth was utterly destroyed – and so was humanity! Satan obliterated everything! Both need a Savior, yet somehow mankind has been deceived by darkness and become so acclimated to chaos that it doesn't even know how wicked evil is. We need a Savior. We desperately need to be saved and restored to newness of life by Jesus to walk in the kingdom of God.

Beloved, you were placed in the midst of a battle where two kingdoms are at war; your mind is the battlefield – and your soul is the prize!

"Saints, this world is demonic, sensual and sinful because the prince of darkness has corrupted it with lies, confusion, doubt and fear resulting in unbelief and rebellion in order to pervert truth in our mind and thwart faith from taking root in our heart. We were all born through water into this demonic world of darkness and sin, yet we have a way of escape: be born anew through the Spirit and be saved by Grace… from death into life… through faith in Jesus Christ."[24]

How do we escape this world? You must be born again… by the Spirit of God!

The Kingdom Of God

How can I describe the kingdom of God? The best way – is to describe the nature of God first.

In the book "Image" (#3) we are able to perceive the identity of Jesus based upon the messages He taught us – as being one with the Father. But… who is the Father? A better question to ask is:

---

[24] Excerpt copied from "Gateways" section titled: "Thoughts, Purposes and Plans."

"what" is the Father? Who the Father is… is based upon what He does. The Father is: the Mind of the Godhead. By the thought of His intellect, the Father brings things into existence that did not exist.

> "God, who gives life to the dead and calls those things which do not exist as though they did" (Rom. 4:17).

> "The LORD of hosts has sworn, saying, "Surely, as I have thought, so it shall come to pass, and as I have purposed, so it shall stand" (Isa. 14:24).

Our doctrines correctly teach God spoke things into existence. God said… "Let there be light" and so it was. God said… "Let us make man in our Image according to our likeness… and give them dominion over the earth" (Gen. 1:26-28 condensed) and so it was. Man's commission for the earth has always been to have dominion as the Lord's emissaries, but for some mysterious reason the church is reluctant to teach about dominion. Why? I perceive an enemy's hand in this! God created mankind as the host of earth for dominion over the earth, but the enemy deceived us into thinking our true home is heaven and we will go home to heaven when our body dies. This is a lie from the deceiver to prevent us from seeing the big picture… and overtaking the kingdom of darkness on this planet with light. Earth is our eternal home!

We were bamboozled out of our rightful birthplace and inheritance in the heavens: Earth!

Jesus said: "You are the light of the world" (Matt. 5:13). Now, go… and be light!

Mankind has a tradition: you become a citizen of whatever country you are born in. This truth also applies to the spiritual dimension: you were born on earth. And yet, you are also a citizen of heaven… having been spoken into existence by God (Gen. 1:26-28; 2:1; Eph. 1:4) long before your physical substance (body) was formed over your soul. The host of earth (men) are dual citizens of Heaven and Earth! Yet your rightful place, habitation and domain – is earth.

Now, start fighting to recover what was stolen from you by the enemy – in the name of Jesus!

God spoke things into existence. There is an interesting way to describe what the Father does as proceeding forth… by the thought of His intellect:

"The creative thoughts of God and the creative power of His word always precede creation. In this manner, "word is two-fold: λόγος ἐνοιάθετος – word conceived; and λόγος προφόρικος – word uttered. The λόγος ὁ ἔσω and ὁ ἔξω, ratio and oratio – intelligence and utterance."[25]

What is the Father? The Father is the Mind of the Godhead! The thoughts of God '*logos*- λόγος' are the authority of the Father, the Maker of all things; and creation is under the authority and domain of the Creator, Jesus Christ, through whom all things were created – by '*logos*' – His utterance as the Word of God.

> "In the beginning was the Word, and the Word was with God, and the Word was God. [2] He was in the beginning with God. [3] All things were made through Him, and without Him nothing was made that was made" (John 1:1-3).

> "For by Him all things were created that are in heaven and that are on earth, visible and invisible, whether thrones or dominions or principalities or powers. All things were created through Him and for Him" (Col. 1:16).

All things were created – by and for – Jesus Christ our Lord.

---

[25] Matthew Henry's Commentary on the Whole Bible, an exposition on John 1:1; Volume VI, p. 848; MacDonald Publishing Company, McLean, Virginia.

Why is it so important for us to comprehend this very complex history of creation? Because it goes to the core of our being – as well as understanding the Lord's will for man on earth! Since God made us and created us to be like Him, **we need to understand "what" He is – in order to understand what we are.** Why? Because we get our identity from Jesus, who created us as a likeness of Him – in order to live in oneness with the Father – just as Jesus demonstrated.

- The Father is Spirit (John 4:23, 24)
- The Father is invisible, His attributes are invisible (Rom. 1:20)
- Jesus said: "No one has seen the Father at any time" (John 1:18)
- John said: "No one has seen God at any time" (1 John 4:12)
- "Not that anyone has seen the Father, except He who is from God" (John 6:46)
- "He who has seen Me has seen the Father" (John 14:9).
- "I and My Father are one" (John 10:30).

This is why it's critical for us to understand and comprehend "what" the Father is!

Jesus is God, but if "no one has seen God at any time" then our doctrines seem to have a disconnect regarding the Divinity of Jesus. To be certain – Jesus is God! Jesus is the Manifested One – who appears and reveals Himself to men, but the Father remains known only to Jesus... and for good reason... because God's thoughts are invisible. And so are yours.

"What is man that you are mindful of him?" This question goes to the core of knowing what we are – which can only be comprehended by knowing "What" the Father is (who made us). By the thought of His intellect, He made us – on purpose for a purpose.

Form follows function.

What He does is based upon what He is… and this is true for mankind as well. We were thought into being as a soul existing in His presence – "In Christ before the foundation of this world" (Eph. 1:4) – for this purpose: to be the host of Earth (Gen. 2:1). Next, we were formed upon the earth, and then the Spirit of life breathed life into us and we became… a living being (Gen. 2:7). You are a spiritual being… and then you became a living being. Do not go further into this book or in your walk of faith with Christ Jesus until you thoroughly comprehend this point because it will liberate you from terminal humanity – as taught to you by others deceived long ago by the world of darkness that surrounds us and keeps us enslaved in ignorance to darkness. **You are a spiritual being that is having a human experience**! Jesus came to set us free to walk in the liberty of the Spirit, but somewhere along the way… we misunderstood His message and we became captives once again to fatalistic, humanistic doctrines taught by men.

The kingdom of God operates according to God's authority. The Supremacy and Preeminence of God operates all creation in accordance with His authority and power to govern His kingdom – in Heaven and on Earth. We were created for this purpose: to operate earth under His authority – and have dominion. Earth is our domain. Any authority we have – was given to us by God to govern this world and establish the kingdom of heaven on earth. If you have received any authority or power in this life, you got it from God.

If you have any complaints about all the problems on earth, then know this: God gave you His authority to change it with truth. The person God sent to change this chaotic world – is you!

Focus on Jesus and dwell in the present. Faithfully do what you are called to do – today.

Jesus said to His disciples before His ascension:

> "It is not for you to know times or seasons which
> the Father has put in His own authority" (Acts 1:7).

Some people say Jesus didn't know the will of the Father which somehow makes Him less than the Father. How ridiculous! Jesus is God!!! Jesus is the Father who sent Himself as a Son in order to teach us how to live as sons and daughters of our heavenly Father.[26] Jesus can manifest Himself however and whenever He wants! The reason Jesus said this (above) is not because He didn't know – and it's not because it wasn't within His own authority to know – it's for two reasons:

1. Disciples don't need to know times or seasons in order to faithfully do the will of God here and now (and this is true for us today), and
2. Dynamic fluidity allows God to orchestrate things based upon man's response to His command to walk according to His will (or negatively – under demonic influence)

The times and seasons within the Father's authority are known to Jesus because Jesus orchestrates and manifests the will of God, but it is "we" who do not need to know. It's on a "need to know basis" the will of God is made known (revealed) to men. If we knew the truth about seasons in the future, we would focus more on the future instead of walking in the present... which is what has been happening the past 100 years. Preachers and prophets have been telling us about end times and seasons and (specifically) the rapture wherein we focus more on the rapture to escape evil darkness rather than walking with dominion authority to come against it – today! We've been tricked to focus on future things... which hinder us from staying focused on our daily mission: have dominion over darkness!

> Jesus said: "Therefore do not worry about
> tomorrow, for tomorrow will worry about its own
> things. Sufficient for the day is its own trouble"

---

[26] Read "Image" to thoroughly comprehend this statement

(Matt. 6:34).

God knows the end from the beginning because – He orchestrated everything from beginning to end – whereby He walks men through it day by day. Our beginning and end were predetermined by God – before the foundation of the world, so I encourage you to enter into the flow of the Spirit and let the Spirit guide you along the path God prepared and pre-purposed for you.

> Jesus said: "I am the Alpha and the Omega, the Beginning and the End," says the Lord, "who is and who was and who is to come, the Almighty" (Rev. 1:8).

> "Remember the former things of old, for I am God, and there is no other; I am God, and there is none like Me, [10] ***declaring the end from the beginning***, and from ancient times things that are not yet done, saying, 'My counsel shall stand, and I will do all My pleasure,' [11] Calling a bird of prey from the east, the man who executes My counsel, from a far country. Indeed I have spoken it; I will also bring it to pass. I have purposed it" (Isa. 46:9-11)

The Holy Spirit is our intercessor between God and man to push us and pull us into alignment with the will of God… even when we completely mess things up (which we notoriously do effortlessly). Free will allows mankind to do well or mess up… yet dynamic fluidity enables the Spirit to correct our mistakes on the fly. We are being guided by the Holy Spirit to help us do the will of God even as the reins of man's mind are being influenced by the Spirit on a regular basis to keep us on the straight and narrow way.

> "What is man, that You should exalt him, that You should set Your heart on him, [18] ***that You should visit him every morning***, and test him every moment?" (Job 17:17, 18).

The Mind of God, our Father, thinks things into existence (the

Authority of our Maker) and then the Heart of God, Jesus our Lord, manifests and performs the will of God (the Authority of our Creator) to bring things into existence. This is what God is and this is what God does… and they are ONE! And this is true with man as well; we think things into existence… and then we bring them into existence through the actions of our heart. How incredible is that! You do it all the time… and now you know why!

Thoughts of our mind…are seeds… which we plant in the garden of our heart… to produce fruit.

Man's intellect enables him to accomplish anything. This is not my theory; these are God's words, so read the Tower of Babel story (Gen. 11). Man can live in oxygen-free environments within submarines and space stations, and fly through the air within cylindrical aluminum tubes (jets). Man's ability to accomplish many exceedingly good things is counterbalanced by his infinite ability to commit evil atrocities on other people – and unborn children through abortion.

But I must interject and ask: whose will are you doing: God's… or yours? Who is sitting upon the throne of your heart as Lord of your life… is it Jesus or is it you?

Jesus created us in "His Own image" according to His likeness; we were created by Jesus to act like Him and operate exactly like Him. The problem with mankind is: we forgot who we are, we forgot we're suppose to operate like Jesus, and we forgot how to do it. So Jesus came to teach us all over again. Study the life of Jesus carefully if you want to know the will of God and do it. This is not a great mystery: study Jesus and imitate His example. He came to establish the kingdom of heaven on earth, and He sent you here to go and do likewise.

> "As the Father sent Me, I also send you" (John 20:21).

Jesus came as the Son of/from God to teach us how to live as sons and daughters of God.

Jesus said He did the works of the Father… and so must we! Jesus said the Father was dwelling in Him… and this is also true for you and me! The Father has been dwelling within you the entire time you've been alive, but you've probably been taught otherwise… as was I.

When Jesus told us: "The Father dwells in Me" – He was telling us something quite ordinary and yet quite profound (because we forgot the truth): the Father dwells in your spirit. Jesus is our Divine Example who is teaching us and showing us how to acknowledge the Father dwelling in us, and in so doing… is teaching us how to hear God's voice and do His will. The "Father of all, who is above all, and through all, *and in you all*" (Eph. 4:6) dwells (temporarily) in "you all" but the Father wants us to build a permanent abode (*mone*-home) for Him in our heart (John 14:23).

> "Do you not believe that I am in the Father, and the Father in Me? The words that I speak to you I do not speak on My own authority; but the Father who dwells in Me does the works" (John 14:10).

The Father dwells in you. Allow this truth to resonate in you – and live in the knowledge of this truth to honor your heavenly Father as He dwells in you.

"Does the works" is an interesting statement… because it speaks of the "words" the Father speaks through Jesus… as the Living Word of God. The word "work(s)" – '*ergon*-2041' means: "an effort or occupation; by implication, an act; deed; labor; work."[27] Jesus is telling us the Father in Him is doing the work, and likewise when we submit our authority to Jesus as we have been instructed when we declare Jesus is Lord (1 Cor. 12:3), the Father will do the same to us and through us – in order for us to act like Jesus and become a likeness of Him – whereby we only say what we hear God

---

[27] Strong's Concordance.

saying, and do what we see God doing (John 5:19).

Jesus is Lord. Jesus is God Almighty (Gen. 17:1; Rev. 1:8). Jesus didn't need to pray or hear from God in order to do the will of God: Jesus *IS* God Incarnate! He taught these things in order to teach us what to do!!! Yet we need to differentiate something here with great scrutiny. Jesus was not saying this because He was less than the Father; Jesus was demonstrating to us, as our heavenly Example, this realigned and realized "work" of the Father through each of us... so we know what to do by teaching us how to do it.

Jesus prayed aloud to teach us how to pray; Jesus cast out demons to teach us how to have authority over the enemy; Jesus healed the sick to teach us how to liberate souls taken captive by the enemy to various illnesses, diseases and infirmities; Jesus performed miraculous signs and wonders for three reasons: A) to teach us... that man has been delegated to act on His behalf to accomplish the will of God, B) to lead captive souls to liberty in Christ Jesus, and C) establish the kingdom of heaven on earth... in His name!

> "Therefore My Father loves Me, because I lay down My life that I may take it again. [18] No one takes it from Me, but I lay it down of Myself. I have power to lay it down, and I have power to take it again. This command I have received from My Father" (John 10:17, 18).

Jesus had Divine Authority the entire time He walked in the flesh, but He said these things to teach us what we are to do... and why we must do it... as men aligned under the authority of God to do the works of God... which starts by hearing God's voice. Jesus had power to lay His life down and pick it up again... and by grace through faith... so do you. The way of Christ – is to surrender and yield your life to do the will of the Father.

However, Jesus being God creates a minor problem: Jesus said we have not seen the Father or heard His voice at any time (John 5:37). What did Jesus mean by this? The substance of the Father is invisible and immaterial... as being within the realm of spiritual thought. In this regard, we cannot experience the Father in a tangible manner, but we can experience the Father through the One who manifests the Father – Jesus Christ – and the Spirit He sent to guide us and tutor us. The Presence of God we feel is Jesus and the Voice we hear is the Holy Spirit – who does not speak on His own authority (John 16:13). Can Jesus be the voice of God? Yes, because He is the Word of God (John 1:1). Can the Spirit be the presence of God? Yes... because they are One, so let's not get tripped up by who does what. "The Lord our God, the Lord is One" (Deut. 6:4). Focus on Jesus – the One we are able to hear and see.

- "*Now the Lord is the Spirit*; and where the Spirit of the Lord is, there is liberty" (2 Cor. 3:17)
- "No one can say that Jesus is Lord except by the Holy Spirit" (1 Cor. 12:3)
- "For through Him [Jesus] we both have access by **one Spirit** to the Father" (Eph. 2:18)
- "*But he who is joined to the Lord is one spirit with Him*" (1 Cor. 6:17)

The God of Oneness – is One with His Spirit. And one with you – through your spirit!

When Peter declared Jesus as "The Christ of God" (Luke 9:20), Jesus credited the "Spirit of the Father" as the one who revealed this to Peter. Likewise, if we say or do anything, we must credit the Spirit of God who dwells in us – who is working His will through us.

> "But when they deliver you up, do not worry about how or what you should speak. For it will be given to you in that hour what you should speak; [20] for it is not you who speak, but *the Spirit of your Father* who speaks in you" (Matt. 10:19, 20).

It is the Spirit of the Father (the God of Oneness) who speaks through you! Is this beginning to make sense? When we surrender our life (lay it down) and become obedient to the Father through faith in Jesus Christ, we are yielding the operation of our body and spirit (which belong to God; 1 Cor. 6:20), to become another manifestation of Jesus upon the earth. When we declare Jesus Lord of our life, *we are yielding our will to operate under His authority in order to accomplish His will*. This may seem complicated, but it isn't. If you don't know what this means, then simply do this: focus on Jesus and imitate His example.

Jesus is the Image of God. Jesus is our Great Example! He spent His entire life teaching us how to live according to the manner in which we were created. Imitate Jesus… and you will be glorifying your Father in Heaven.

KINGDOMS

Kingdom of Paradox

Do you want to know what man's biggest problem is on planet earth other than not remembering? Poor planning!

We work and toil in this life without the slightest clue of what we'll be doing when we get to the other side. So I ask: since you will be dwelling in eternity, would you want to know where it is and what you'll be doing? Do I have your attention now? Ok! So I ask: if your actions in this life determined what you'd be doing for all eternity and where you'll be doing it, would you want to know more in order to alter (and improve) your prospects in life eternal?

The sad thing is: I'll tell you everything you need to know, but only a very few will change or alter their current identity in order to affect their future reality!

You are becoming even now... the identity of your future self.

Pay close attention to this parable by Jesus:

> "He [Jesus] also said to His disciples: "There was a certain rich man who had a steward, and an accusation was brought to him that this man was wasting his goods. ² So he called him and said to him, 'What is this I hear about you? Give an account of your stewardship, for you can no longer be steward.' ³ "Then the steward said within himself, 'What shall I do? For my master is taking the stewardship away from me. I cannot dig; I am ashamed to beg. ⁴ I have resolved what to do, that when I am put out of the stewardship, they may receive me into their houses.' ⁵ "So he called every one of his master's debtors to *him,* and said to the first, 'How much do you owe my master?' ⁶ And he said, 'A hundred measures of oil.' So he said to him, 'Take your bill, and sit down quickly and write

fifty.' ⁷ Then he said to another, 'And how much do you owe?' So he said, 'A hundred measures of wheat.' And he said to him, 'Take your bill, and write eighty.' ⁸ So the master commended the unjust steward because he had dealt shrewdly. For the sons of this world are more shrewd in their generation than the sons of light. ⁹ "And I say to you, make friends for yourselves by unrighteous mammon, that when you fail, they may receive you into an everlasting home. ¹⁰ He who *is* faithful in *what is* least is faithful also in much; and he who is unjust in *what is* least is unjust also in much. ¹¹ Therefore if you have not been faithful in the unrighteous mammon, who will commit to your trust the true *riches?* ¹² And if you have not been faithful in what is another man's, who will give you what is your own? ¹³ "No servant can serve two masters; for either he will hate the one and love the other, or else he will be loyal to the one and despise the other. You cannot serve God and mammon" (Luke 16:1-13).

Most preachers key into the mammon aspect of this story without comprehending the real message supporting the mammon topic: what are you looking forward to? How are you preparing for eternity? Are you planning ahead? What on earth are you doing??? Study this parable very closely. Jesus said the people of "this world" are wiser than the sons of light! Jesus commended (literally: praised) the unjust steward because he acted shrewdly. Why would Jesus praise someone for acting in an unbiblical way? O, my friend... yet he was! However, that man was doing it in an unethical manner. Let me explain.

We are all stewards on this planet for a very short time. Everything belongs to King Jesus... and we were sent here as stewards of His stuff to build the kingdom of heaven. But sadly, much like the unjust steward, we take the Master's things and use them for our own personal gain. This part of the story we comprehend, but the afterlife is the whole point of this message by

Jesus. Huh? Yes, the afterlife message includes "planning ahead" when you get to the other side.

You can't take earthly riches with you... but you can make deposits into your faith account for your use when you get to the other side. THAT – is the focus of the Lord's message!

The sons of "this world" are at least wise enough to forward resources into their future existence to take care of their projected needs, yet the sons of the kingdom are clueless in this regard. The Lord considers them unwise and unfaithful stewards!

> "And if you have not been faithful in what is another man's, who will give you what is your own?" (Luke 16:12; above)

Indeed, if you haven't been faithful with God's stuff, then who will give you what is your own? Ponder this statement carefully. What is your own? Who (or what) are you putting your trust in?

The church spends so much time teaching people to live well so you can enter into heaven, but I've never heard a message about performing deeds of righteousness which are forwarded into your faith account when you get to the other side. If your body died while you sleep tonight, what would be in your faith account? When you awaken, what you've got now is all that you'll have in eternity. Ponder it! What have you got? The church needs to preach "this" message rather than the health and wealth gospel pertaining to things which turn to dust. Strive to earn true riches and lay up an inheritance for your use that no moth, rust or thief can despoil.

Now, go back and read verse 9 because I want you to see something quite remarkable: Jesus speaking sarcastically. He is telling them: if you're going to do it, then do it exceedingly excellently. We are all going to an eternal home. Are you planning ahead? That is the message of this parable. My message to you is: if you aren't living your life as a disciple of Jesus to steward everything you've got to advance the kingdom of heaven on earth, then you aren't even on the same sheet of music with Jesus. Unjust stewards wind up in a place called Outer Darkness – where there is weeping and gnashing of teeth.

Parable Take-a-ways

Truism #1: the deeds of righteousness you sow in this life get forwarded into your faith account for your use when you get to the other side.

Truism #2: anything you do or accomplish in this life which does not have glory attached to it – that gives glory to God – will be burned in the judgment fire.

Truism #3: you reap what you sow… in this life into the next.

Truism #4: there are no do-overs! This life right now is your second chance… to get right! Jesus is the One who was able to make it right, and now it's up to you to get it right!

Truism #5: free will is the greatest gift in God's creation. It allows us to choose love or hate. It allows us to choose grace or sin. And it allows us to make unwise choices – for which we pay the penalty – or act wisely to operate according to grace and receive an inheritance for good works and deeds of righteousness accomplished with divine help from God's Spirit.

This last Truism is what the soul of man has been searching for since the beginning. King Solomon, the second wisest man of earth (second only to Jesus) sought it out, but was unable to comprehend it. He determined that life was futile and a chasing after wind. Actually, his messages in Ecclesiastes unknowingly found the answer that eluded him without him knowing it. Solomon asked a multitude of questions from a human perspective, yet not once did he ever ask the Holy Spirit. He never inquired of God or the Holy Spirit why things happen on earth.

Operating from a different perspective… the author asked the

Author and Finisher of faith for the answers you are now reading about.

Truism #6: the best of who you are in this life... is who you will be for all eternity. Choose wisely!

Truism #7: are you willing to trade up? Are you willing to exchange the life you have for the life you always imagined? (Matt. 16:26) Stop wishing it – and start believing for it! Faith is not the belief that something can happen, but rather... faith is something that is birthed in truth – it will happen – because God said it will happen – when you act upon it!

> "For what profit is it to a man if he gains the whole world, and loses his own soul? Or what will a man give in exchange for his soul?" (Matt. 16:26).

Truism #8: the water-born man must die to self before he can be reborn by the Spirit – to life eternal – in Christ Jesus.

Truism #9: live without any regrets.

Even as I write this missive, having forced myself to get up from a restless sleep, I wrestle between the man of flesh and the disciple dedicated in service to Jesus. This push-me/pull-you dynamic tension of faith in the midst of the reality we see and experience in this life is merely a shadow of the eternal reality we shall live in – which is determined by what we are willing to sacrifice upon the altar of self sacrifice in reverent adoration to Jesus. To put this into context: I've been fasting two weeks and wrestled in all attempts to sleep yet because of many divine thoughts running through my mind prior to teaching a class in the morning for the benefit of one person – who needs to be set free from institutional Christianity – I pull my beggarly self out of bed to write truth upon truth for this one person. What... are you willing to do for the "one?" At midnight... are you willing to get up and pray or write or do whatever the Spirit leads? Are you willing to get up in the middle of the night to give bread to the person who keeps knocking at your door? (Luke 11:5-8). Set your priorities on things above! This one person will govern nations and establish houses of peace wherever he goes when he hears this message... which you are about to read. What are you willing to sacrifice in this life... which will be rewarded in life eternal... for the sake of the one? Whatever you do for the one... you do it in service to the One!

> "Now he who plants and he who waters are one, and each one will receive his own reward according to his own labor" (1 Cor. 3:8).

> "He who receives a prophet in the name of a prophet shall receive a prophet's reward. And he who receives a righteous man in the name of a righteous man shall receive a righteous man's reward" (Matt. 10:41).

We may be very surprised by some things we find in our faith account – in eternity.

> "For if I do this willingly, I have a reward; but if against my will, I have been entrusted with a stewardship" (1 Cor. 9:19).

Much of what we do is required of us as a stewardship entrusted to us, as an obligation based on our original mandate from God as the salt of the earth – which will be rewarded, but those deeds done sacrificially as unto the Lord... will be rewarded exponentially.

> "For the Son of Man will come in the glory of His Father with His angels, and then He will reward each according to his works" (Matt. 16:27).

Truism #10: whatever you've sacrificed in this life will be recompensed 30/60/100-fold. No worldly investments offer this rate of return which will last into eternity.

Truism #11: why wait for eternity when you can live like an angel now?

Truism #12: only fools hear truth yet do nothing to change the future – even if only to help themselves.

So I ask: what are you willing to do right now in order to effect (make happen) your future place and position in life eternal? This question should actually be an endless loop of consciousness in your soul to seek and do "greater than" rather than "less than" for the kingdom of God.

> "But ***the meek shall inherit the earth***, and shall delight themselves in the abundance of peace" (Psa. 37:11; also in the Beatitudes said by Jesus, Matt. 5:5).

Recently, and many times prior as well, I've heard preachers talk about what we will be doing in eternity. All I've ever heard anyone say is: we will worship God. Pardon the irreverence but… give me an unsanctified break! If all I'll do is worship, worship, worship … for ten billion years… sounds more like hell to me. So, do you want to know what you'll be doing in eternity? Then keep reading. It is absolutely incredible! How do I know this? Because it's all written down in the Bible! Here is a summary. Go read the rest of it yourself!

Tell me: what are you doing now that is worth dying for? If it's worth dying for – then it's worth living that way now! Plan ahead! Do it now… and get ready… there's a paradigm shift ahead!

The key to unlocking the mysteries of life eternal is a four letter word: PARA. If you aren't proficient in Greek, this word means nothing, and if you are proficient in Greek, this word probably has you scratching your head.

PARA – Is A Four Letter Word

What will you be doing when you get to the other side of temporary in eternity?

The word '*para*-3844-παρὰ' means: "near, from beside;" alongside.[28] This word retains its basic meaning in the English language and is able to convey much information when placed alongside (*para* +) other words. For example:

Paraclete – '*parakletos*-3875' means: "an intercessor." This is one of the names for the Holy Spirit, our Intercessor, the one who is called (or summoned) to come alongside us; in this case – to guide us on this spiritual journey and help us know God's truth and live according to truth.

Parable – '*parabole*-3850' a spiritual story placed alongside (side by side) a complimentary truth or commonly known reality to teach a religious principle or moral lesson through comparison and contrast; one such classic is: The Parable of the Sower – which includes the words '*para hodos*' (translated wayside) with a very deep meaning as "the way alongside the true way."

Paradox – *para* + '*doxa*-1391' *doxa* in its basic sense means: an opinion; translated glory. Paradox is truth placed alongside a complementary or contradictory truth to reveal deeper truth through comparison/contrast, for example: "My power is perfected in weakness" (2 Cor. 12:9); "He who saves his life will lose it, but he who loses his life will save it" (Matt. 16:25). A similar Greek word '*paradoxos*-3861' translated "strange (Luke 5:26) is used to describe miracles not previously seen, and literally means: contrary to expectation; i.e. extraordinary."[29] Many Parables by Jesus employ paradox ideas to cause the reader to grasp the deeper meaning within the message (much like the Parable of the Unjust Steward mentioned above).

Paradise – '*paradeisos*-3857' translated: a park; an Eden (place of future happiness); refers to the garden place for Adam alongside Eden – in Eden.

---

[28] All term and definitions from Strong's Concordance; except "alongside" a word introduced by the author.
[29] Strong's Concordance.

- The future place Jesus told the penitent thief on the cross next to Him where he would go (Luke 23:43)
- The place where the Apostle Paul experienced a heavenly event (2 Cor. 12:4)
- The place in the New Earth where the tree of life is located (Rev. 2:7) also mentioned as being found in Eden (Gen. 2:8) as the place the Lord planted for Adam to dwell

As I've said many times before, Jesus never promised us heaven. He told the thief on the cross next to Him where we are all going, which should be incredibly great news to all of us. "Heaven is My throne" (Acts 7:49). The New Earth, however, is the '*topos*' place (John 14:3) alongside the Father's "*oikia*" house in His "*oikos*" estate where we shall dwell eternally with Him. This will become crystal clear when we study the first garden given to Adam – by the Lord – as a forward operating position from Heaven to advance the kingdom of heaven on earth.

> "And the LORD God formed man of the dust of the ground, and breathed into his nostrils the breath of life; and man became a living being. [8] The LORD God planted a garden eastward in Eden, and there He put the man whom He had formed. [9] And out of the ground the LORD God made every tree grow that is pleasant to the sight and good for food. The tree of life was also in the midst of the garden, and the tree of the knowledge of good and evil. [10] Now a river went out of Eden to water the garden, and from there it parted and became four riverheads.
> [11] The name of the first is Pishon; it is the one which skirts the whole land of Havilah, where there is gold. [2] And the gold of that land is good. Bdellium and the onyx stone are there. [13] The name of the second river is Gihon; it is the one which goes around the whole land of Cush. [14] The name of the third river is Hiddekel; it is the one which goes

toward the east of Assyria. The fourth river is the Euphrates. [15] Then the LORD God took the man and put him in the garden of Eden to tend and keep it" (Gen. 2:7-15).

Follow these steps very carefully, as they apply to each of us as well:

- Verse 7: The Lord formed Adam of the dust of the ground (i.e. of earth)
- Verse 8: Then the Lord planted a garden eastward in Eden and He put the man there. The place where Adam was formed is called Eden – the Garden of God (Ezek. 28:13); and then the Lord planted another garden for Adam eastward in Eden – and called it Eden as well. This point is revelatory: whenever God extends His kingdom, He calls it by that name. The Father dwells in Heaven, and we are like Jesus in our mission mandate to occupy earth; wherever we go, with Christ dwelling in us, we advance the kingdom of heaven in the name of the King of Heaven. Jesus said: "Repent. The kingdom of heaven is at hand (near, from beside; alongside)" (Matt. 4:17). Wherever the King of Heaven goes, He takes back enemy territory… **and then calls it** "the kingdom of heaven."
- Verse 9: two trees are in the garden: the tree of life and the tree of knowledge (which will be another important topic of discussion later)
- Verse 10: "Now a river went out of Eden… to water the garden." Stop for a moment and try to visualize a river going out of Eden to water a garden in Eden. This makes no sense unless you understand the garden which the Lord planted for Adam was given the same name that is located eastward "**in**" Eden. Adam's garden is located "alongside" God's Garden – and this garden is called Paradise (i.e. the garden alongside of God's Garden). Wherever God goes, He establishes a forward operating position called "a garden" for us to dwell as we inhabit and take back more enemy territory. This message is about two types of

- gardens: as a territory (topos place) on earth and as a house in your heart.
- Verse 11-14: (all scripture is important, yet these are irrelevant to this message)
- Verse 15: God planted a garden eastward in Eden where He put Adam (v. 8), so how can God take "the man and put him in the garden of Eden to tend and keep it" if Adam is already in a garden in Eden? Because they are two separate gardens! The Garden "OF" Eden (which is God's) is different than the garden "in" eden (sic) which is Adam's. Adam's garden is near/beside/alongside the Lord's garden. Let the epiphany happen in your mind. The garden in eden is near at hand… and it's located in your heart.

The undiscovered territory called heaven that man has been searching for – is the garden of your heart – which is alongside Heaven – where the Father dwells (in your spirit) – alongside your soul – within your earthen tabernacle.

Home is where your heart is! Let the epiphany happen and let revelation enlighten your mind.

So I ask: what have buildings got to do with any of this? Now go… and tend the garden of your heart and produce an abundant crop that gives glory to God… and bless your neighbor as well.

So, do you want to know what you will be doing in eternity? You just read it. The Lord will establish a garden in the New Earth and give it to you to tend and keep. And here is the most interesting part: the size of your garden is commensurate (equal to) the garden of your heart which includes – all true riches you forwarded into your faith account.

You shall reap what you sow. Is this making sense?

How large of a house or territory in the Father's estate do you desire in the New Earth?

> "Then the King [Jesus] will say to those on His right hand, 'Come, you blessed of My Father, inherit the kingdom prepared for you from the foundation of the world" (Matt. 25:34).

You get out of it... what you put into it!

Be a wise steward of God's things and use them to establish the kingdom of heaven on earth. In the New Earth, this is what we will be doing:

- We are gardeners tending the garden of our heart to produce glory fruit now
- We will be gardeners of Eden and given territory *in eden* (i.e. Paradise) to produce nations and cities (like Nimrod, as one example, but not like him – for his own glory)
- And one day out of seven, the Lord will take us out of our garden and put us in His Own Garden to maintain intimacy with Him – wherein we will bring our glory and honor into it (Rev. 21:24-26)

We were put in a wilderness (the kingdom of darkness) to produce a crop (fruit), but first you need to remove any stones in your heart that prevents you from cultivating and growing the righteousness of faith. Stones, in this regard, represent any sin or offense (especially unforgiveness) which created a hardened heart which prevents you from operating with a contrite heart. The thief on the cross understood this... yet the people of Noah's day did not.

The Parable of the Sower has much truth to teach us about the condition of our heart and is considered by many a classic (Mark 4). The four types of soil represent four conditions of the garden in our heart which produce four types of understanding:

1. The hardened heart (seed that fell by the wayside) produces no understanding
2. The rocky heart produces limited understanding until trials cause faith to whither

3. The worldly-focused heart has fertile soil (some understanding) but the crop fails to grow faster than weeds choking it and thus little or no fruit is produced
4. The fertile heart produces much understanding – and much fruit as well

Let's focus our attention on the hardened heart. It says some seed fell by the wayside and this could be misconstrued as bad aim by the sower (which would be inaccurate). The literal phrase in Mark 4:4 is: καὶ (And) ἐγένετο (it came to pass) ἐν τῷ (as he) σπείρειν (sowed) ὃ (-) μὲν (some) ἔπεσεν (fell) παρὰ (*para*-alongside) τὴν (the) ὁδόν (*hodos*-3598-way). Preachers have interpreted this to mean the shoulder of the road, but upon close examination, the term *para + hodos* represents a place "alongside the way." Let me paint a word picture: there are two roads running side-by-side; one is the way of the Lord and the other is a way that seems right to a man (which I call the way known as religion). The seed that fell on the other way alongside the Lord's way – produced NO understanding… because Satan quickly snatched truth before any understanding could take root. The para-way alongside (yet apart from) the Way of Truth (Jesus is the Way and the Truth; John 14:6) produces no understanding to explain why things happen the way they happen on earth, nor does it understand what we will be doing in eternity. Got it?

> "And Jesus said to him, "Assuredly, I say to you, today you will be with Me in Paradise" (Luke 23:43).

The word "today" is somewhat mistranslated. The Greek word '*semeron*-4594' means: now, as of this day; to-day (not "today" as a point in time but rather as a moment when faith produced some new, not according to time (*chronos*-5550) but new according to character (*kainos*-2537)). *Semeron* is better translated "now" thus indicating a determination by Jesus regarding this man's eternal destination – in that instant – will be in Paradise – in the garden near/beside/alongside of Heaven… with Him! A conversion happened in his mind – and the Lord saved him.

Through faith in Jesus, we have much to hope for. Even as we are made new in character like the thief, we are also promised "now" (from the point of conversion going forward)… we are promised a *topos* place in Paradise… with Jesus. This is the good news of the gospel!

Beloved, if you are unsure of your eternal destination, then stop what you're doing and ask Jesus what He wants you to do! Hear His voice and understand the message! Set your priorities in order. Do the "one thing" Jesus wants from all of us: abide with Him… intimately… in oneness with Him. The afterlife message includes "planning ahead," so don't just hope you get there… live your life in such a way "now" so your faith account is overflowing when you get to the other side. Truth is liberating. The kingdom of heaven is near at hand! It is closer than we imagined.

The kingdom of heaven is neither up nor down – it's IN – and now it's time to let heaven out.

Kingdom of the Spirit

> "Let your light so shine before men, that they may see your good works and glorify your Father in heaven" (Matt. 5:16).

What does this mean: to glorify your Father in Heaven? How can we do this... if God our Father dwells in us? It will be impossible to comprehend the answer to this question if you think of God our Father in physical terms.

God is Spirit. Embrace the realm of the Spirit!

For starters, God is everywhere! God is not limited to being in any one place, nor is He diminished when He is. God can manifest Himself anywhere at any time – and He can do so simultaneously everywhere – because God is Spirit.[30]

You, however, are a finite spiritual being that is limited by the restrictive nature of your earth suit (physical body). Your soul is eternal, but your body is mortal. The spirit God formed within you (Zech. 12:1), however, operates according to "grace" by the Spirit of Grace to accomplish supernatural (spirit-normal) events such as when Jesus and Peter walked on water. Furthermore, the spirit within you is "the light" Jesus mentioned:

> "You are the light of the world" (Matt. 5:14).

Our spirit is the lamp God placed within us to be His "sons of light" – to disperse the darkness of this world, to be a light before men (Dan. 5:14; Matt. 5:14-16), and to assist our soul.

> "The spirit of a man is the lamp of the Lord, searching all the inner depths of his *heart* [being]"

---

[30] Study the Theophanies in "Image."

(Prov. 20:27).[31]

The lamp of the body is the eye… the lamp of man's soul is the spirit.

"The spirit within us is the light (lamp) that was given to us by the Lord that is being strengthened by the Spirit of God that changes our focus (way of seeing things) and renews our mind … so that we may operate as sons of light… in order to transform this darkened world into the kingdom of Christ with two good eyes full of light."[32]

By faith, you are sons of God and sons of light! This is "who" you really are!

> "You are all sons of light and sons of the day. We are not of the night nor of darkness" (1 Thess. 5:5).

Secondly, the Spirit of the Father dwelling in your spirit does the works. Meditate on that!

> "… for it is not you who speak, but the Spirit of your Father who speaks in you" (Matt. 10:20).

Thirdly, the kingdom of God is within you. This key helps comprehend much spiritual truth.

> Jesus said: "For indeed, the kingdom of God is within you" (Luke 17:21).

Since God is everywhere and the Father dwells in you, then the kingdom is there as well. Yet God gave us free will to live according to His kingdom within us – or the other that surrounds us.

---

[31] Heart (translated belly-KJV) is '*beten*-990' meaning: "to be hollow; body (8x)." Strong's Concordance. Thus, body (or being) may be a better translation within this context, since men are earthen vessels.

[32] Excerpt from "Commission" section titled "Eyes For The Mind."

Fourthly, the angel that sees your Father's face is the spirit within you.[33]

> Jesus said: "... for I say to you that in heaven their angels always see the face of My Father who is in heaven" (Matt. 18:10).

Jesus told us "in the resurrection... [we will] be like angels" (Matt. 22:30) as we dwell on earth. And Jesus called Judas "a devil" (John 6:70). Therefore, we have the option – today – to act like either angels or demons (which will be explained in much greater detail). This is the probationary test that sanctifies us and proofs us in preparation for eternity. What you are becoming now is what you will be in eternity. Ponder that! And since your angel (which is the spirit within you) always sees your Father's face in heaven, then where is heaven?

The Kingdom of Heaven is neither up nor down... the journey is in!

> "He has made everything beautiful in its time. Also ***He has put eternity in their hearts***, except that no one can find out the work that God does from beginning to end" (Eccl. 3:11).

> ***The Kingdom of God is within you...***
> ***and now it's time to let heaven out!***

And finally, the Spirit of God dwelling with you and in your spirit enables you to accomplish exceedingly incredible supernatural (spirit-normal) deeds. You are a soul. You have a spirit. And you have an earthen body for this season of eternity – which is temporary – and then you get a new one in the regeneration – which is eternal. And here is the kicker: God created you and me

---

[33] This is a complex mystery that required five years of study under the guidance of the Spirit. For further proof, read "Gateways" section titled: "The Final Chapter" and read 40 pages of proof.

in His image according to His likeness (Gen. 1:26-28). God created us – as a likeness of Him. We are like God according to His likeness. This is not heresy, I can assure you. This truth is as plain as the nose on your face (John 10:34, 35). We are soul with spirit because that is what God is: Soul with Spirit. God even came to earth in a temporary earth suit – like us. Jesus is His name! And when Jesus comes again, "We shall see Him as He is… and we shall be like Him."

> "… it has not yet been revealed what we shall be, but we know that when He is revealed, we shall be like Him, for we shall see Him as He is" (1 John 3:2).

You are an angel, by faith… through confirmation, by the Spirit.

You are a pre-planned, predestined, predetermined participant in the Kingdom of the Spirit. The knowledge of this truth should cause a paradigm shift in how you see yourself… and clarify your mission on earth: to have dominion.

The spirit within you is the divine nature God formed within you – in order to partner with Him in the restoration of earth – as you partner with others in the gospel of Jesus Christ.

> "Grace and peace be multiplied to you in the knowledge of God and of Jesus our Lord, [3] as His divine power has given to us all things that pertain to life and godliness, through the knowledge of Him who called us by glory and virtue, [4] by which have been given to us exceedingly great and precious promises, that *through these you may be partakers of the divine nature*" (1 Pet. 1:2-4).

When you allow your mind to be renewed by the Spirit, you will be transformed by God's truth to become again what you were in the beginning – *elohims* – sons and daughters of God Most High. **Truth makes available what the Spirit makes possible.**

Therefore, it is mission critical for the saints of God to understand "what" they are according to the spirit within them. We are spiritual beings having a human experience – in the Kingdom of the Spirit (Gen. 1:2)! Everything we were created for and born to accomplish is intricately interwoven within our spiritual DNA as soul with spirit. *What the soul makes available, the spirit makes possible.*

What grace makes available, faith makes possible! We are connected to the Father – through faith in Jesus – in oneness of the Spirit – as a spiritual family in the Kingdom of Heaven through the Spirit. All for One – and One in all.

Your angel is your spirit. Now pay close attention to these scriptures placed alongside one other and perceive this marvelous mystery: angels are spirits.

> "*I, Jesus, have sent My angel* to testify to you these things in the churches. I am the Root and the Offspring of David, the Bright and Morning Star" (Rev. 22:16).
>
> "The Revelation of Jesus Christ, which God gave Him to show His servants—things which must shortly take place. And *He sent and signified it by His angel* to His servant John" (Rev. 1:1).

What, then, do you think the Lord's Angel is? The answer is simple: the Spirit!!! The Lord's angel (the Spirit) was sent to testify to John – "I was in the Spirit on the Lord's Day" (Rev. 1:10) – and the Spirit was also sent to testify to the churches. The word '*angelos*-32' (angel) means: messenger – so perceive what Jesus is saying through His Messenger (i.e. the Angel of the Lord), which is His Spirit – and *hear what the Spirit says to the churches*:

- "To the angel of the church of Ephesus write, 'These things says He' [Jesus]" (Rev. 2:1)
- ➤ "He who has an ear, *let him hear what the Spirit says* to the churches" (Rev. 2:7)
- "And to the angel of the church in Smyrna write, 'These things says the First and the Last' [Jesus]" (Rev. 2:8)
- ➤ "He who has an ear, *let him hear what the Spirit says* to the churches" (Rev. 2:11)
- "And to the angel of the church in Pergamos write, 'These things says He [Jesus] who has the sharp two-edged sword'" (Rev. 2:12)
- ➤ "He who has an ear, *let him hear what the Spirit says* to the churches" (Rev. 2:17)
- "And to the angel of the church in Thyatira write, 'These things says the Son of God' [Jesus]" (Rev. 2:18)
- ➤ "He who has an ear, *let him hear what the Spirit says* to the churches" (Rev. 2:29)
- ➤ "He who has an ear, *let him hear what the Spirit says* to the churches" (Rev. 3:6)
- ➤ "He who has an ear, *let him hear what the Spirit says* to the churches" (Rev. 3:13)
- ➤ "He who has an ear, *let him hear what the Spirit says* to the churches" (Rev. 3:22)

The Lord's angel – is the Holy Spirit. The Spirit is speaking these seven messages which were given to seven ministers (called angels) for seven churches (called lampstands) by the angel of the Lord, which is His Spirit! This is how the Kingdom of the Spirit operates under the guidance, governance and direction of King Jesus. The Spirit – speaks – and the Spirit continues to speak to all churches, even today – yet how many listen?

> "The mystery of the seven stars which you saw in My right hand, and the seven golden lampstands: The seven stars are the angels of the seven churches, and the seven lampstands which you saw are the seven churches" (Rev. 1:20).

Mystery solved. The seven stars... are angels sent to the seven churches. These angels are ministers. The angel of the church in Ephesus – is Timothy.

> "Who makes His angels spirits, His ministers a flame of fire" (Psa. 104:4).

"Timothy was a minister of the gospel, an evangelist by ordination, who became the leader of the church in Ephesus, which was established by the Apostle Paul, and the Apostle John ministered there as well. John was fully aware of Timothy and the church of Ephesus, and, even though Timothy overcame many personal shortcomings to accomplish many incredible deeds, it seems he forgot something: his first love."[34] He forgot his first love – and so has the church!

Wake up Church! Listen up!!! We are in the midst of a major course correction for the church because she stopped listening – and she abandoned her First Love, so listen up! Listen to the Spirit of Christ!

We are standing at the precipice! The church age is over – the kingdom age has begun![35] ***One kingdom, one God, one King, and one Lord – Jesus Christ!***

> "But you are not in the flesh but in the Spirit, if indeed the Spirit of God dwells in you. ***Now if anyone does not have the Spirit of Christ, he is not His***" (Rom. 8:9).

The Holy Spirit is the Spirit of the *Lord* (i.e. *Jesus*), whose names are attributed to Jesus: "the Spirit of Christ" (Rom. 8:9); "the Spirit of Jesus Christ" (Phil. 1:19); "the Spirit of Jesus" (Acts 16:6); and "the Spirit of His Son" (Gal. 4:6) because it is the Spirit of Christ

---

[34] Excerpt from "Gateways" section titled: "We Are Sons of God."
[35] Between every major spiritual shift, there is always a period of transition – and we are in transition now.

who reveals Christ to us. The Voice we hear is the Spirit of the Lord (and Jesus is Lord). The Voice we hear is the Spirit of God (and Jesus is God). So I ask: why have we made this so complicated – from a theological perspective – when a simple gardener without seminary training can figure this out.

When John the Baptist proclaimed the coming of the Messiah, he said of Jesus: "This is He who baptizes with the Holy Spirit" (Matt. 3:11; John 1:33), so therefore, the Baptism of the Holy Spirit is commissioned by Jesus Himself.

God is Spirit. Is there a big distinction between the Holy Spirit, the Spirit of the Father and the Spirit of Christ who dwells in you? At this present time, I understand them to be the same.

> "Do you not know that you are the temple of God and that the Spirit of God dwells in you?" (1 Cor. 3:16)

What is the purpose of the human body… and what is the purpose of the spirit God formed in man? The body (from '*skenos*-4636' a hut or *temporary residence*) is the **abode** of the spirit… and the body is the **tabernacle** of the soul (2 Cor. 5:1, 4).[36] The Father dwells in the abode of our spirit and Christ abides in the heart-house (tabernacle) of our soul (Eph. 3:17).

Read that again and again… because the flesh profits nothing. Meditate on it!

Our body is the tabernacle of the soul. And our body is the abode of the spirit where God abides <u>with</u> us (John 14:23). The word '*mone*' (*abode*) which was spoken by Jesus (John 14:2) "In my Father's house are many (*mone*) *abodes*" (also translated "*mansions*") literally means: are many dwelling places.

> "And the glory which You gave Me I have given them, that they may be one just as We are one: [23] *I*

---

[36] Strong's Concordance.

> ***in them**, and **You in Me**;* that they may be made perfect in one, and that the world may know that You have sent Me, and have loved them as You have loved Me" (John 17:22, 23).

Not only are they One in each other, on earth and in heaven, they desire to be One in us! And it gets even better than this! You are one of their dwelling places! The Father and the Son want to manifest themselves in you, in unity of the Spirit, to become Christ's likeness and kingdom ambassadors on the earth. Jesus gave us His glory for one primary reason: to make us one with Him (John 17:22). And why did Jesus send the Holy Spirit? So the testimony of Jesus dwells in you richly!!! (Rev. 1:19; 19:10).

This is very important: God will never leave or forsake us. The Spirit of the Father dwells with us in our spirit, and Christ abides in our heart house, such that... even when the body dies and our spirit returns to God who gave it (Eccl. 12:7), the Lord abides with us in our heart. How amazing is this! And likewise yet regrettably... how fearful are those who do not comprehend this and refuse to live by faith. Jesus, our Immanuel – God with us, will never leave us '*orphanos.*'

God is our heavenly Father. God is Spirit. God's Spirit dwells in our spirit – which means – the Father dwells in our spirit. We've never been alone on this mission from heaven sent by the Father to have dominion on earth with the Spirit guiding us every step of the way.

The Spirit is the key! The river of living water... is the Spirit of God. Go with the flow!

Through faith in Jesus Christ, we are adopted into God's spiritual family wherein God becomes our heavenly Father... according to the Spirit.

> Jesus said: "But when the Helper comes, whom I
> shall send to you from the Father, the Spirit of truth
> who **_proceeds from_** the Father, He will testify of
> Me" (John 15:26).

Jesus sent the Holy Spirit… who proceeds from the Father. Ponder this carefully!

> Jesus said to unbelieving Jewish leaders: "If God
> were your Father, you would love Me, for I
> **_proceeded forth_** and came from God; nor have I
> come of Myself, but He sent Me" (John 8:42).

Jesus proceeded from God – and the Spirit of truth proceeds from the Father. These spiritual truths were spoken to teach us… Jesus and the Father – are One. The Father and Spirit – are One! Jesus is Lord – and "The Lord is the Spirit" (2 Cor. 3:17) – and They are One.

Take a moment… and let that truth wash over you… and renew your thought process.

God is Spirit – and the Holy Spirit is the Father of Jesus who overshadowed Mary (Luke 1:35). This is such a marvelous mystery to comprehend. Jesus said: "I and My Father are One" – which means: Jesus is the Father who sent Himself as a Son to teach us how to live as sons and daughters of our Father in heaven (who dwells in our spirit). Absolutely amazing!

> "No one has seen God at any time. The only
> begotten Son, who is in the bosom of the Father, He
> has declared _Him_" (John 1:18).

The Spirit of God, the Spirit of the Father, the Spirit of Christ, the Spirit of the Lord, the Spirit of truth, the Spirit of grace, the Holy Spirit, the Inner Witness, the Spirit of holiness, the Spirit of wisdom and understanding, and all other names for the Spirit are teaching us: God is Spirit! Yet God manifests Himself in a multitude of ways, such as: a Son, a Father, a Friend, the Ancient of Days, the Prince of Peace, an Army Commander, a Conquering King, the Lion and the Lamb, our Kinsman and Redeemer, our Savior, and as Lord, Lord God, Lord God Almighty and God Most High as He reveals Himself to you – on a intimate, experiential, personal relationship level. Why does God do this? To help us know and understand this: God is God Almighty… and God loves you!!! God is the One True Living God! The Lord our God, the Holy One – is God – and there is no other.

> "Now to our God and Father be glory forever and ever. Amen" (Phil. 4:20).

God is Spirit – yet He reveals Himself in a multitude of ways to help us comprehend Him.

God is Spirit! When we perceive Him as Trinity, even this expression minimizes His all encompassing identity! Our understanding of who God is – begins by comprehending what Jesus told us: God is Spirit (John 4:24). First and foremost: God is Spirit. Yet man has trouble identifying with God as Spirit, so God manifests Himself in a multitude of ways which He can comprehend. Many of us can describe Jesus and some of us may be able to describe the Father as "Origin and Source – as the impetus, originator, giver and source of everything,"[37] but the vast majority of us cannot describe the Holy Spirit… yet this aspect of His divine nature is who God truly is. And yet the church fails miserably to understand the Holy Spirit – or the reason why Jesus sent this expression of God Himself to us: to empower us to become a likeness of Jesus.

What we need most… it the mind of the Spirit!

> "Now He who searches the hearts knows what the mind of the Spirit is, because He makes intercession for the saints according to the will of God" (Rom. 8:27).

---

[37] Excerpt from "Image" section titled: "The Father of the Son."

Mind Of The Spirit

Imagine this for a moment by closing your eyes to see this in the spiritual dimension: your soul and spirit reside (side-by-side) within your earthly tabernacle (body). Your spirit hosts the presence of God, and this is what Jesus meant by: "the kingdom of God is within you." Your soul must decide to rely on the nearness of God – or it can act independently of Him. When you establish the presence of Jesus (who is the King of Heaven) upon the throne of your heart, you are able to proclaim what Jesus proclaimed: "The kingdom of heaven is at hand!"

The kingdom of heaven is neither up nor down – it's in – and now it's time to let heaven out!

The problem with institutional Christianity is: we focus on physical representations rather than the realm of the Spirit. Catholics focus on Mary, Pentecostals focus on Father God, Baptists focus on evangelism, Fundamentalists focus on the written word, yet every denomination has some particular focus that takes their eyes of their true focus: Jesus. Jesus sent the Holy Spirit – the Spirit of Christ – to teach us truth and help us walk in the truth, but the pulpit of man is eerily silent on the Holy Spirit who was sent as the Administrator of His Church to guide us in all wisdom, righteousness, and truth – in order for us to be born again and imitate Jesus.

At great redundancy, I repeat myself: the Spirit – the Spirit – the Spirit!!! Walk according to the Spirit – and you will not gratify the desires of the flesh. Imitate Jesus – and you will glorify your Father in heaven (who – by the way – dwells with you and in you).

It's all about Jesus – and God gets the glory!

God is not diminished in any way or manner He chooses to reveal Himself.

Consider this: He chose YOU to reveal Himself through YOU!

What a marvelous mystery: Christ in you – the hope of glory!

> "Yet for us there is one God, the Father, of whom are all things, and we for Him; and one Lord Jesus Christ, through whom are all things, and through whom we live" (1 Cor. 8:6).

> "Hear, O Israel: **The LORD our God, the LORD *is* one**! ⁵ You shall love the LORD your God with all your heart, with all your soul, and with all your strength" (Deut. 6:4, 5).

Love God with everything you've got! Praise Him with all that is within you!

> "Praise the LORD! Praise the LORD, O my soul! ² While I live I will praise the LORD; I will sing praises to my God while I have my being" (Psa. 146:1, 2).

Regardless of where you are or what you've done in life… God can redeem it and get glory from it. Either we magnify the Lord and make Him larger in our perception of Him or we can diminish and disregard Him altogether as irrelevant. Free will allows this choice. Whatever you focus on… gets bigger. Yet your choice regarding your perception of God doesn't diminish His Sovereignty and Preeminence over all creation! God chose to manifest Himself 2,000 years ago and Jesus is – the Revelation of God Himself:

King of kings and Lord of lords

Whether you accept this truth and change your ways to walk in His way – is a choice we must all make. Knowing this yet refusing to walk by faith with Jesus as your Lord – is a deadly choice.

King Jesus is Lord God! God loves you! And God formed a spirit within you so He could walk with you and be with you. How amazing! God wants to be with us; He has never left us or abandoned us. Why would God do this? A: The Spirit is the key!!

> Jesus said: "You do not know what manner of spirit you are of" (Luke 9:55).

There are two types of spirits: heavenly and earthly. The manner of spirit you are of is earthly (for the earth) and operates according to your mission as the host of earth (Gen. 2:1) to have dominion on earth. You were sent here (as was I) for two primary reasons:

1. As "the salt of the earth" (Matt. 5:13) and as co-redeemers with Christ – as life-giving spirits (1 Cor. 15:45) to save souls alive!
2. As "the light of the world" (Matt. 5:14) and as co-laborers and partners with Christ – to come against the kingdom of darkness and establish the kingdom of heaven on earth

Your "light" is the spirit (sic) in you – which belongs to God (1 Cor. 6:20) and your spirit is a habitation for the Spirit of the Father who tabernacles _with_ you! Your heavenly Father dwells _in_ your spirit – and alongside (_with_) your soul. Truly I say – the Spirit of God is the key to unlocking the mysteries of the kingdom! Seek and pursue Him, seek and find Him, seek and walk with … the Spirit of life (Rom. 8:2).

> "… and we will make Our home _with_ him" (John 14:23)… in the "unity of the Spirit (Eph. 4:3, 4).

What, then, is the spirit within man? This spiritual aspect of "what we are" is one of the most monumental aspects we must comprehend about man in order to live victoriously "in Christ" as the means whereby we are able to operate on earth like Jesus did in order to do the same works He did… and greater works as well. The spirit within us hosts the presence of the Holy Spirit, which is the tabernacle of the Father, to accomplish the Lord's will – and God's plan. The Father and Spirit – are One – and through faith in Christ – they are one _in_ you and one _with_ you!

Immanuel means: God with us. God's Spirit – dwells <u>with</u> us and dwells <u>in</u> us (John 14:17). Jesus said many things… in order to teach us God "the Father of us in heaven" has been alongside us every moment of every day. Jesus said of Himself and the Father:

- "I am in the Father and the Father in Me" (John 14:10)
- "I am in the Father and the Father in Me" (John 14:11)
- "… ***the Father is <u>in</u> Me***, and I in Him" (John 10:38)
- "I and My Father are one" (John 10:30).
- "I am not alone, because ***the Father is with Me***" (John 16:32)
- "I am <u>***with***</u> the Father who sent Me" (John 8:16).
- "And He who sent Me is <u>with</u> Me. The Father has not left Me alone, for I always do those things that please Him" (John 8:29).
- "The Father who dwells <u>*in*</u> Me does the works" (John 14:10)
- "At that day you will know that I ~~am~~ in My Father, and you in Me, and I in you" (John 14:20; "am" was added and should read: "I in My Father, and you in Me")
- "… that they all may be one, as You, Father, are in Me, and I in You" (John 17:21)

It is important to read and re-read these declarations by Jesus because – "As He is, so are we in this world" (1 John 4:17). Jesus came to teach us what is happening <u>in</u> us… and <u>with</u> us!

> "Do you not believe that I am in the Father, and the Father in Me? The words that I speak to you I do not speak on My own *authority;* but ***the Father who dwells <u>in</u> Me*** does the works" (John 14:10; read Matt. 10:20 above to perceive this truth).

The Father dwelt in Jesus (in His spirit – small 's') and likewise, the Father dwells in your spirit! This truth is liberating! And exhilarating! The problem we have comprehending this truth is because the earth suit prevents us from perceiving our true spiritual reality... as spiritual beings having a human experience... and also much toxic theology as well.

The Father Of Us

Jesus is Lord God. Jesus said "the Father" sent Him, so <u>*carefully*</u> consider this next scripture:

> "Come near to Me, hear this: I have not spoken in secret from the beginning; from the time that it was, I *was* there. ***And now the Lord God and His Spirit have sent Me***" (Isa. 48:16).

The God of Oneness reveals and manifests Himself in manifold myriad ways to guide the affairs of men for this purpose: to implement the plan of God on earth. The Spirit of God is a rushing wind. The Spirit of God is a rushing river, so get ready to dive and go – all in.

> "... ***the Lord God and His Spirit have sent Me***" (Isa. 48:16).

> Jesus said: "As the Father has ***sent Me***, I also send you" (John 20:21).

Did you sense a shift in your thought process when you read these? Jesus is Lord! Jesus is "Lord God Almighty" (Rev. 4:8; 11:17; 15:3). The Lord God sent Jesus and Jesus said the Father sent Him! Therefore, the Father is Lord God. And since Jesus is Lord God, that means Jesus is the Father... who sent Himself as a Son. This is absolutely incredible!

> "...that God was in Christ reconciling the world to Himself" (2 Cor. 5:19).

Jesus is the Lord our God. And just as "the Father of us" sent Jesus, our Father also sent you! And get this: He sent you the same way He sent Jesus... by the overshadowing of the Holy Spirit upon your mother. Can you say paradigm shift?[38] Thus, it happened unto Him (Jesus) to teach us what has happened unto us.

> "Inasmuch then as the children have partaken of flesh and blood, He Himself likewise shared in the same" (Heb. 2:14).

Now I beseech you: honor your mother and your father. This is the reason behind the commandment. God used them to send you – here.

Now do you see why Jesus told us the Father was greater than all? (John 10:29) Because the Father sent Himself as a subordinate version of His glorified self – as Jesus Christ, the only begotten one – to do what no man could ever accomplish in a million lifetimes!

The Father dwells in our spirit who not only sent us on a mission, but the Father came with us – as the Spirit in our spirit alongside our soul – to reveal Christ to us in order for Christ to dwell in the heart of our soul through faith. We've been invited to live in oneness with the Spirit to accomplish the will of God in the sameness/likeness/newness/oneness of Jesus. However, in order to maintain this relationship with the Father of us who dwells in us, we must maintain our spiritual relationship with Jesus as Lord – in oneness with the Spirit. The Spirit is the key!

And just as Jesus was sent to accomplish the will of God, likewise… so were you! This is why Jesus came: to teach us what to do – and how to do it! Remember the testimony of Jesus!

> "The Spirit of the Lord God is upon Me, because the Lord has anointed Me to preach good tidings to the poor; He has sent Me to heal the brokenhearted, to proclaim liberty to the captives, and the opening

---

[38] To fully comprehend this awesome mystery, read: "Image – The Revelation of God Himself" (book #3).

> of the prison to those who are bound; and the opening of the prison to those who are bound; [2] to proclaim the acceptable year of the LORD, and the day of vengeance of our God; to comfort all who mourn, [3] to console those who mourn in Zion..." (Isa. 61:1-3).

The realm of the Spirit must be known, understood and embraced – because you were destined from the beginning to be born anew by the Spirit – in order to operate according to the Spirit – and walk according to the spirit (sic) within you. The Spirit is the key!

> "For what man knows the things of a man except the spirit of the man which is in him? Even so no one knows the things of God except the Spirit of God" (1 Cor. 2:11).

Where does the Paraclete (the Holy Spirit) take residency in you? The term paraclete (3875) means: intercessor; one who comes alongside. The Holy Spirit dwells *in* your spirit – who comes alongside "the heart-house of your soul" to dwell *with* you in the earthen temple called: __state your name__. Is this beginning to make sense?

> "Do you not know that you are the temple of God and that the Spirit of God dwells in you?" (1 Cor. 3:16)

The Spirit dwells *with* you – *in* your spirit – as a Paraclete – alongside your soul.

Yet Christ dwells in the heart of your soul,[39] through faith (Eph. 3:17; Col. 3:16), so that wherever you are – both now and eternally – Christ Jesus goes with you.

---

[39] The soul consists of mind and heart. To learn more, read "Commission" and Gateways."

"Christ in you, the hope of glory" (Col. 1:27). Amen!

Through faith, you are already dwelling eternally with Christ right now. There is an aspect of "being in heaven" with Him that you are able to experience – right now. So I ask: why wait for eternity when you can "go all in" and live with Jesus now – on earth as it shall be in heaven? Think about the way you want to live in eternity with Jesus – and start doing it now! Do it now!

Two Kingdoms – Two Spirits

"And the Spirit of God hovered" (Gen. 1:2).

It is mission critical to comprehend this very short message. There are two kingdoms on earth and they are at war with one another: the kingdom of God vs. the kingdom of darkness. The battle is between good and evil and the result is either life or death. These kingdoms have different operating systems: grace vs. sin. Two princes govern them: the Prince of Peace (Jesus) and the prince of the powers of the air (Satan). And two competing spirits guide the sons of men to believe in one prince or the other to serve one kingdom or the other.

> "By this you know the Spirit of God: Every spirit that confesses that Jesus Christ has come in the flesh is of God, [3] and every spirit that does not confess that Jesus Christ has come in the flesh is not of God. And this is the *spirit* of the Antichrist, which you have heard was coming, and is now already in the world. [4] You are of God, little children, and have overcome them, because He who is in you is greater than he who is in the world" (1 John 4:2-4).

There is a spirit in a man… yet the soul of man has free will to choose one spirit over the other.

> "And you He made alive, who were dead in trespasses and sins, [2] in which you once walked according to the course of this world, according to the prince of the power of the air, **the spirit who now works in the sons of disobedience**, [3] among whom also we all once conducted ourselves in the lusts of our flesh, fulfilling the desires of the flesh and of the mind, and were by nature children of wrath, just as the others" (Eph. 2:1-3).

Our mind is able to listen to and communicate with three entities: God, self, the enemy. Some walk according to the Spirit, but not everyone listens to the Spirit of Christ. Many have been deceived to follow a wayward spirit, yet God gave us a simple way to test the spirits to see who they are aligned with. Ask them two questions: "Who is your Lord?" This determines – if they know Jesus is Lord and they serve Him – or if they serve someone else.

> "You believe that there is one God. You do well. Even the demons believe—and tremble!" (James 2:19)

If they say Jesus, then test them by asking: "Do you believe Jesus came in the flesh?" Deep theology is not needed to live by faith, nor a complete understanding of who Jesus is, yet these two questions are sufficient to separate goats from sheep. Be wise, and do not partner with just anyone. All of us were born in darkness, and some of us found the light, yet many are still in some state of transition between darkness and light, so be kind and merciful with patience and longsuffering – just as your Father in heaven was – while faith was taking root in you.

> "But there is a spirit in man, and the breath of the Almighty gives him understanding" (Job 32:8).

Godly wisdom and understanding is what we need more than anything else because – truth itself is under attack by the spirit of this world... which is evil! Two kingdoms operating under two different spirits also have two different versions of truth. God's truth is under attack by godless truth... and this is evidenced in the news today: people see the same event yet perceive it from two entirely different perspectives because they are using two different versions of truth – to discern reality. We see it declared even now... and battle lines are being drawn:

Darkness will call the light – darkness; and darkness will call itself – light.

> "Woe to those who call evil good, and good evil;
> who put darkness for light, and light for darkness;
> who put bitter for sweet, and sweet for bitter!" (Isa. 5:20).

We are living on the precipice of the most tumultuous period of time in human history. Truth has become relative to whatever you want to believe. We call these: agenda. Biology has become irrelevant within a culture that seeks to change a person's identity using 27 different gender classifications. Science and religion have become irrelevant as well because truth was rewritten to accommodate error – to worship created things and this world. Even the light within many (which is the spirit) grows darker in this evil age… which Jesus warned us about:

> "But if your eye is bad, your whole body will be full of darkness. If therefore the light that is in you is darkness, how great is that darkness!" (Matt. 6:23)

Consider the current state of affairs in the world. It gets worse, then it seems to get a little better, but it continues to get evil and it seems the darkness is winning. Faithful ones in Christ – remain vigilant: our King has overcome this world! Keep your eyes focused on Jesus!

The church created a doctrine of last days to understand what the great tribulation is – and then it created a scenario where those with faith in Christ are safely raptured before this happens. Oh really? Jesus told us many will fall way when persecution happens, and the scriptures also tell us there is a great multitude in heaven that came out of the great tribulation (Rev. 7:14), so I ask: which is it? How can there be a great multitude who came out of great tribulation (Matt. 24:15-22)… if the elect are raptured before it happens? Also, how do those on earth on the last day get raptured if the rapture has already happened? Our doctrine is illogical! Jesus said we will be persecuted (John 15:20). Yet those who remain faithful until the end will be rewarded (Matt. 5:12). Through patient endurance, a disciple will never bring a negative accusation against God… or bend the truth to accommodate manmade doctrines.

> "You therefore, beloved, since you know this beforehand, beware lest you also fall from your own steadfastness, being led away with the error of the wicked" (2 Pet. 3:17; see also 2 Thess. 2:3).

Go, therefore, in grace and peace, in the love of Christ Jesus, but "be wise as serpents and gentle as doves" (Matt. 10:16)... and "see then that you walk circumspectly, not as fools but as wise, [16] redeeming the time, because the days are evil. [17] Therefore do not be unwise, but understand what the will of the Lord is" (Eph. 5:15-17).

> "And from the days of John the Baptist until now the kingdom of heaven suffers violence, and the violent take it by force" (Matt. 11:12; and violence against God's Truth continues today).

This is a cautionary message! The days we live in... are evil. Truth has been perverted and distorted. Lawlessness abounds (Matt. 24:12)... and greater evil is on the horizon. Do not be unaware. The great tribulation is coming, yet many believers will be caught unaware because understanding God's truth has not taken root in their life (Mark 4:17; 13:19).

> "But know this, that in the last days perilous times will come" (2 Tim. 3:1).

> "Yes, the time is coming that whoever kills you will think that he offers God service" (John 16:2).

Know the truth. Love Jesus. Be lovers of God's truth. Listen to the Spirit. Stay in the truth.

Created As Worshippers

> "But the hour is coming, and now is, when the true worshipers will worship the Father in spirit and truth; for the Father is seeking such to worship Him. [24] God *is* Spirit, and those who worship Him must worship in spirit and truth" (John 4:23, 24).

This scripture is monumental in importance to comprehend the realm (kingdom) of the Spirit and its relation to the Father. Jesus Himself makes a correlation between God as Father… and God as Spirit. Woven between these precisely crafted words is the truth of the gospel: God is seeking worshippers. God created us as worshippers – as instruments of worship – yet most people cannot perceive this aspect of what they are. We've become human doings rather than spiritual beings having a human experience… and true worship became compromised as a result.

God is seeking worshippers "in spirit and in truth." The message Jesus conveyed to the Samaritan woman at the well is the same message for everyone around the world: ***the hour now is!*** Jesus instituted this hour through His visitation to draw all people to Himself to reveal the love of the Father to us… by appearing as Him. The hour has come and continues even now – for all people to worship the Lord neither on this mountain nor that mountain nor in this temple/church/mosque or any other house of God. God is everywhere. God is Spirit. The only way anyone is able to accurately and effectively worship God is – in spirit and in truth!

This was a dramatic departure from how Judaism worshipped God with repetitious religious ceremonies and how other cultures worshipped God with much observance to physical actions and vigorous emotional appeals to appease their gods.

To worship the One, True, Living God… one must become acquainted with truth… and Jesus is the Truth!

Knowing the truth and being set free by the Truth… liberates us to worship God as He desires to be worshipped. Once again at the risk of great redundancy... unless you have been born anew by the Spirit, it is impossible to worship God "in spirit and in truth." How dare we claim to know how God desires to be worshipped – as if glory can be manifested through hymnals, choirs, shofars or electric guitars. Over the years, I've witnessed a great many spectacles using symbols, venerated objects and religious (even mystical) techniques to help people enter into "the presence of God." Think about that for a moment. God is everywhere – and dwells in you. Does your church use a lot of hype and exuberant expressions of faith in order to conjure the Spirit in order to experience the presence of God in worship? Well, this my friends... is exactly what pagans do... because they lack knowledge of the truth.

How about long-winded prayers that employ God's name in an irreverent manner? We are cautioned not to take the Lord's name in vain because the culture of pagans and heathens is to use vain repetition in a vain effort to get God's attention. During one particular prayer meeting, the Spirit instructed me to start counting the number of times one individual said "Father" during his prayer – approximately 250 times! How this man was taught to pray this way goes to the core of the spiritual disconnect we have within the Christian church; we do many things knowing neither the truth... nor the Spirit of Truth. When Jesus taught us to pray, He taught us "how to" and "how not to" (Matt. 6:7). He said "Father" once... and I strenuously encourage all disciples of Jesus to follow His example... and insert the word "um" the other 249 times!

> Jesus said: "And when you pray, do not use vain repetitions as the heathen do. For they think that they will be heard for their many words" (Matt. 6:7).

I've also heard saints pray in this manner: "Dear Heavenly Father, Lord God, Jesus, Father God" in an attempt to call out to God – with all His names – to make sure their prayer gets delivered to the right person. Really? I'm not being hyper critical, but we really have a very shallow understanding of who God is... and whose

Name is above every name (Phil. 2:9). Pray to Jesus.

> "And whatever you ask in My name, that I will do, that the Father may be glorified in the Son. [14] If you ask anything in My name, I will do it" (John 14:13, 14).

Worshipping God in the realm of the Spirit is rarely if ever experienced within the institutional church. This may sound outrageous, but I assure you it is not. When we come into a building to worship God, do we worship Him based upon the traditions taught to us by others who were taught by their father's fathers... or shall we ask the Spirit of Jesus how the Father desires to be worshipped. There will always be numerous expressions of worship throughout the world, but the worship of God must originate "in spirit" and depend upon the Spirit of Truth to lead us and empower us in the worship of God – in truth.

How is anyone supposed to know how to do this? This may seem like an improbable mystery to comprehend... because we have believed many inaccurate doctrines about the Father... and even fewer doctrines are taught regarding the Holy Spirit of God and His effectual and permanent presence within the Church (not church buildings, per se) to guide worshippers in worship. If your church has an order of worship that is routine and predictable, then it is not being led by the Spirit. The worship leader will always be – the Spirit!

Jesus set us free from the legalisms of religious institutional traditions and vain worship.

Jesus is God. God is Spirit. Worship God... in spirit and in truth.

Worship – is the imitation of that which someone values most. If a worship leader values a good and orderly service with three songs and then a solo while the offering is conducted, let me sharpen my sword to say... how is God glorified in this? Stand up, sit down, stand up, kneel, bow, kneel, sit, kneel... "now stand and repeat after me the articles of our confession." The church service has become so well choreographed that the Spirit is stifled and quenched and nary is a hand upraised in reverent awe of God... in obedient surrender to Him.

"In the nature of worship... Christians shall worship God, not in ceremonial observances of the Mosaic tradition, but in spiritual ordinances, consisting less in bodily exercise, and animated and invigorated with divine power and energy. The way of worship which Christ has instituted is rational and intellectual, and refined from those external rites and ceremonies with which the Old Testament worship was both clouded and clogged. This is called true worship, in opposition to that which was typical."[40]

> "For we are the circumcision, who worship God in the Spirit, rejoice in Christ Jesus, and have no confidence in the flesh" (Phil. 3:3).

The offering of Jewish sacrifices to the Lord had become repugnant to Him because they were obligatory observances that lacked obedience... and intimacy. Offering sacrifices was instituted by the Lord to teach everyone one thing: the true offering is the sacrifice of oneself upon the altar of God in service unto Him.

> "I beseech you therefore, brethren, by the mercies of God, that you present your bodies a living sacrifice, holy, acceptable to God, which is your reasonable service [act of worship; KJV]. ² And do not be conformed to this world, but be transformed by the renewing of your mind, that you may prove what *is* that good and acceptable and perfect will of God" (Rom. 12:1, 2).

Jesus came to satisfy the requirements of the Mosaic Covenant as the sacrificial Lamb of God whereby the Old Covenant with

---

[40] Matthew Henry's Commentary on the Bible; John Chapter 4; section 3.2.2.b titled: "The blessed change itself."

sacrifices on altars was rendered "obsolete" (Heb. 8:13) in order to institute a new manner of worshipping the Lord "in spirit and in truth" within a New Covenant established by Him that He offers freely to anyone – through faithful obedience to His gospel. Yet the Catholic Church continually offers sacrifices in every Mass upon an altar whereby everyone joins together in saying: "May the Lord accept <u>this sacrifice</u> from your hands to the praise and glory of His name." They have forgotten all remembrance of what Jesus taught – choosing rather to imitate obsolete and ineffectual Jewish ceremonies performed by religious men who refused to listen to the Voice of the Spirit. Special garments are never needed for worshippers "in truth" – except the garment of praise.

The pendulum swings both ways. Pentecostals claim to operate in a higher realm of the Spirit, especially during worship, but they also have an achilles heel: silent adoration. They fear silence. When the Spirit causes a heavenly hush to fall upon their congregation, too often I've observed "coaches" get up to coach; they tell believers to sense the move of the Spirit or explain what the Spirit is doing… which oftentimes gets long winded (because they sense the power of the Spirit and get invigorated by Him). So I say: just shut up and hover in the spirit… and act like the Holy Spirit who hovers. You may be surprised by the unction of the Spirit when this happens: prophetic utterances, tongues with interpretation, words of knowledge and many other giftings by the Spirit as well, but the one thing that happens most often is the soft, glorious, whispered voices of saints in "a capella" oneness… worshiping the Lord without instrumental assistance. My entire body quivers in electric wonder by the Spirit's presence in these rare moments.

We were created by God – to be worshippers of God. Worship God in spirit and in truth.

God Is Spirit

This phrase "God is Spirit" occurs only once in scripture, yet because Jesus said it – an entire doctrine can be made from it. Jesus is God. God is Spirit. Jesus is Lord and…

"The Lord is the Spirit (2 Cor. 3:17).

Meditate on that for a month and see what happens to your faith life!

Let me say this a little differently. The nature of the spirit within us makes us worshippers. Regardless of time in history or place on earth, men worship because it's in our nature (our divine nature) as spiritual beings to worship. We "are" instruments of worship! Intuitively, all men know they were created to worship… something. We worship something (not always God) because we were created for worship. Our spirit is the divine nature within us (2 Pet. 1:4) which God gave to us where the Father dwells – to host His presence – so we would never be separated from Him. Our spirit enables us to worship the God of grace and mercy wherever we are. However, many try to live life separated from him… but this is technically impossible… even when they construct an alternate reality to believe He is distant from them and dwells in the outer cosmos. How primordial! Yet we reinforce this alternate reality with some church doctrines so we may continue to live sinful lifestyles thinking He does not see us – or hear our thoughts.

Utterly ridiculous!!!

"*If* I ascend into heaven, You are there; *If* I make my bed in hell, behold, You are there" (Psa. 139:8; these are rhetorical "if" statements).

"Where can I go from Your Spirit? Or where can I flee from Your presence?" (Psa. 139:7).

One thing I've learned: regardless of where you go, you can't get away from this Jesus.

The Father With/In Us

> "Or do you think that the Scripture says in vain,
> "The Spirit who dwells in us yearns jealously"?"
> (James 4:5)

This is an incredible mystery which will make more sense in the following scripture:

> Jesus said: "Take heed that you do not despise one of these little ones [very young children], for I say to you that in heaven their angels always see the face of My Father who is in heaven" (Matt. 18:10).

"Assemble these facts in your mind: you have an angel; your angel sees your heavenly Father's face; and your Father is in Heaven. So, now, there is only one condition whereby these facts may be unified: the Father is in you! And so is heaven! And so is eternity (Eccl. 3:11)! ***Your angel is none other than your spirit that was given to you by God – to host His* presence with *your heart* –** everywhere you go on planet earth. Let the epiphany happen in your mind!"[41]

Some may reject this teaching because I associated the term angel to the spirit within us (even though Jesus referred to the Spirit as His angel), so let's take this one step further... [42]

- Are angels referred to as spirits? Yes (Psa. 104:4; Heb. 1:13, 14).
- Are angels referred to as stars and sons of God? Yes (Job 38:7).
- Are angels associated with light? Yes (Matt. 28:3; Luke 24:4; Acts 12:7; 2 Cor. 11:14). Jesus is the Light of the world and Jesus referred to us as "the light of the world" (Matt. 5:14) which pertains to the lamp (spirit) that was placed within us.

---

[41] Excerpt from "Gateways" section titled: "We Are Sons Of God."
[42] Excerpts copied from "Gateways" section titled: "The Final Chapter."

> "The spirit of a man is the lamp of the Lord, searching all the inner depths of his heart [being]" (Prov. 20:27).

Now then, are angels referenced in scripture as lamps? Yes (below)...

> "And from the throne proceeded lightnings, thunderings, and voices. Seven lamps of fire were burning before the throne, which are the seven Spirits of God" (Rev. 4:5).

For heavenly angels, the spirit garment is upon them; for humans, the spirit is in them with a human garment superimposed upon them. We are angels in disguise!

"The light of the Lord was placed within us – as one type of glory, yet the light was placed upon angels – as yet another type of glory.

> "He counts the number of the stars; He calls them all by name" (Psa. 147:4).

"Angels in heaven are called "sons of God" in the Old Testament and men are called servants; yet this is reversed in the New Testament whereby men are called sons of God and angels are servants. This has everything to do with the glory Jesus gave us (John 17:22).

"Are angels in heaven referred to as our "brethren"? Yes (Rev. 19:10). And they are also ministering spirits sent here to assist us as "heirs" of salvation (Heb. 1:4) and even deliver us from danger (Acts 5:19; 12:7; 27:24)! "What is man" if angels in Heaven are our brethren?"[43]

This word, which was revealed to me, is incredibly awesome to comprehend! For five years I researched the scriptures to

---

[43] Excerpt from "Gateways" section titled: "The Final Chapter."

comprehend "what is man" and learned much about our complexity. The Father dwells <u>with</u> us <u>in</u> our spirit. Read "Gateways – The Final Chapter" to learn this: we are angels in disguise. The fullness of this revelation was slowly revealed to me over 18 months, so don't expect to completely comprehend it in three minutes. Read it, meditate on it, search the scriptures and let the Spirit walk you through it. Some will receive it, some will not.

This puts an entirely fresh nuance to how Jesus taught us to pray:

> "Our Father in heaven..." (Matt. 6:9).

"Our Father" – is the Father of us. We know where the Father is – He is in Heaven and Heaven is His throne, so where is heaven? Perhaps the better question to ask is: "what" is Heaven? Heaven is – the presence of Jesus. Therefore, the kingdom of heaven is wherever the King of heaven is. Jesus said: "The kingdom of God is in you" (Luke 17:21), and if Jesus abides in your heart through faith, then the kingdom of heaven is neither up nor down... it's IN... and now it's time to let heaven out! Heaven – is the presence of God – in Christ Jesus – who dwells *in* you!

The Lord taught us to pray two ways; He said to pray "Father in heaven" and He told us to pray in your secret place. And now you know where this is: in your heart. And this is how the Father is able to hear all your thoughts and prayers because He dwells alongside your soul – in the spirit He gave you. You are a tabernacle for God that He uses to redeem the earth, and build nations and kingdoms – through you!

> "He who dwells in the ***secret place*** of the Most High Shall abide under the shadow of the Almighty. I will say of the Lord, "He is my refuge and my fortress; My God, in Him I will trust" (Psa. 91:1)

> "But you, when you pray, go into your room, and when you have shut your door, pray to your Father who is in the ***secret place***; and your Father who sees in secret will reward you openly" (Matt: 6:6).

Now do you see why the Father is able to hear your thoughts? You do not need to verbalize words or make any sounds because God can hear our thoughts (Gen. 18:12-13) and knows the intents of our heart (1 Chron. 28:9; Luke 5:22). And now you know why... because He dwells <u>with</u> you... in the spirit alongside your soul!

> ***"Am I a God near at hand," says the LORD,***
> ***And not a God afar off? (Jer. 23:23).***

> Jesus said: "If anyone loves Me, he will keep My word; and My Father will love him, and We will come to him and make Our home <u>*with*</u> him" (John 14:23).

Not <u>in</u> – but <u>with</u>! Momma was right! Home is where your heart is!

It is incredibly important to illuminate how one word of scripture creates subtle yet enormous differences in how we interpret scripture. Does God make His home <u>in</u> us – or <u>with</u> us? Jesus said: "with us!" The Father dwells temporarily <u>*in*</u> our spirit (which is yielded when the body dies), but through faith – we are told by God to build a permanent '*mone*' home in our heart so that God's glory and presence can dwell <u>with</u> us – eternally! We are master builders (1 Cor. 3:10) and master craftsmen (Prov. 8:30)... in the realm of the Spirit... to establish the kingdom of heaven on earth... through the host of earth called the sons of men (i.e. you and me)!!!

Do you want to know what your purpose in life is? You just read it. Now ask Jesus for His specific details on what He wants you to do.

> "Heaven is My throne, and earth is My footstool.
> What house will you build for Me? says the Lord,
> or what is the place of My rest?" (Acts 7:49)

"But Solomon built Him a house" (Acts 7:47)... and so have the rest of us.

We keep building temples and churches and mosques to inhabit space and take territory yet never mention the most holy place where we need to build – is a house in our heart for God to dwell – where we shall dwell together – eternally! Let the epiphany happen in your mind!

The territory we need to take in obedience to Jesus... is our own heart!

The spiritual dimension of man within the Spirit realm of the Father is incredible to comprehend. Nothing is impossible <u>with</u> our God. Yet for most of humanity, this is too impossible to comprehend and believe... so we rely on manmade doctrines preached in houses made with human hands.

> ***God does not dwell in temples made with human hands***
> ***(Acts 17:24)***
> ***God dwells in temples that have human hands!***

The Spirit With/In Us

Your spirit is a safety net for your soul to prevent you from falling into the Pit (Psa. 49:9). The Father loves you very much and He wants to tell you this Himself, but you need to sit still and listen. Wherever you are, close your eyes, call to Him from your secret place... and listen.

"Be still... and know that I am God" (Psa. 46:10).

The spirit within you is the divine nature God gave you (2 Pet. 1:4) that enables you to:

A) to abide with God eternally
B) to be "the light of the world" (Matt. 5:14) to disperse darkness

C) to be "the salt of the earth" (Matt. 5:13) to flavor it with grace
D) to activate faith within you – and operate through your spirit
E) to accomplish all the same miraculous works Jesus did
F) to be a tabernacle to host the presence of your Father in heaven
G) to help us walk in uprightness
H) to act as a safety net for the soul
I) "The spirit of a man is the lamp of the Lord" (Prov. 20:27) to guide his soul for this reason:

> Jesus said: "Watch and pray, lest you enter into temptation. The spirit indeed is willing, but the flesh is weak" (Matt. 26:41).

Our mission as "disciples under a commission" is to operate through our spirit in the same manner Jesus did. We accomplish this grace – through faith.

We know that "Heaven" is God's throne, but we've made a great many assumptions about where it is and what it is... and "what" type of house God wants us to build. Build it... in your heart... and build it on the solid rock: faith in Jesus as Lord, God and King.

Our mission as "disciples under a commission" is to operate through our spirit in the same manner Jesus did... and the spirit within us if infinitely more capable of accomplishing this mission than the flesh.

> "And He who sent Me is with Me. The Father has not left Me alone, for I always do those things that please Him" (John 8:29; see also verse 8:16; 16:32).

The Father sent you and the Father is <u>with</u> you – also! The Father dwells in your spirit, so allow this truth to completely conquer and saturate your soul. Our God has always been near at hand! This ability to imitate Jesus and do what He did is supercharged once we are baptized by the Holy Spirit – and fire. Jesus was baptized this way! But Jesus is God, so why would Jesus need to be baptized by the Holy Spirit to walk in the power of the Spirit – if Jesus is God (Luke 1:14)? That is precisely the right question to ask!!! Jesus did not need to be empowered by the Spirit so He could perform miracles – but it happened this way to show us what we must do if our intention is to imitate His example. The born again experience gives us a new spirit and a new heart – to begin anew – and live according to grace! The Spirit makes this happen.

> "Therefore… "Do not be conformed to this world,
> but be transformed by the renewing of your mind,
> that you may prove what is that good and
> acceptable and perfect will of God" (Rom. 12:2).

Jesus was baptized by the Holy Spirit. It happened thus unto Him in order to show what must happen – unto us. Newness – through truth, change and oneness – is the reason why!

"What, then, is the purpose of any building if the Father is already in us? That is precisely the right question to ask. The Father has a temporary place of staying that He wants converted into a permanent '*mone*' home in our heart – through faith in Jesus Christ. To be candid, we do not need to go anywhere or to wait any longer because the process of our salvation has been made complete in Christ. We are already – not yet; however, we must tarry in these earthen vessels through sanctification before we experience glorification in order to increase the size of our eternal house and estate. The type of "new man" house you are building in your heart becomes your eternal '*oiketerion*' habitation dwelling in the New Earth. How large or small your new man becomes – is entirely up to you."[44]

Seek first the kingdom of God – and His righteousness – and do the will of the Lord.

---

[44] Excerpt from "Here" section titled: Oneness With The Father."

Operate According To Faith – And Glory

> "Most assuredly, I say to you, he who believes in Me, the works that I do he will do also; and ***greater works than these he will do***, because I go to My Father" (John 14:12).

How can we operate according to this pattern? Jesus taught us to operate according to faith. If you have the faith of a mustard seed, you will say to this mountain – move – and it will move (Matt. 17:20). When we operate according to faith, there is nothing we cannot accomplish. But first, you must thoroughly believe this truth – before you can enter into faith because faith means: being thoroughly persuaded and convinced these words of truth... are the truth.

Jesus was teaching us to live according to truth. Children of faith – must live according to truth – and the truth will set you free! And secondly, in order to activate faith:

> "You must be born again!" (John 3:3-8)

Now do you see it? Jesus showed us what to do so that we can continue the works He did. Do you see the connection between living like Jesus in the power of the Spirit – and living by faith through the spirit (sic) within you? The operational means to accomplish what God purposed for us – is according to the Spirit dwelling in our spirit – through faith!

We are taught to glorify God, but what does this mean? Having visited a multitude of churches, I am been perplexed when people shout "GLORY" without really knowing what it means. They know that glory is attributed to God, which is true, but ask them to explain it and you will hear a diversity of explanations.

What is glory? Glory '*doxa*-1391' signifies: "an opinion."[45]

---

[45] Strong's Concordance.

Within the context of God, it signifies a good opinion. When we give glory to God, we are rendering a good opinion that – God is good! When all your thoughts of God are good and you are exalting His goodness, this is when you, my friend, are glorifying God. Your good opinion (*doxa*) gives glory to God. You are rendering a good opinion unto God – which glorifies God and gives Him glory.

Goodness is related to glory. Glory is all that God is, good is all that God is – and goodness is all that God does… because God is good always. God's nature is good – all the time. All the time – God is good. There is never an exception in this regard: goodness is attributed to God.

> Jesus said: "Why do you call Me good? No one is good but One, that is, God" (Luke 18:19).

Jesus is teaching us something about God and Himself in this moment. Jesus is implying: do not call Me good… unless you are also willing to call Me God.

If you do good things, it's because "God in you" is doing it – in you and through you. Ponder that statement for a moment… or millennia. Any good that is done on earth is because the God of all Goodness and Glory and Might is accomplishing it through you. This is the will of God – do good (i.e. do well; Gen. 4:7)! Therefore, the will of God is to render a good opinion that is based upon the truth – and in doing so – you will give glory to God.

The kingdom of God is good, is established by good, will always be good and operate according to goodness. There is not any aspect of God's kingdom that isn't good, so if you are in full agreement with this, then there's only one thing to do if you want to do the will of God: do good!

> "And we know that all things work together for good to those who love God, to those who are the called according to His purpose" (Rom. 8:28).

"All things" spoken of by the Apostle Paul refers to: suffering. Regardless of our current circumstance or situation – or our past mistakes – God can redeem it and get glory from it. Yet we teach our children in Sunday School: "All things work together for good" without any comprehension whatsoever this scripture pertains to suffering… and they grow up not knowing what to expect along the path of life as a faithful, mature soldier for Christ. We must not create fear at an early age, but we must also prepare our children to survive the evil set against them!

> "He who is in you is greater than he who is in the world" (1 John 4:4).

The New Earth church must embrace two things: A) forgetting the past to press forward, and 2) a biblical understanding of pain, suffering and persecution – to advance the kingdom of God.

> "My brethren, count it all joy when you fall into various trials, ³ knowing that the testing of your faith produces *patience*" (James 1:2, 3; *or endurance*).

> "… but rejoice to the extent that you partake of Christ's sufferings, that when His glory is revealed, you may also be glad with exceeding joy" (1 Pet. 4:13).

> "… that I may know Him and the power of His resurrection, and **the fellowship of His sufferings**, being conformed to His death" (Phil. 3:10).

> Jesus said: "***Blessed are those who are persecuted*** for righteousness' sake, for theirs is the kingdom of heaven" (Matt. 5:10).

Those who are persecuted… inherit the kingdom of heaven… in the New Earth!

Pain and suffering is one way of sanctifying and humbling our soul. This world cannot comprehend this nor deduce any good reason for it, yet it's part of our human condition to endure biblical pain and suffering – and the great equalizer as well: death. Some pain actually helps us get to our preferred destination – the presence of God – when we let go of selfish and earthly things and cling to God for divine assistance. Saints, when you suffer:

> "Rejoice and be exceedingly glad, for great *is* your reward in heaven" (Matt. 5:12).

Regardless of what you are patiently enduring… persevere and maintain the course of faith. The pain and suffering you endure – and overcome – may become the testimony to help someone else get through the storm they are in. God can redeem anything, including trials and tribulations!

> God takes our mess – and it becomes our message.

> God takes our test – and it becomes our testimony.

The Kingdom Of Glory

God's kingdom will give Him all the glory – because all glory belongs to Him. However, God placed a seed of His glory in all of us to produce one thing: more glory. God created us "good and upright, and crowned us with glory and honor" (Eccl. 7:29; Psa. 8) for us to produce more glory in the earth. Some well-meaning religious clerics will quote Isaiah "My glory I will not give to another" (Isa. 42:8), so allow me to rephrase my statement above; we are to be good stewards of the glory God has given to us.

And yet, if God does not give us His glory, then how do you explain Jesus giving us His glory – and Jesus is God?

> "And the glory which You gave Me I have given them, that they may be one just as We are one" (John 17:22).

The whole point of life on earth – is to restore the oneness we had with the Father – as sons of God who were "daily in His presence" (Prov. 8:30) before we were sent to earth. Glory – is about Oneness with the Father!!! United in oneness with the Father – with one heart and one mind – in oneness with the Spirit! This is what our faith journey is all about!!!!!!

> ***"But he who is joined [glued] to the Lord is one spirit with Him" (1 Cor. 6:17).***

Therefore, fellow saints, disciples and beloved brethren of Christ, I admonish you:

- "...be renewed in the spirit of your mind" (Eph. 4:23)
- "... stand fast in one spirit, with one mind striving together for the faith of the gospel" (Phil. 1:27)
- "For through Him [Jesus] we both have access by one Spirit to the Father" (Eph. 2:18)

Oneness of the Spirit in the spirit of our mind – is one of the keys of the kingdom! In this, God is glorified – in us – and through us. Newness happens – through truth, change and oneness!

> "Now He who searches the hearts knows what the mind of the Spirit is, because He makes intercession for the saints according to the will of God" (Rom. 8:27)

The problem we continue to have in church is we think glory means something that only God has... and we're wrong. Does all glory belong to God? Absolutely, yes! Will we be held accountable for misusing God's glory that He gave us to build our own kingdom? Ponder that question deeply, as everyone on earth is guilty of this crime. Jesus said, "The kingdom of God is within you" (Luke 17:21), but all of us have kicked God off the throne of our heart and exalted "self" upon it – or worse – exalted someone else upon it.

Whenever we act independently of God, we are using God's glory to accomplish our own sinful agenda. Adam and Eve behaved this way in Eden, and billions have been tempted as well.

Glory – relates to operating in oneness with God to establish His kingdom – in you and through you – as you sojourn for one season of eternity on earth. At some point, we've all squandered our stewardship responsibility of God's glory and used it for irreverent means. In order to see this more clearly, let's examine how Eve was deceived by Satan and see what he was tempting her to do.

> "Now the serpent was more cunning than any beast of the field which the LORD God had made. And he said to the woman, "Has God indeed said, 'You shall not eat of every tree of the garden'?" [2] And the woman said to the serpent, "We may eat the fruit of the trees of the garden; [3] but of the fruit of the tree which *is* in the midst of the garden, God has said, 'You shall not eat it, nor shall you touch it, lest you die.' " [4] Then the serpent said to the woman, "You will not surely die. [5] For God knows that in the day you eat of it your eyes will be opened, and you will be like God, knowing good and evil" (Gen. 3:1-5).

Satan began the conversation by challenging the truth she believed, then challenged God's truth, and then got her to believe something God never said – according to her own word – by adding her own words onto God's truth. The whole point of Satan's temptation is to get Eve (and us) to doubt God's truth and then act independently of God to take matters into our own hands.

Satan was tempting Eve to be something she already was – in order to get something she already possessed! And we (as *elohims*) are no different than Eve in this regard.

Let's examine the tree and the type of fruit on this tree. The tree is called: "The knowledge of good and evil." The fruit upon this tree is glory fruit. Satan was tempting Eve (and us) to take this glory-fruit and use it in any manner other than as God intended. If we take it without having God's permission, we've committed evil; if we've received glory (by permission) but use it for any means other than those prescribed by God, we've committed evil; if we give this glory to another, we've committed evil (and this is what Adam and Eve did – they gave their glory to Satan (Luke 4:5, 6). This tree in the midst of the Garden represents the knowledge of using God's glory – either for good or for evil. So I ask: how are you using the glory God placed within you? Are you operating under God's authority to promote the kingdom of God within you and to establish the kingdom of heaven on earth? Are you acting as a good steward of God's glory – or are you building your own kingdom according to your best laid plans?

What, then, is the other kingdom like? It is evil! The kingdom of darkness is rooted in evil... and it is based upon an irreverent sinful lie and a sinful supposition: you can take God's glory and use it to establish your own kingdom. This, my friends, is what many have done – including myself. For many years I received numerous awards and recognitions for the work I did, but the problem was: I took all the credit for the good God did through me. I was praising the work that my mind accomplished and I had become a little devil just like Satan himself... which is why the Lord had to completely crush me and change my thought process so I could operate according to His kingdom purpose... and be His writer. This is a very subtle sin, but this type of arrogance is a stench in the nostrils of God. I repulsed even myself by the stench of what I had become... and I held myself in contempt!

My friends, we have all been duped into thinking we are the master of our ship. Our souls have been in jeopardy since day one as we wander in the wilderness in the kingdom of darkness! We teach our children about the most important things in life, like being happy, yet have no clue the goodness within us that enables us to be happy – was given to us by God to accomplish His plan.

Kingdoms are all about taking territory. It time to start building the one kingdom that matters... the kingdom of God in our heart. Focus on taking this territory – and all thoughts – captive to the obedience of Christ!

Where Does Glory Originate

Where does glory originate? In the Mind of God! All of God's thoughts are good, which means all His opinions and plans are good. The LORD said: "I know the thoughts (plans; NIV) that I have for you" – and if He has thoughts and plans '*machashabah-*4284' "purpose, plan, thought, intent,"[46] then He wants to tell you about those plans. If you want to hear "your" message, then you must go to the Source!

> "*I want to know the thoughts of God – all the rest are details.*" – Albert Einstein

God wants us to know Him, know His thoughts and His ways. This is not a divine mystery but an open invitation – to know and understand His character and to walk in His ways.

> "How precious also are Your thoughts to me, O God! How great is the sum of them! [18] If I should count them, they would be more in number than the sand; when I awake, I am still with You" (Psa. 139:17, 18).

Since we were created like God in His image, where does your glory originate? Yes, in our mind! How could it be otherwise! So where do you think the enemy will attack first? Yes, the mind. Once the enemy has created some type of schism or foothold of doubt or confusion or despair or whatever, it doesn't take long for the enemy to continue to chisel away good opinions with irreverent lies and conflicting ideas. We believe them – which compromises our spiritual ability to render good opinions.

The mind of man is the most vulnerable component of his soul. There are major segments of the church that refuse to consider these aspects of the mind – choosing rather to focus all effort on

---

[46] Strong's Concordance.

dealing with the heart of the matter, but how did the heart develop the issues it has? Unintelligent thoughts and ideas were planted in our heart by the mind. Think about this next scripture carefully in regards to your crown:

> "What is man that You are mindful of him, and the son of man that You visit him? [5] ***For You have made him a little lower than the angels, and You have crowned him with glory and honor.*** [6] You have made him to have dominion over the works of Your hands; ***You have put all things under his feet***" (Psalm 8:4-6).

The crown on your head... is glory... and honor. The crown on your head (the mind of your soul) was intended to render good opinions (glory) and exalt God above the rulers of this world (honor). If you were to pick one part of your body to protect the most, which one would it be? I suggest the helmet of salvation.

> "... above all, taking the shield of faith with which you will be able to quench all the fiery darts of the wicked one. [17] And take the helmet of salvation, and the sword of the Spirit, which is the word of God" (Eph. 6:16, 17).

When we protect our mind (the thinker) and wash it with the regenerating truth of the Spirit (Titus 3:5), we will logically and intelligently protect our heart (the knower) with the breastplate of righteousness and the shield of faith. Sadly, though, we've traded logic and reason for small-minded thinking and itchy ears... whereby our hearts have become an immoral wasteland.

And another point as well... what does the word obedience mean? Literally:

- The Hebrew word for obey (8085) '*shama*' – means, "to listen intelligently;"

- The Greek word for obey (5219) *'hupakouo'* – means "to listen attentively."
- The Jewish profession of faith, "Hear O Israel" – the Shema (a derivative of shama) simply means: hear – and obey (Deut. 6:5).
- Obedience simply means: to listen intelligently – and do it. We are not puppets – we are listeners who hear His voice!

All glory originates with God within the Mind of the Father, and man was crowned with glory and honor to imitate his Creator and produce glory... just like Him... by thoughts of our mind. The renewed mind within born anew disciples willingly desire to be sanctified and washed and changed by God's truth to render good opinions. The renewed mind that operates with a sound mind is constantly being washed by truth to operate with revelation understanding in revelation splendor... whereby thought processes of the revelation mind will become radiant as when lightning flashes across the sky. And many mysteries of the kingdom will be revealed to them.

> "And one cried to another and said: "Holy, holy, holy *is* the Lord of hosts; the whole earth *is* full of His glory!" (Isa. 6:3).

How shall I describe the kingdom of God? For starters, it is filled with the glory of God. All glory was generated by God – and some of this glory was produced by creation, of which you are one part. All creation exists to produce two things: more life and more glory. Find an exception to this and you will find an enemy's hand at work. Satan's kingdom is hell-bent on robbing and taking captive God's glory wherever it is by creating chaos and confusion... and destroying everything that is life-giving in the process while doing so.

In the Genesis account, two trees are in the midst of the garden: the tree of life (Jesus) and the tree of knowledge. In order to live and stay alive spiritually, both trees are needed. Knowledge of the Lord and the wisdom to walk uprightly are essential for godly character if you desire to render good opinions with a sound mind.

Can I describe the kingdom of God another way? Yes. The kingdom of God in the New Earth will be filled with people that know how to use God's glory for good.

God's glory will be used – according to God's purposes and according to God's good pleasure – or His message was misunderstood. It's God's kingdom! How could it occur otherwise?

Do we not do the same? We create relationships, habitations, businesses and communities according to what pleases us, and we align ourselves with those people and things that are good and pleasurable to us by building strong relationships within strong communities.

That principle applies to everyone and may be one of the litmus tests used for-or-against us in the Judgment: did you advance the kingdom of good? Did you use God's glory for good or evil? Did you render good opinions about God and your neighbor? Did you learn to love or hate? Did you promote a culture of life or death? In other words: what did you accomplish on earth that produced more glory for God that exalted Him higher than the heavens in your own mind – and the world around you? Did you build God's kingdom in your heart? If you didn't, then you were working against God… and you became part of the problem as: a soul in rebellion.

Where do you think I'm going with this? (Honestly, I have no clue… I'm just writing what I hear.) If you are not magnifying the Lord in your soul to produce more glory that exalts God above everything, including heaven itself, then what (honestly) are you magnifying and what are you giving glory and honor to?

Magnify the Lord in your soul until there is nothing greater than Jesus in your heart.

Money isn't the problem; the love of anything that puts God #2 in your life is the problem. The love of anything, which oftentimes includes money, is called: mammon. Search your heart with your conscience to see if God is even in the top three.

> "Jesus answered him, "The first of all the commandments is: 'Hear, O Israel, the LORD our God, the LORD is one. [30] And you shall love the LORD your God with all your heart, with all your soul, with all your mind, and with all your strength.' This is the first commandment. [31] And the second, like it, is this: 'You shall love your neighbor as yourself.' There is no other commandment greater than these" (Mark 12:29-31).

For some of us, we refuse to acknowledge God's existence. Yet some of us, when bad things happen, will oftentimes blame God for it, which is so twisted on so many levels because Satan caused it yet you are blaming God for it! Can anything be more perverse than that? God is good all the time – and only thinks good thoughts toward you all the time, yet you bring an accusation against Him? This is the power of Satan's deception – to trick us into blaming God for something Satan did.

Adam and Eve had their own glory which was given to them by the Lord, but they forfeited it to a serpent whose only purpose was to subjugate them within his kingdom of sin, rebellion and depravity to live in fear. Pay careful attention to this next point: you let the same thing happen to you. You may not remember the moment when this happened because it was so long ago, but there was a moment when you did something that was against the moral compass in your heart – and your conscience convicted you. Sadly, though, you may not have repented from it. If your parents were aware of it, their responsibility was to instruct you and discipline you. Making excuses at that time was part of the sin identification problem to avoid the obvious condition of your heart. The correct response to sin should be: "I was wrong. Forgive me." You can't go back and change that moment in time – and for some of us it might be better not to search it out – but you can begin anew right now, in repentance, by asking the Lord to forgive your sin, your rebellion, your rejection of Him, and every wrong you've ever done.

Can God truly forgive every sin you've ever done? Absolutely! When you repent with a contrite heart, He forgives your sin and then... He remembers it no more (Jer. 31:34). He wants us to walk in newness of heart and mind and the liberty of the Spirit... to do greater works.

Forgiveness is something Adam and Eve never asked God for... and we are their offspring. Start over... and ask the Lord to forgive you.

> "Or do you despise the riches of His goodness, forbearance, and longsuffering, not knowing that the goodness of God leads you to repentance? [5] But in accordance with your hardness and your impenitent heart you are treasuring up for yourself wrath in the day of wrath and revelation of the righteous judgment of God, [6] who "will render to each one according to his deeds": [7] eternal life to those who by patient continuance in doing good seek for glory, honor, and immortality; [8] but to those who are self-seeking and do not obey the truth, but obey unrighteousness—indignation and wrath, [9] tribulation and anguish, on every soul of man who does evil, of the Jew first and also of the Greek; [10] but glory, honor, and peace to everyone who works what is good, to the Jew first and also to the Greek. [11] For there is no partiality with God" (Rom. 2:4-11).

The kingdom of good will be inhabited by people that produce good thoughts and render good opinions in order to produce goodness and glory. Goodness is related to glory, and the kingdom of God will be filled with both. Crowns of glory and honor await the righteous in life eternal in the New Earth... and they will bring their glory and honor in it (Rev. 21:24, 26).

> "For the Lord God is a sun and shield; the Lord will give grace and glory; no good thing will He withhold from those who walk uprightly" (Psa. 84:11).

We have a major problem within the world today: good has become relative. A similar problem exists: truth has come relative. A very simple diagnosis of this problem reveals: truth is not a condition... Truth is a person: Jesus is the truth (John 14:6). Ancient Greeks were obsessed with knowing the truth, but the truth of the matter which they widely debated was dwelling as a Door in their heart that they were reluctant to seek – or open. The right facts in any situation are merely facts based upon human opinion. If you want to know the truth, then seek Jesus. A good opinion will always declare Jesus: King of kings and Lord of lords. Jesus is Lord of all!

The answer to every condition or every problem known to man will always take us back... to Jesus. In order to have peace, you must go to the Source of all life, peace and godliness.

If you desire world peace, then seek Jesus – the Prince of Peace (Isa. 9:6).

Goodness is not a mystery we need to search for. God wrote the moral code of goodness and uprightness upon the tablets of our heart before we took our first breath. Like everything spiritual in this life, it seems we need to go back to the beginning and become like little children when we operated in grace... before we attained the knowledge of good and evil. Our goal as followers and disciples of Jesus – is to repent and live according to grace. When we operate according to grace, the Spirit strengthens us and empowers us to sin less. What Grace makes available, faith makes possible! Grace enables us to become again what we were before we fell into sin: little children (Matt. 18:3; 19:14)... as sons and daughters of our heavenly Father.

Grace – the attributes of God's character – makes this happen in us and through us by the Spirit of Grace – in the kingdom of goodness, glory and grace.

Our sojourn on earth is to become again what we were to begin with: like angels in heaven (Mark 12:25). After the judgment and the resurrection, the regeneration will happen wherein God makes all things new again – and the saints will dwell upon the New Earth for all eternity – in the kingdom of heaven… on Earth as it is in Heaven.

> "The kingdom of God is within you" (Luke 17:21).

The kingdom of God is the realm of the Spirit… who dwells within you!

You must be born again in order to enter the realm of the Spirit – the kingdom of God.

> "Jesus answered and said to him, "Most assuredly, I say to you, **unless one is born again, he cannot see the kingdom of God**." ⁴ Nicodemus said to Him, "How can a man be born when he is old? Can he enter a second time into his mother's womb and be born?" ⁵ Jesus answered, "Most assuredly, I say to you, **unless one is born of water and the Spirit, he cannot enter the kingdom of God**. ⁶ That which is born of the flesh is flesh, and that which is born of the Spirit is spirit. ⁷ Do not marvel that I said to you, '***You must be born again***.' ⁸ The wind blows where it wishes, and you hear the sound of it, but cannot tell where it comes from and where it goes. ***So is everyone who is born of the Spirit***" (John 3:3-8).

You must be born of the Spirit in order to understand the realm of the Spirit!

The kingdom of God that you continue to establish and build within your heart even now… will still be there after everything has been shaken in the judgment. What house are you building in your heart right now for the Lord to abide? (John 14:23) What kingdom are you building in your heart? I tell you the truth: nations will proceed from your heart because you trusted in the Lord your God.

The far away country… is in your heart.

What grace makes available, faith makes possible!

God has given us the keys of the kingdom. Walk with the Spirit. Live according to grace. Operate from faith.

> Jesus said: "And I will give you the keys of the kingdom of heaven, and whatever you bind on earth will be bound in heaven, and whatever you loose on earth will be loosed in heaven" (Matt. 16:19).

We are kingdom builders sent from heaven to establish the kingdom of heaven on earth, so loose more of heaven onto earth. We should not be looking anywhere else – except toward Jesus, the Author and Finisher of our faith. Grace and peace be yours in abundance.

It's all about Jesus – and God gets the glory! Amen!

The Father's Dominion

On October 27, 2014, while in prayer, I asked Jesus to explain the dominion to me. I spent the next four days in His presence and much was revealed to me. After He was done speaking, I asked Him why He was telling me all this information, He simply said: "No one asked before."

During this four day encounter, I asked Him to explain the Father's dominion to me. It's short and sweet – and it's also included in the book "Dominion" in the Image Bearer series.

"One morning while in prayer, I asked the Father, "What does the dominion of your kingdom look like?" (And then I smelled overcooked toast)

"The dominion of My kingdom reflects My glory. It does not appear in a manner as you would understand. It becomes life and motion and stillness in a moment. It enables the highest good to prevail. It loves unconditionally, it rejoices exuberantly, it forgives generously, it keeps no record of offense, it delights in everything good that was made according to My glory.

"The enemy will entice multitudes with many attractive looking life-way offers to see if they can rob Me of My children. Indeed, some will be lost, but those who are Mine will always be Mine. I know who are Mine; I know the thoughts of their heart.

"What can I tell you that you have not already read, but do not yet comprehend, or understand. Consider all the parables by Jesus and consider all His lessons: the kingdom of heaven is like...

"Think about things above, and not about things on earth, and your perspective will change."

END

The Father's dominion enables the highest good to prevail... and it delights in everything good that was made according to His glory (which is everything He made). This is one instance in which I had little knowledge of what was being written, yet when compared to what appears in this chapter – it echoes the same sentiment. Goodness prevails... in the kingdom of God's glory! Meditate on goodness – and you will give glory to God.

"The Lord Jesus Christ be with your spirit.
Grace be with you. Amen" (2 Tim. 4:22).

It's all about Jesus – and God gets the glory! **Amen.**

Honor The King

"If I am a King, where is My honor?"

This chapter title and word from the Lord came to me during Christmas Eve worship. The church makes much ado about sweet baby Jesus and clings to the hope of redemption through faith in Him, yet rarely do we grasp the fullness of His true character... as a King who rules and reins over His church, the earth, and the cosmos as well.

Jesus is Lord (1 Cor. 2:3). This is the benchmark of salvation for all people on earth, not just Christians. Jesus is Lord of all (Acts 10:36). So I ask you: who is the King of Heaven? Is Jesus King or is the Father King? This chapter will explain this question from God's perspective.

During the sermon following worship, the preacher talked ever so briefly about Jesus being "like" a heavenly Father. This preacher misunderstood who Jesus really is. Carefully read this well-known scripture displayed prominently during Christmas and ponder deeply yet another aspect of our Lord's Divine character... as "Everlasting Father."

> "*For unto us a Child is born,*
> *Unto us a Son is given*;
> And the government will be upon His shoulder.
> *And His name will be called*
> Wonderful, Counselor, Mighty God,
> *Everlasting Father*, Prince of Peace" (Isa. 9:6).

Most of us do not see Jesus as "Everlasting Father" – and yet He is! He is also the Prince of Peace, Wonderful, Counselor, and Mighty God. So I ask: do we regard Jesus as Lord? Our doctrines teach us – yes – so every time the word "Lord" and "Lord God" is mentioned in scripture in both Old and New Testaments (i.e. "the Lord said")... is applicable to Jesus.

Do you see Jesus this way? If not, then you have been taught to believe a less-than version of "who" Jesus really is! Jesus is more than just "the Son of God" who was sent to save us. Jesus is Lord! Jesus is King of Heaven and Earth! And since Jesus is a King, He is also worthy of all honor and glory, but our way of thinking within the church somehow fails to embrace Jesus as God and King who is worthy of all glory… and honor.

> "But now the Lord [Jesus] says: 'Far be it from Me; for those who honor Me I will honor, and those who despise Me shall be lightly esteemed" (1 Sam. 2:30).

Does the church reverence Jesus in this manner? On the surface, our typical response is – yes – but if we truly understood Jesus as God and King, we would elevate the "Name above every name" to more than the authorized footnote in our pious prayers offered to the Father. Jesus is Lord. Jesus is God and King, and because He is God and King, Jesus is also our heavenly Father… who sent Himself as a Son… to teach us how to honor God as the Father of us all.

Allow that last statement wash over your soul and regenerate your mind – with revelation truth!

Jesus taught us how to pray – and also to reverence God as "the Father of us" in heaven:

> "The Father of us in the heavens, Hallowed be Your name" (Matt. 6:9).

"The literal Greek for the Lord's Prayer is: "Πάτερ (Father) ἡμῶν (of us) ὁ (the one) ἐν (in) τοῖς (the) οὐρανοῖς (heavens)." God is – the Father of us. This slight yet enormously vast distinction on the identity of Jesus is able to put clarifying light between – Jesus who is God – and God who is the Father of us all… who sent all of us here as Our Father in heaven. Jesus is God, who sent Himself as a Son, to teach us how to live in relationship with the Father of us – so that by faith in the Son we are adopted as spiritual sons and daughters into the spiritual kingdom of our Father – the one in the heavens."[47] If you have a hard time comprehending this, then read: "IMAGE."

The Father of us in heaven (i.e. all of us in human form, including Jesus)... has been calling out to as many who will listen, hear His voice, know Him, follow Him... and come home to the Father (John 10:27; 14:6).

Therefore, Jesus said:

> "If anyone serves Me, let him follow Me; and where I am, there My servant will be also. If anyone serves Me, him My Father will honor" (John 12:26).

> "... that all should honor the Son just as they honor the Father. He who does not honor the Son does not honor the Father who sent Him" (John 5:23).

Jesus taught us to honor the Son equally with the Father... for this reason:

> Jesus said: "I and *My* Father are one" (John 10:30).

Perhaps you are able to grasp what Jesus is teaching: by honoring the Son (as He dwelt in the flesh), we will honor Him after His ascension... as the Father of us... in Glory! This is a remarkable mystery which somehow became shrouded along the pathway of religion.

> "If you had known Me, you would have known My Father also; **and from now on you know Him and have seen Him**" (John 14:7). "Jesus said to him, "Have I been with you so long, and yet you have not known Me, Philip? **He who has seen Me has seen the Father**; so how can you say, 'Show us the

---

[47] Excerpt from "Image" section titled: "The Last Word."

Father'?" (John 14:9).

The words Jesus spoke to His disciples were worded in a very specific manner – as revelatory truth revealing His Divine identity while in their presence – which also holds up under tremendous scrutiny centuries later!

> "I and *My* Father are one" (John 10:30).

Honor sown unto Jesus now… shall become honor given by the Father in glory.

As followers and disciples of Jesus, we need to operate within this mindset that Jesus is God and King – and Jesus is our heavenly Father who searches for worshippers in spirit and in truth to serve Him as adopted sons and daughters in His kingdom… on earth as it is in heaven.

> "But the hour is coming, and now is, when the true worshipers will worship the Father in spirit and truth; for the Father is seeking such to worship Him. [24] God *is* Spirit, and those who worship Him must worship in spirit and truth" (John 4:23, 24).

Jesus was teaching us "God is Spirit" and we are to "worship the Father" yet we struggle to perceive Jesus as both God and Father due to many manmade doctrines. God is the "expression" and the Father and Son are manifestations of God. Truly, God is Spirit, and Jesus is God, which means: if Jesus is God, then Jesus is Spirit as well. Amen!

> "Now the Lord is the Spirit; and where the Spirit of the Lord is, there is liberty" (2 Cor. 3:17).

Jesus is Lord! The Lord is the Spirit! God is Spirit! This deep theology is very difficult to understand and virtually impossible to perceive unless a person has been born again and their mind has been renewed by the Spirit of God to comprehend spiritual truth. Jesus was God the entire time He walked on earth! Jesus is

"Immanuel – God with us" (Matt. 1:23) to tangibly show us God has always been with us since the beginning.

There is one God (the expression) and multiple manifestations of His Divine character.

Our Sojourn To Comprehend – God

We began this sojourn in darkness, but through faith in Jesus we are adopted into the Father's spiritual family as heirs of His kingdom.

> "Listen, my beloved brethren: Has God not chosen the poor of this world to be rich in faith and heirs of the kingdom which He promised to those who love Him" (James 2:5).

This promise was made to each of us – by Jesus Himself:

> "Do not fear, little flock, for it is your Father's good pleasure to give you the kingdom" (Luke 12:32).

> "And I [Jesus] will give you the keys of the kingdom of heaven, and whatever you bind on earth will be bound in heaven, and whatever you loose on earth will be loosed in heaven" (Matt. 16:19).

Yet the church fails the Father's children miserably by not educating them regarding Jesus as God and King who alone "is worthy to receive all honor and glory" (Rev. 4:11) who has entrusted us with dominion to establish the kingdom of heaven on earth... in His Name!

Jesus is King. Reverence King Jesus! Honor King Jesus!

> "And He has on His robe and on His thigh a name written: KING OF KINGS AND LORD OF LORDS (Rev. 19:16).

So I ask: are you a child of God? Through faith in Jesus, you truly are. Through faith, God is your Father. The church teaches this, but do you see your heavenly Father as a King… and also as your Master or Lord? Probably not! There are not two Kings of Heaven; there is only one because – God is One! Too often, we perceive our heavenly Father as a sugar-daddy Santa Claus who gives wonderful gifts despite being naughty or nice children, yet we will all be held accountable for this: did we reverence the Master? Did we honor the King?

> "A son honors his father, and a servant his master. If then *I am the Father*, where is My honor? And if I am a Master, where is My reverence? *Says the Lord* of hosts to you priests who despise My name. Yet you say, 'In what way have we despised Your name?" (Mal. 1:6).

During the time Jesus ministered on earth, the priests failed to comprehend Him as the Messiah and sought to murder Him. They were expecting a conquering King – and thus they got exactly what they deserved – the end of an obsolete Covenant whereby Jesus instituted a New Covenant whereby anyone can be saved… not through vain sacrifices, but through faith in Jesus as the Son of God – and – the sacrifice of "self" upon the altar of repentance and obedience (Rom. 12).

Beloved in Christ, we somehow suffered a serious doctrinal disconnect with regard to honoring King Jesus with the same intensity and reverence by which we honor the Father – which I perceive as a knee-jerk Protestant and Pentecostal reaction to centuries of Maryology. For this reason I was called to write… to show the Church who Jesus is… so the bride gives all glory, honor, praise and worship to Jesus… and Jesus only!

Jesus is the Manifested One who appears – as and on behalf of – God to effect salvation on earth. God is the expression… within a manifold diversity of manifestations. God manifests Himself:

- As a Son
- As a Child
- As a Father
- As a Messiah
- As a Christ
- As a Redeemer
- As a Deliverer
- As a Savior
- As a Lion and a Lamb
- As a Friend
- As a Teacher
- As a Master
- As Lord of lords
- As King of kings
- As a Conquering King
- And as a Judge

Everything we shall ever need is found in the God of Oneness.

> "Hear, O Israel: *The LORD our God, the LORD is one*! ⁵ You shall love the LORD your God with all your heart, with all your soul, and with all your strength" (Deut. 6:4, 5).

Whatever we need from God is found in the Oneness of Him. Mystery solved!

Jesus is our Everything!

This is why Jesus said: "And the Father Himself, who sent Me, has testified of Me. *You have neither heard His voice at any time, nor seen His form*" (John 5:37). Any time we claim to have seen God or heard His voice – be assured – we've seen Jesus and we've heard a Message from one of two Messengers: Jesus or the Spirit of Jesus (aka Holy Spirit, Spirit of God, Spirit of Jesus Christ, Spirit of the Lord, etc.).

In Revelation, Jesus revealed Himself to John (and us) by using seven "I am" statements:

1. "I am the Alpha and the Omega, *the* Beginning and *the* End," says the Lord, "who is and who was and who is to come, the Almighty" (Rev. 1:8)
2. "I am the Alpha and the Omega, the First and the Last" (Rev. 1:11)
3. "I am He who lives, and was dead, and behold, I am alive forevermore. Amen. And I have the keys of Hades and of Death" (Rev. 1:18)
4. "I am He who searches the minds and hearts. And I will give to each one of you according to your works" (Rev. 2:23)
5. "Behold, I am coming as a thief" (Rev. 16:15)
6. "And behold, I am coming quickly, and My reward *is* with Me, to give to every one according to his work" (Rev. 22:12)
7. "I, Jesus, have sent My angel to testify to you these things in the churches. I am the Root and the Offspring of David, the Bright and Morning Star" (Rev. 22:16)

"Perhaps the most interesting aspect of Jesus – is *nowhere* found in the book Revelation: the physical appearance that John knew. When Jesus reveals Himself to John, the disciple whom Jesus loved (John 13:23; 19:26), who was an eyewitness to both the Transfiguration and the Resurrection, John should have recognized Him, but He didn't. Seven times Jesus reveals Himself, but never as Jesus "according to the flesh":"[48]

1. Rev. 1:12-14 – "and in the midst of the seven lampstands One *like* the Son of Man" whose head and hair "were white like wool." There is no doubt that this is Jesus, but John does not seem to recognize Jesus when He reveals Himself as "the Ancient of Days" (Dan. 7:9, 13)

---

[48] Excerpt with seven points from "Image" section titled: "The Spirit with the One."

2. Rev. 4:1-3 – "and behold, a door standing open in heaven… and behold, a throne set in heaven, and One sat on the throne. And He who sat there was *like* a jasper and a sardius stone in appearance; and there was a rainbow around the throne, in appearance like an emerald." Here is Jesus as we are to envision Him now, as He is in heaven 'according to His glory' in Oneness with the Father and abiding with Him, because He reveals Himself as "the Lord of Glory" (1 Cor. 2:8; James 2:1)
3. Rev. 5:6 – "and behold, in the midst of the throne and of the four living creatures, and in the midst of the elders, stood a Lamb as though it had been slain, having seven horns and seven eyes, which are the seven Spirits of God sent out into all the earth." This image of Jesus is a clear and unveiled message that John himself can identify with, whereby Jesus reveals Himself as "the Lamb of God" who took away the sin of the world! (John 1:29)
4. Rev. 14:1 – "and behold, a Lamb standing on Mount Zion." Jesus is revealing Himself by various images to communicate who He is in glory – who is worthy to receive worship… "Yet I have set My King on My holy hill of Zion. I will declare the decree: the LORD has said to Me, 'You are My Son, today I have begotten You" (Psa. 2:6, 7), whereby Jesus reveals Himself as the One who is worthy to stand upon God's Holy Mountain, i.e. "His dwelling place" (Zech. 14:4-9; Psa. 132.13; Isa. 8:13-18; John 4:21)
5. Rev. 14:14 – "and behold, a white cloud, and on the cloud sat One *like* the Son of Man, having on His head a golden crown, and in His hand a sharp sickle." Jesus reveals Himself as "the Lord of the Harvest."
6. Rev. 19:11 – "and behold, a white horse. And He who sat on him was called Faithful and True, and in righteousness He judges and makes war." Jesus reveals Himself as "the Conquering King" and as the One who sits as Judge upon the judgment seat of Christ.
7. Rev. 22:16 – "I, Jesus, have sent My angel to testify to you these things in the churches. I am the Root and the Offspring of David, the Bright and Morning Star." Jesus

concludes the revelation of Himself *in Word only*, as the Word of God (Rev. 19:13), not in prophetic physical form, by declaring more names attributed to Him of which these are just a few of over 111 names for Jesus in the Bible… with 42 in Revelation alone. [49]

Jesus revealed Himself to John seven different ways: as the Ancient of Days, the Glorious One, the Lamb of God, the King on God's holy mountain (Zion), the Lord of the harvest, the conquering King, and finally… as the Word of God. Jesus operates within dynamic fluidity rather than static reality[50] and can appear however He wants to whoever He wants, so when people describe seeing the face of God in a vision, dream or whatever, we can be sure that they have seen another aspect of Jesus because… Jesus is the only one who has seen the Father (John 6:46)… ***and He is the only visible manifestation of God that can be seen***.

The reason Jesus can say "If you've seen Me you've seen the Father" and also "I and My Father are One" is because… Jesus is

---

[49] There are at least forty-two names for Jesus in Revelation: Jesus Christ (1:1), the Faithful Witness (1:5), the Firstborn from the dead (1:5), the Ruler over the kings of the earth (1:5), the Alpha and the Omega (1:8); the Beginning and the End (1:8; 21:6; 22:13), the Almighty (1:8), the First and the Last (1:10, 17), Son of Man (1:12; 14:14), He who lives (1:17), He who has the keys of Hades and of Death (1:18), Son of God (2:18), He who has the key of David (3:7), the Amen (3:14), the Faithful and True Witness (3:14), the Beginning of the creation of God (3:14), One sitting on the throne (4:2), Lord God Almighty (4:8), O Lord (4:11), the Lion of the tribe of Judah (5:5), the Root of David (5:5), the Lamb (5:6, 8), the living God (7:2), our God (7:10), Him who lives forever and ever (10:6), the God of the earth (11:4), the God of heaven (11:13), our Lord and of His Christ (11:15), Lord God Almighty (11:17), Child (12:4, 5), King of the saints (15:3), The One who is and who was and who is to be (16:5), Lord of lords and King of kings (17:14), the Lord our God (19:1), the Lord God Omnipotent (19:6), Faithful and True (19:11), The Word of God (19:13), Almighty God (19:15), KING OF KINGS AND LORD OF LORDS (19:16), Christ (20:4), the Root and the Offspring of David (22:16), the Bright and Morning Star (22:16).

[50] Static reality represents those things in the physical dimension which seldom change or change very slowly. The spiritual dimension, however, is always fluid and changes often and quickly at times, hence, dynamic fluidity represents those elements that change often, especially the things of the Spirit.

God... and Jesus is the Father who sent Himself as a Son. He did this in order to teach us how to live as sons and daughters of our heavenly Father. Yet we continue to minimize the excellence and magnificence of our God by keeping Jesus, the Manifested One, as eternally locked into that Messianic image... and sadly, some leave His butchered body hanging upon a cross as emblematic of their true perception of Him: a murdered Messiah who claimed to be King of the Jews.

The Jews dishonored the King of Glory, yet the Church also dishonors the Lord of Glory for this reason: they know not who He is. Jesus is King of kings, and Jesus is Lord of lords, but it seems we've forgotten what it means to revere, honor, and fear the King of Heaven who is also the Lord who Judges in Righteousness and Truth.

Jesus is King. Honor the King!

> "Now to the King eternal, immortal, invisible, to God who alone is wise, be honor and glory forever and ever. Amen" (1 Tim. 1:17).

Three wise kings came from the east to pay homage to this newborn King; however, the church doesn't acknowledge Jesus as King until the celebration of His rising from the dead at Easter. Doesn't this seem oddly strange?

Jesus is King of kings. Jesus is King of His kingdom, King over every people group (including the Jews), and Supreme Commander over Heaven, Earth, and all Creation as the Word... "through Whom the worlds were created" (Heb. 1:2).

> "By faith we understand that *the worlds were framed by the word of God*, so that the things which are seen were not made of things which are visible" (Heb. 11:3).

> "In the beginning was the Word, and the Word was with God, ***and the Word was God***. ² He was in the beginning with God. ³ All things were made through Him, and without Him nothing was made that was made" (John 1:1-3).

Jesus is the Word of God! It's the last revelation revealed to John (#7 above) by Jesus that is most incredible because it takes us back to the beginning of our common point of origin where our journey begins – and where we shall return: the Garden of Eden in the Paradise of God.

> "And they [Adam and Eve] heard the voice of the LORD God walking in the garden" (Gen. 3:8; KJV).

"The voice… walked." This is absolutely remarkable!

Honor the King! Honor every Word uttered by the King. Yet somehow we think honoring the Word of God (which some traditions misconstrue to be the Bible) as words of/from Jesus – is negotiable. Truly, we shall be held accountable for every word which we failed to honor. Think about this for a moment: if your boss told you to do something but you refused to do it, what would happen? You would be terminated from employment! If a soldier disobeys a direct order, they are court-martialed and perhaps discharged. First century believers were admonished to honor the words (teaching) of the apostles (1 Tim. 5:17), so, why do we think we can pick and choose which words from Jesus to believe when we are commanded to obey ALL of them?

> "You are My friends **if** you do whatever I command you" (John 15:14).

Honor the King! The reason we refuse to Honor King Jesus is due to the fact we've believed a "less-than" version of His true Identity. Jesus is "the Preeminence" and "the Express Image" (***charakter***-5481) of the invisible God! And no other earthly examples of '*charakte*r' exist!

> "... who being the brightness of His glory and the *express image* of His person, and upholding all things by the word of His power, when He had by Himself purged our sins, sat down at the right hand of the Majesty on high" (Heb. 1:3).

Honor the King. Jesus is Lord and He is King over all creation... and everything on this planet belongs to Him, yet our understanding of His identity remains shrouded by the institutional church so they can continue to use His things without His permission.

Honor the King. This includes taking care of creation. This is His planet! Woe to anyone who destroys, corrupts, or pollutes this planet (Rev. 11:18). "The earth is the Lord's, and all its fullness" (Psa. 24:1; 1 Cor. 10:26) which includes all resources He's made available for our use.

Honor the King, and honor earthly kings to whom God has positioned as rulers to govern the nations.

> "Honor all people. Love the brotherhood. Fear God. Honor the king" (1 Pet. 2:17).

This includes honoring your earthly father and mother through whom you were created.

> "Honor your father and your mother, that your days may be long upon the land which the LORD your God is giving you" (Ex. 20:12)

Consider this: if you cannot honor your earthly father and mother by whom you were conceived through whom God chose to usher your soul onto this planet, then let me ask: how can you honor the Lord if you cannot honor your parents? Here is a slightly different perspective: if you cannot forgive others, then your heavenly Father cannot forgive you.

"But if you do not forgive, neither will your Father in heaven forgive your trespasses" (Mark 11:26).

How we treat our parents – and others – for better or worse – is how God will treat us on the Day of Judgment! This is one of the Kingdom's principles: you reap what you sow!

At some point, we've all gotten lost and strayed away from the path of righteousness and truth. The scriptures have numerous examples of people who walked away from God – and then returned to exalt God as Lord and King. One classic example is King Nebuchadnezzar:

> "And at the end of the time I, Nebuchadnezzar, lifted my eyes to heaven, and my understanding returned to me; ***and I blessed the Most High and praised and honored Him who lives forever***:
> For His dominion *is* an everlasting dominion,
> And His kingdom *is* from generation to generation.
> [35] All the inhabitants of the earth *are* reputed as nothing;
> He does according to His will in the army of heaven
> And *among* the inhabitants of the earth.
> No one can restrain His hand
> Or say to Him, "What have You done?"
> [36] At the same time my reason returned to me, and for the glory of my kingdom, my honor and splendor returned to me. My counselors and nobles resorted to me, I was restored to my kingdom, and excellent majesty was added to me. [37] ***Now I, Nebuchadnezzar, praise and extol and honor the King of heaven***, all of whose works *are* truth, and His ways justice. And those who walk in pride He is able to put down" (Dan. 4:34-37).

We are all being tested and proofed to determine our future place in eternity – in the New Earth. What you have and what you'll receive on the other side in life eternal is whatever you've placed as deeds of righteousness into your faith account during this life.

Consider the manner in which you are currently living because… it determines your eternal outcome! Little or much – is all determined by you! Did you love the Lord with all your heart and mind? Did you love others? Did you honor the King! What – will you have – when you enter the Kingdom of Glory?

> "And the nations of those who are saved shall walk in its light, and the kings of the earth bring their glory and honor into it" (Rev. 21:24).

We will dwell eternally with King Jesus in the New Earth and we will come into the King of Glory's presence in the New Jerusalem to bring our glory and honor to Him. Take a moment to image this because… this is the true reality that Jesus promised us: Paradise with Him!

What did you think you would be doing in Paradise once you got there (which BTW Jesus never promised us heaven)? Floating on clouds, playing harps, eating Bon-Bons? You will be serving the King of Heaven for six days and then you will bring your glory and honor to Him on the seventh day. What we are doing now on earth is merely a type and shadow of what we shall be doing in eternity in the New Earth after the regeneration.

So I ask: what do you think you will be doing in Paradise? Truly I tell you… you are deciding your fate even now. Your soul shall continue to dwell eternally (Psa. 49:8, 9) even as you are dwelling now. Free will enables us to live either according to grace – or disgrace!

What do you want to be for all eternity: a beggar, laborer, manager, magistrate – or as a prince in the King's court? We shall all occupy a '*topos*' place and perform some duty in the New Earth, so I challenge you: strive to be a pillar in the House of God! Live like a disciple – now!

Honor the King. Now that you know how important this statement is for all believers walking in obedience to become disciples of

Jesus, the term 'honor'[51] has much truth for us to embrace.

- '*kabad*-H3513' – weightiness, to be heavy; either "in a bad sense (burdensome) or a good sense (numerous, rich, honored)." Thus, we become more heavier/weightier – either grievous or gracious – based upon our heart's response to the truth we believed
- '*timao*-G5091' – "to prize, i.e. to fix a valuation upon" as done: toward the Father by the Son (John 5:23), by the Son to the Father (John 8:49), by the Father to those who serve Jesus (John 12:26), toward earthly kings and authorities (1 Pet. 2:17), and widows (1 Tim. 5:3), and ministers of the Gospel (Acts 28:10)

Honor is how we place weightiness and value on everything. King David refused to kill Saul because he believed in this principle: honor the king – regardless of what they do even if they attempt to kill you twice. Honor your parents for who they are – not according to what they have or haven't done. Honor is our earthly response to a heavenly duty and responsibility to live as an image bearer, as a manifested likeness of Jesus Christ on earth, and as one of the King's kids.

Honor: the value you get out of it… is the value you put into it. Sow and reap!

Reverence God. Fear God. Love the Lord. Honor the King. Give God all the glory.

God crowned you with glory and honor (Psa. 8). What you do with it… is up to you. Live as someone who was graced with honor.

Ultimately… the choice is yours.

Why wait for eternity when you can live like an angel now!

---

[51] All terms from Strong's Concordance.

Honor the King!

*It's all about Jesus – and God gets the glory!
Forever and ever, Amen!*

Kingdom of Christ

> "To them God willed to make known what are the riches of the glory of this mystery among the Gentiles: which is **Christ in you**, the hope of glory" (Col. 1:27).

The term Christ '*Christos*-5547' means: anointed. The simplicity of this marvelous word that implies – an anointed one – is the term by which we identify Jesus and also those belonging to Him (Christian – little anointed one)

"Christ in you" represents yet another anointed person in service to the Lord which unlocks the mystery of man on earth with another key: what you believe in – creates the world you live in.

The Jewish nation waited expectantly for the Messiah, yet this word appears only twice in the Old Testament (Daniel 9:25 and 26) – and only twice in the New Testament (John 1:41; 4:25).[52]

> "And when he had gathered all the chief priests and scribes of the people together, he inquired of them where the Christ was to be born" (Matt. 2:4).

There is a subtle distinction between Messiah and Christ (which is a New Testament term); Messiah was an expectation solely for the Jewish nation yet Christ is an expectation for all people through faith in Jesus as the Son of/from God. New Testament texts were written by Jewish converts to faith in Jesus, and these Godly men referred to Jesus as the "Christ" to indicate His unique role to Israel as the Messiah (Deliverer) – also to Gentiles as a Savior.

> "Indeed He says, 'It is too small a thing that You should be My Servant to raise up the tribes of Jacob, and to restore the preserved ones of Israel; I

---

[52] The word Christ was erringly translated in the NIV as "Messiah" 72 times, yet failed to designate two references in Daniel; when added to 310 times the NIV mistranslated "host" should cause this version to be retired permanently.

will also give You as a light to the Gentiles, that
You should be My salvation to the ends of the
earth' " (Isa. 49:6).

Finding one person to accomplish perfectly the role of Messiah is extraordinary, yet finding one person to accomplish the role as Christ to the Gentiles who also fulfilled over 68 Messianic prophecies[53] – as well as 27 prophecies fulfilled during His death and crucifixion alone – is astronomical. The probability (or chance) of just eight prophecies being fulfilled by one person – has been mathematically performed. "Multiplying all these probabilities together produces a number (rounded off) of 1×10^{28}. Dividing this number by an estimate of the number of people who have lived since the time of these prophecies (88 billion) produces a probability of all 8 prophecies being fulfilled accidentally in the life of one person. That probability is 1 in 10^{17} or 1 in 100,000,000,000,000,000. That's one in one hundred quadrillion!"[54]

These prophecies were written over a 1,550 year period and yet it happened exactly as prophesied... to one man: Jesus Christ!

The probability of being killed by a shark worldwide (average 6-7 persons/yr) is 1 in a billion (1,000,000,000); or winning the lottery is 1 in 14 million (14,000,000); or being struck and killed by lightning worldwide (est. 24,000 persons) is 1 in 292,000. Thus, you are one-hundred million times more likely to be killed by a shark than Jesus fulfilling prophecy... accidentally! See what I mean? It happened the only way it could have happened: by God Himself becoming a man to do what no one else could. And this is why Jesus told us "not" to seek after anyone else claiming to be Christ – or to go anywhere to find Him. Trust Jesus! All others are counterfeits! He knows what He's talking about!

---

[53] Some place the number around 200 and even as high as 456. Source: Ray Konig; About-Jesus.org.
[54] Mathematical calculations produced by Peter Stoner; Science Speaks; Moody Press, 1958.

Jesus is – the only One!

> Jesus said: "Then if anyone says to you, 'Look, here is the Christ!' or, 'Look, He is there!' do not believe it" (Mark 13:21).

Jesus is the only One. No others will be sent. If you belong to a religion that claims to have been visited by Jesus or follows a prophet sent by God to build upon what Jesus did, you've got to understand this: it's fake. It's counterfeit. Jesus commissioned the Holy Spirit to continue speaking His message… and all other messages which contradict His… are invalid!

The word 'Messiah-H4899/G3323' means: anointed one. God… sent Himself as a Son, as the Chosen One, as the Messiah, as the Savior of the world, as the Christ – as the Messenger to authenticate the message of God's love, redemption and eternal salvation – to mankind. Jesus is the *"express image"* (*character*; Heb. 1:3) of God who came to liberate us from the kingdom of darkness – and there is no other way or any other Name by which we are saved! (John 14:6; Acts 4:12). Jesus is the Way and the Truth! Avoid all counterfeit expressions. **Cling to Jesus only**!

> "God, who at various times and in various ways spoke in time past to the fathers by the prophets, ^{2} has in these last days spoken to us by His Son, whom He has appointed heir of all things, through whom also He made the worlds; ^{3} who being the brightness of His glory and **the express image of His person**, and upholding all things by the word of His power, when He had by Himself purged our sins, sat down at the right hand of the Majesty on high, ^{4} having become so much better than the angels, as He has by inheritance obtained a more excellent name than they" (Heb. 1:1-4).

A more concise and precise illustration of who Jesus is – cannot be found anywhere else in scripture.

In Christ

Many people have heard of Jesus. Some people know about Him. Yet few take time to know Him experientially and intimately. Most have heard gospel messages, but what does it mean to be "in Christ"? Firstly, it means different things to different people. From my perspective – it means: oneness with Him. Consider this analogy: when salt encounters food, the food becomes salty (it becomes one with the food); when food encounters salt, the character of the food is altered and it becomes more like salt.

Jesus said: "You are the salt of the earth" (Matt. 5:13). Christ in you will make you Christ-like, but your immersion in Christ will alter your reality to change you and transform you to become more like Christ. Conversion should result in immersion (baptism is a type and shadow)… which is essential, according to the Spirit, in order for born anew newness to happen.

> "Therefore, if anyone is in Christ, he is a new creation; old things have passed away; behold, all things have become new" (2 Cor. 5:17).

When the truth of Christ dwells in you, you assimilate His truth and begin acting like Him; when you abide in Christ, your identity becomes lost in the oneness of who Jesus is (and you assimilate His character).

> "For you are all sons of God through faith in Christ Jesus. For as many of you as were baptized into Christ have put on Christ" (Gal. 3:26, 27).

"Christ in you" is fundamentally different than being "in Christ." Through faith in Jesus, Christ abides in us – as we dwell in Christ. This aspect of faith is marvelous to consider. To the extent you allow Christ to rein as Lord in your mortal body… it affects and effects the environment around you that you live in. Perspectives produce paradigms… and kingdoms. So I say: surrender to the sanctifying work of the Holy Spirit and yield to become more like

Christ.

> "To the church of God which is at Corinth, **to those who are sanctified in Christ Jesus, called to be saints**, with all who in every place call on the name of Jesus Christ our Lord, both theirs and ours" (1 Cor. 1:2).

Christ in you creates the kingdom of Christ around you… alongside many anointed ones called saints… all around the world.

> "Now He who establishes us with you in Christ and has anointed us is God" (2 Cor. 1:21).

When Christ in you – becomes your everything – then nothing outwardly will alter your perception of self – or your reality of being in the kingdom of Christ. Consider the gravity of this statement said by Jesus:

> "The kingdom of God is within you" (Luke 17:21).

The kingdom of God is all around you… and in you. Think about this for a moment. Ponder your reality within the realm of the Spirit. Embrace the realm of the Spirit! God is Spirit. The kingdom of the Spirit is all around you… and dwells in you. God's Spirit – dwells <u>with</u> us (in our spirit) and dwells <u>in</u> us (in the tabernacle of our heart; John 14:17). Once you understand the totality of this, it will reshape your understanding to embrace a new paradigm of faith. The Spirit is – around you and within you to accomplish much in the heavenly realm to advance the kingdom of heaven on earth. You are shifting atmospheres and reshaping this planet when you fully comprehend your mustard seed of faith is able to move mountains – in the realm of the Spirit. Pray in the spirit… and see what happens next.

> "Now thanks be to God who always leads us in triumph in Christ, **and through us diffuses the fragrance of His knowledge in every place**" (2 Cor. 2:14).

Christ dwells in us – as we dwell in Him. Seems impossible to fathom or reconcile; how can we be in Christ – when Christ is in us? This is the realm of the Spirit – who makes us one with Him – and one with everyone else abiding in Him.

> ***"But he who is joined [glued] to the Lord is one spirit with Him" (1 Cor. 6:17).***

Christ in us – enables us to dwell abundantly and triumphantly in the kingdom of Christ. When we are untied in one spirit with the Spirit, the saints will release a new level of glory – through the unity of the Spirit – to activate revival in our communities all around the world. The Spirit of Glory in us… makes this happen.

> Jesus said: "And the glory which You gave Me I have given them, that they may be one just as We are one" (John 17:22).

Christ In You

"Christ in you" is the fundamental basis of saving faith… even as you live and move in the kingdom of Christ in the realm of the Spirit to accomplish God's will on earth. But when we (who are the church) are united in one spirit with the Spirit, greater works will result. Greater works will not occur until unity of the body is embraced – and division is discouraged.

Perhaps the most perplexing aspect of faith as we dwell in captivity on earth is: we are in Christ as Christ dwells in us. And here is another one: "We are in the world – but not of it."

> "I have given them Your word; and the world has hated them because they are not of the world, just as I am not of the world. [15] ***I do not pray that You should take them out of the world, but that You should keep them from the evil one.*** [16] They are not of the world, just as I am not of the world.
> [17] Sanctify them by Your truth. Your word is truth.

> [18] As You sent Me into the world, I also have sent them into the world." (John 17:14-18).

By God's grace through faith in Jesus – we are set free from slavery in darkness and bondage to sin... even as we continue to dwell in captivity in "this world" on earth until the day we are set free through death to continue our journey – from out of temporary (the exit) – into eternity. Life is a paradox: technically, we are free even as we dwell in captivity. My advice is: learn to praise Him and dance before Him in the presence of suffering even as you dwell (temporarily) in captivity. Blessed are you when you embrace this reality!

God said: "Heaven is My throne. What house will you build for Me? And where is the place of My rest?" The throne of your heart is what the Lord of glory is after, and the house He wants us to build is in your heart as well. God wants to be Lord over you – and Lord in you! But first, He must be Lord in the tabernacle of your heart! And to guarantee you will always have access to the Father – according to faith – Jesus establishes Himself as a Door in your heart (where eternity exists; Eccl. 3:11; John 10:19) so that you may dwell eternally with the Father regardless of what happens to your body or your spirit. Truly, I say:

> "For I am persuaded that neither death nor life, nor angels nor principalities nor powers, nor things present nor things to come, [39] nor height nor depth, nor any other created thing, shall be able to separate us from the love of God which is in Christ Jesus our Lord" (Rom. 8:38, 39).

To be "in Christ" implies (initially) we have been grafted "into" the Vine and have been adopted into the family of God. The scriptures do not say grafted onto (as is the common practice of gardeners and vinedressers)... Jesus said "in" and this point is exceedingly important. Just as the kingdom is in you, you are in the kingdom. This is such a marvelous mystery. The inside-out and outside-in operation of our spirit in oneness of the Spirit – makes us one with Him on many levels. Truly, I say: you've never been alone on this sojourn through temporary (with one exception: the false reality you created in which He wasn't Lord over you and in you).

> "I am the true vine, and My Father is the vinedresser. ² Every branch in Me that does not bear fruit He takes away; and every *branch* that bears fruit He prunes, that it may bear more fruit. ³ You are already clean because of the word which I have spoken to you. ⁴ Abide in Me, and I in you. *As the branch cannot bear fruit of itself, unless it abides in the vine, neither can you, unless you abide in Me.* ⁵ "I am the vine, you *are* the branches. He who abides in Me, and I in him, bears much fruit; *for without Me you can do nothing.* ⁶ If anyone does not abide in Me, he is cast out as a branch and is withered; and they gather them and throw *them* into the fire, and they are burned. ⁷ If you abide in Me, and My words abide in you, you will ask what you desire, and it shall be done for you. ⁸ *By this My Father is glorified, that you bear much fruit; so you will be My disciples*" (John 15:1-8).

The Lord is seeking worshippers – in spirit and in truth – who have dedicated themselves as disciples of Him for this reason: to make more disciples. Yet many will refuse His invitation.

> Jesus said: "For judgment I have come into this world, that those who do not see may see, and that those who see may be made blind" (John 9:39).

Whatever happens to us in this life... and then life eternal... happens because you either choose to perceive the reality of Christ around you and within you – or you choose to remain blind.

However, when we remain "in Christ" and stay attached "in" Him, the Spirit works in us "as a new creation"... to change us until we are formed and conformed into the image of the Original Pattern:

Jesus Christ. As we grow "in Christ" we shall begin to look and sound more like Jesus; and as we abide "in Christ" we shall be known as His disciple – as "operating in oneness" with Him – and as Him. This is what Paul meant by "until Christ is formed in you" (Gal. 4:19): the Spirit of Christ will continue to change you and renew you and enlarge His presence "in you" until it's no longer you.

> "There is therefore now no condemnation to those who are in Christ Jesus, who do not walk according to the flesh, but according to the Spirit" (Rom. 8:1).

Jesus is your example: imitate Jesus! Walk according to the Spirit! Christ in you is making you mature, complete and perfect in the oneness of who Jesus is – whereby you've become another manifest expression of the Father as Christ dwells in you. To "be perfect" (*teleios*-5046) means: "complete; mature." Now consider this: you and I are *elohims* – (John 10:34) which means: lacking little of God. When we combine these words together, the fullness implies: you are being perfected – to become a mature and complete expression of who Jesus is according to His likeness. So I say again: imitate Jesus!!!

Christ in you – is not membership into a secret society of saved souls (though salvation is one of the benefits). Christ in you – connects you into the Vine (Jesus) along with many other grafted branches who exist for one purpose: to bear fruit. If you claim an association with Jesus but you cannot express unending love, adoration and devotion in worship of Jesus as Lord of your life, then perhaps you trusted a gospel other than His. If you are not producing spiritual fruit (good works) nor taking care of others less fortunate than you nor making disciples, then you never understood His message.

> The message you will hear, but not understand.
> And looking you will see, but not perceive spiritual things,
> Nor comprehend how the kingdom works.[55]

---

[55] The author's translation of Matt. 13:14, 15.

> *"Lest they should understand with their hearts and turn"*
> *(Matt. 13:15).*

The word "understand" is '*suniemi*-4920' and means: to put together mentally, to comprehend, be wise, to consider, to unite perception with what is perceived (Luke 24:45; Matt. 13:15). Jesus wants us to comprehend mentally – and do this in combined union "with" – our heart…for this purpose: be converted! The word turn is '*epistrepho*' and means: to turn; convert; to have a revolution. Jesus wants to start a revolution in your mind that causes you to convert your heart and passionately pursue spiritual things – namely – Christ Jesus – and His righteousness – and His kingdom. (Matt. 6:33) Is this beginning to make sense?

The greatest Revolutionary this world has ever seen… wants to start a revolution in your mind!

What is the message Jesus wants us to embrace? Love God and love one another as Christ loved you (John 13:15)! There are three basic things we need to understand as we move forward in faith: 1) focus on Jesus, 2) imitate His example, and 3) teach others to do likewise.

> Jesus said: "For I have given you an example, that you should do as I have done to you" (John 13:15).
>
> "For to this you were called, because Christ also suffered for us, leaving us an example, that you should follow His steps" (1 Pet. 2:21).

If you think you will not experience pain or suffering when you come to faith in Christ (because the preacher told you so), then you were sold a false gospel. If you think you will not suffer persecution or poverty or various tribulations because Christ dwells in you, then you were taught a false gospel message. Jesus emptied Himself – for our sake – and became poor (2 Cor. 8:9) – and suffered on our behalf (1 Pet. 2:21). Are you willing to surrender all for the cause of Christ? Study the life of the apostles and you will learn two things: they all experienced suffering (and martyrdom) and received a great reward for faithful obedience. So I ask: if the Lord asked you to give up your wealth, would you? (Mark 10:21) Think about this question: if you had only one year to live... what would you do? Would you travel the world – or act like Christ and change it! From personal experience I tell you: if it isn't worth dying for, then it isn't worth living for!

> "Therefore, since Christ suffered for us in the flesh, arm yourselves also with the same mind, for he who has suffered in the flesh has ceased from sin" (1 Pet. 4:1).

Faith in Christ is worth living for – and is worth dying for! Faith enables us to patiently endure much suffering and persecution and affliction even as our soul is being sanctified and perfected – by grace – through faith. Sanctification is the means whereby we are being prepared for eternity. Don't knock it till you've tried it. Imagine the person you want to be on the other side – and start living that way now. It will be difficult at first, but the retirement benefits are out of this world.

So I challenge you: why wait for eternity when you can live that way now!

None of this is possible unless you understand the truth of the gospel that Jesus taught... which is absolutely impossible to comprehend apart from being born anew by the Spirit of God. You may know it (intellectually), but God wants us to own it... and live it (experientially)! You "MUST" be born again (John 3:7) or it will be utterly impossible for you to understand how the kingdom of God operates (John 3:3) or accomplish those things that please the Father.

- Christ in us – enables us to accomplish exceedingly beyond all expectations what we are unable to do in the flesh apart from the Spirit.
- Christ in us – enables the Spirit to sanctify us and change us from death to life

KINGDOMS

- Christ in us – enables the Spirit to change us and conform us into the image of Christ
- Christ in us – enables the Spirit to conduct heavenly business within us
- Christ in us – enables the Spirit to establish the kingdom of heaven through us
- Christ in you – the hope of glory! Live like you mean it!

None of this is possible unless you've been born anew. Are you born again? Did the Spirit give you a gift to authenticate a covenant was entered into by both you and the Lord? If not, then ask the Lord what you need to do.

> "Examine yourselves as to whether you are in the faith. Test yourselves. Do you not know yourselves, that Jesus Christ is in you?—unless indeed you are disqualified" (2 Cor. 13:5).

The Lord gave me the hand of a ready writer – and another hand to swing hammers. Which truth do you want? If you want God's truth, then go to the source and ask Him yourself. Two-way dialogue with the Lord (not a book) is what the Lord desires with each of His children. Second-hand information is never what the Lord intended. Seek Him and ask Him to teach you – line by line – what you are to know and what you are to do. You are His poem. Seek the Poet.

> "For we are His workmanship, ***created in Christ Jesus for good works***, which God prepared beforehand that we should walk in them" (Eph. 2:10).

The word "workmanship" – '*poema*-4161' (lit. a product; fabric; tapestry) is the word from which we get the word poem. You are Christ's poem. I heard a preacher talk about having a custom suit made for him and his application made so much sense; the person in the earth suit that God created was tailor made specifically for one person... and no one else.

The word "create" (*ktizo*-2936) employs this understanding: a fabrication by the manufacturer to conform to the manufacturer's original specifications for His intended use.[56] You were created as a spiritual being in the likeness of Jesus to be found "in Him" and then "be conformed to Him" for His intended use... which is to establish the kingdom of heaven on earth. You are His workmanship; you are His masterpiece; you are His poem – to do His will on earth. If you don't feel a warriors yell rising up within you to live victoriously for Christ, then something is amiss.

> "For this is the will of God, your sanctification: that you should abstain from sexual immorality; ⁴ that each of you should know how to possess [*ktaomai*-2932; the root of *ktizo*] his own vessel in sanctification and honor" (1 Thess. 4:3, 4).

Mature saints will not engage in sexual immorality. Never compromise this point! Verse 4 (above) can also be translated (by Strongs') as: "you shall gain mastery over your souls." This is the message I keep writing about. Your soul (mind and heart) is who you really are (inside), and your soul has a partner alongside you (your spirit) to help you successfully navigate your journey through this world (the kingdom of darkness) that seeks only to obliterate your existence both now and eternally. Whatever you do – as a soul seeking salvation – must yield to the sanctifying work of the Holy Spirit who dwells in the spirit alongside your soul to prevent you from falling into the Pit (Psa. 49:8, 9). The spirit within you – is a safety net to prevent this from happening.

God, who is rich in mercy and abounding in love (Eph. 2:4) – knows that we are dust (Psa. 103:14). For this reason He sent us here on a commission with a companion (a spirit which He loaned to us; 1 Cor. 6:20) to assist us along this journey. The nearness of God has been with us (Immanuel) every moment of our life. How near He is to you... has always been... up to you.

---

[56] Strong's Concordance.

Kingdom of Mercy

> Jesus said: "But go and learn what this means: 'I desire mercy and not sacrifice.' For I did not come to call the righteous, but sinners, to repentance" (Matt. 9:13).

What was Jesus teaching the spiritual leaders of Israel in that hour? A: Understand the message from the Messenger. God is not impressed with sacrifices or offerings. God is after our heart. God knows what we are going through and He wants us (as His proxy) to take care of one another and help others to faithfully endure the journey. When we study the origin of that message (above), we have an excellent roadmap to learn what the Lord wants us to know:

"For I desire mercy and not sacrifice, and the knowledge of God more than burnt offerings" (Hosea 6:6).

Jesus was teaching all of us: do your homework! Know what God wants and remember to do it! Read the scriptures and understand them mentally (*suniemi*) and have a revolution in your mind that affects your understanding to cause a conversion in your heart (to turn away) from wickedness, (to turn toward) pursue righteousness, and (to live it) be merciful to your neighbor and the stranger.

> "He has shown you, O man, what is good; and what does the LORD require of you but to do justly, to love mercy, and to walk humbly with your God" (Micah 6:8).

Do justice. Correct injustice. Be merciful. Show mercy to all. Walk humbly. Honor the King.

Be kind to everyone you meet. Treat them as if they are an angel of God. Be fair and just in all your dealings. You represent the

King of Heaven, so be circumspect in your estimation of what you do in the knowledge of God and in relation to He who dwells with/in you.

It's not enough for the truth of the gospel to make you salty; you've got to want to get into the salt and be changed by the salt – and be preserved by salt – to accomplish all God predestined you to accomplish.

"The Greek word "mercy" used in Matthew 5:7, *eleemon* [1655] means essentially the same as its English counterpart, "merciful." However, in all likelihood Jesus spoke in Aramaic, and the idea behind His statement about mercy comes from Old Testament—that is, Hebrew—usage and teaching. The word He would have used is the Hebrew and Aramaic *chesed*.'

'William Barclay's *Daily Study Bible* commentary on Matthew regarding this word states:

'It does not mean only to sympathize with a person in the popular sense of the term; it does not mean simply to feel sorry for some in trouble. *Chesedh* [sic], **mercy, means the ability to get right inside the other person's skin until we can see things with his eyes, think things with his mind, and feel things with his feelings** [bold italics by the author]. Clearly this is much more than an emotional wave of pity; clearly this demands a quite deliberate effort of the mind and of the will. It denotes a sympathy which is not given, as it were, from outside, but which comes from a deliberate identification with the other person, until we see things as he sees them, and feel things as he feels them. This is *sympathy* in the literal sense of the word. *Sympathy* is derived from two Greek words, *syn* which means *together with*, and *paschein* which means *to experience* or *to suffer. Sympathy* means *experiencing things together with the other person,* literally going through what he is going through. (p. 103)"[57]

---

[57] Excerpt from "Commission" by the author. Citation on mercy, Forerunner Commentary, John W. Ritenbaugh. www.bibletools.org/index.cfm/fuseaction/Topical.show/RTD/CGG/ID/7132/Ele

The gospel message of Jesus is: God dwells alongside you, He sympathizes (suffers) with you, and He is there to help you and carry you through this life in order to experience life eternal – through faith in Him. By grace you are saved – by Jesus, Grace Incarnate – who desires to have an intimate personal relationship with you – daily!

> "Therefore be merciful, just as your Father also is merciful" (Luke 6:36).

"Grace removes guilt; mercy removes misery."[58]

God loves you more than you'll ever know. The God of mercy and grace and compassion dwells with/in you. He knows what you are going through; He feels your pain and loneliness. He also feels your rejection of Him by resisting a deeper level of faith to walk with Him. He experiences everything you go through, including moments of anxiety, depression, despair and suffering … and yet we subject Him to immorality as well. Saints of God, this must never happen!

So you see: the term "in Christ" is far more extensive and comprehensive than its application to Jesus alone. This term applies to anyone that is aligned with the knowledge of God (truth) and the gospel of Jesus Christ – to act like Him! Offer grace to others – and be merciful like Him.

Many will hear the message… but not understand. If you want to understand the message, then you must be guided by the Spirit in your devotion to Jesus to set yourself apart from the things of this world – and become His disciple. Are you willing to designate one hour a day to prayer and study of the word? From a spiritual perspective, the tithe applies to all resources including time *and* finances. The tithe of time for each 24 hour day is 2.4 hours. What most people give the Lord equates to 30 minutes on

---

emon.htm
[58] Strong's Concordance; study on 'eleios-1656.'

Sunday… and then they wonder why they are blown around like a leaf never knowing or comprehending why confusion seems to swirl like a tornado around them. This is because they are not attached "in" the Vine. Examine yourself! Do you have the mind of Christ? Do you have a mindset that thinks like Jesus?

> "Let this mind be in you which was also in Christ Jesus" (Phil. 2:5).

The apostle Paul was facing the exact same things I write about because we continue to fall victim of our own worst enemy: stinking thinking. We want what's best, we think we know what that is, then we go charging ahead with only a shallow understanding of God's truth and an infinite stockpile of worldly advice.

> "For "who has known the mind of the Lord that he may instruct Him?" ***But we have the mind of Christ***" (1 Cor. 2:16).

Think about that statement. Do you have the mind of Christ? The apostles had the mind of Christ. If you had the mind of Christ like the apostle's did, what do you think would happen to you? You would act like Christ. Isn't that the whole point of faith: to imitate Christ! When you think like Christ, you will act like His apostles and likewise become His disciple. Most know what this means and why they don't become disciples: they counted the cost. They claim the cost is too great for them. The cares of this world… has become their friend.

> "And do not be conformed to this world, but be transformed by the renewing of your mind, that you may prove what *is* that good and acceptable and perfect will of God" (Rom. 12:2).

The mind that is transformed and renewed by the Holy Spirit – will embrace a revolutionary thought process that thinks like Jesus – and acts like Him!

Brothers and sisters in Christ, we are failing in our obedience to Jesus if we reject His message to be His disciple and become like Him. Simply put: you cannot act like Him if you cannot think like Him! You may think this an impossible task, yet you know of multitudes of spiritual people (past and present) that you admire for their faithful devotion to Jesus because they acted like Him. Now I say this with the bluntness of a sledgehammer: you are no different than any of them! You have a nature like Elijah (James 5:17). The only difference between you and them is: they put their faith into action. They believed the truth and then realigned their life to live according to the truth they believed. That is the definition of faith: having being thoroughly persuaded and convinced the truth you believed – is the truth... and now you live according to it.

If you are interested in developing a life that is pleasing to God, then spend more time with Him. While training to become a missionary with YWAM in 1987, I was given this simple yet very effective strategy to initiate a prayer life and the study of the Word. One note of caution, however: use this to get started and then allow the Holy Spirit to change it up. Anything done as routine – oftentimes turns into religion.

An Hour With God

1. Preparation Time – Focus on Jesus, declare obedience to Him, and be yourself.
2. Waiting Time – Let God love you and search you. Seek God's wisdom.
3. Confession Time – Let go of the sins of guilt and confess the sins that weigh on you.
4. Bible Time – Read the Word and pray the Word.
5. Meditation Time – Immediately begin to think on what you just read.
6. Intercession Time – Pray for people and their needs, and all in authority.
7. Petition Time – Present your needs and pray, "Thy will be done."

8. Application Time – What are one or two things God desires of me?
9. Faith Time – Thanking God in advance for what you believe will take place.
10. Praise and Thanksgiving Time – Praise God for WHO He is, and thank Him for WHAT He has done.

Here's a suggestion: laminate this... it makes an excellent bookmark for your Bible.

The means whereby this idea becomes reality is predicated upon only one thing: hearing God's voice. Jesus said: "My sheep, hear My voice, I know them and they follow Me" (John 10:27). Do whatever it takes to be able to hear His voice clearly because – once you do – everything in the realm of the Spirit falls orderly into place.

Through Christ

> "God is faithful, by whom you were called into the fellowship of His Son, Jesus Christ our Lord" (1 Cor. 1:9).

Through faith in Christ, we are promised many precious promises. The greatest promise (from my perspective) is to be partners and joint heirs with Christ – in fellowship with Him.

> "… and if children, then heirs—heirs of God and joint heirs with Christ, if indeed we suffer with Him, that we may also be glorified together" (Rom. 8:17),

The Greek word for fellowship (*koinonia*-2842) is related to (*koinoneo*-2841) and "is used in two senses, (a) to have a share in, (b) **to give a share to, go shares with**"[59] and be a partaker of God's things as a partner in His kingdom in communion with Him to advance the Gospel.

---

[59] Strong's Concordance.

In order to have fellowship *'koinonia'* with Christ, you must first communicate *'koinoneo'* with Him. How can anyone expect to have a share in the Vine unless you communicate with Him?

Most of us have never been taught to perceive God from this perspective, that God wants to "go shares with us," but this is precisely what our Jesus wants – He wants to partner with us!

Before God can "go shares with" us and have shares in the things of God, we need to have "a share in" the Divine relationship with God that focuses on loving fellowship by embracing the One thing all "in Christ" have in common: Jesus – the Son of God.

Fellowship with Jesus relies upon intimacy built upon a relationship of love and trust – with understanding. We need to focus all our attention and affection on Jesus Christ, for He alone is the Way, Truth and Life (John 14:6).

"The Father wants "to give us a kingdom" (Luke 12:32), and Jesus gave us "the keys of the kingdom" (Matt.16:19) to reward us – "to have shares in" – and "to share in the inheritance of Christ" (Eph. 1:11, 18; 5:5; Col. 1:12; 3:24) as we "put all things under our feet and His authority" (Psa. 8:6; Eph. 1:22). All things were delivered to Jesus by the Father (Matt. 11:27), and dominion with authority and power were restored to us by Jesus Christ – prior to His ascension."[60]

This is the life of faith we were called into when we believed the message. So I ask: how is any of this supposed to happen? A: According to the Spirit! But it takes faith to activate the realm of the Spirit… even the faith of a mustard seed can move mountains. In the kingdom, size is irrelevant. Numbers are irrelevant. Faith is the currency of the Kingdom of Christ.

---

[60] Excerpt from Listen section titled: "A Failure To Communicate."

"Therefore if there is any consolation in Christ, if any comfort of love, if any fellowship of the Spirit, if any affection and mercy, ² *fulfill my joy by being like-minded, having the same love, being of one accord, of one mind.* ³ Let nothing be done through selfish ambition or conceit, but in lowliness of mind let each esteem others better than himself" (Phil. 2:1-3).

Consider all these precious promises of faith:

- "Blessed be the God and Father of our Lord Jesus Christ, who has blessed us with every spiritual blessing in the heavenly places in Christ" (Eph. 1:3),
- "…that in the dispensation of the fullness of the times He might gather together in one all things in Christ, both which are in heaven and which are on earth—in Him" (Eph. 1:10),
- "…that we who first **trusted in Christ** should be to the praise of His glory" (Eph. 1:12),
- "…and raised us up together, and made us sit together in the heavenly places in Christ Jesus" (Eph. 2:6)

"When Christ who is our life appears, then you also will appear with Him in glory" (Col. 3:4).

With Christ – in glory! What an amazing declaration! We will appear with Him in glory – and we will be seated with Christ in heavenly places. What better promise can be found anywhere?

The word "with" is '*meta*' (3326) meaning – "joined with, accompaniment"[61] pertains to this sojourned life. From Enosh to Jesus to the Holy Spirit's presence today, we see God joined with us and *alongside us* every step of the way. He knows that we are dust and He knows fully the predicament we are in before we even call upon His name – because He is *right there beside us* and dwelling within us every step of the way. Saints, we can take great

---

[61] Strong's Concordance.

solace in the '*parakletos*' (3875) presence of God's Spirit who tells us, "I will never leave you or forsake you" (Heb. 13:5).

Faith in Jesus is worth living for – because it's worth dying for. As partners with Christ and as partakers of the divine nature, whatever you've sacrificed or surrendered in this life will be rewarded in the next. An inheritance is waiting for you when you get to the other side in the Kingdom of Christ. How large your inheritance is… depends on you!

Only one life so soon it will pass; only what's done for Christ will last.

It's all about Jesus – and God gets the glory.

Kingdom of Grace and Truth

> "For the law was given through Moses, but grace and truth came through Jesus Christ" (John 1:17).

What is grace? What is truth? If we try to define these terms without considering Jesus Christ and His Divine character as God Incarnate (in the flesh), then all our definitions will always fall short of the mark. Grace and truth – came through Jesus Christ!

> "I do not set aside the grace of God; for if righteousness comes through the law, then Christ died in vain" (Gal. 2:21)

Many songs have been written about grace – even amazing grace – which we sing so often that it seems to have become a nauseous code-word for a mystical expression within Christianity sung at all funerals for wretched sinners (yet 'gratefully' not during celebrations of life for saints saved by grace). From my perspective, grace represents all the character attributes of God which He exhibits as expressions of Himself in story after story throughout the Bible – to help us comprehend grace – and comprehend God's nature – and comprehend our purpose for being.

> "And the Child grew and became strong in spirit, filled with wisdom; and the grace of God was upon Him" (Luke 2:40).

My personal definition of grace is: God's righteous attributes exemplified by Christ. Jesus personified grace more than anyone – past, present, and future – and we have much to learn from Him by imitating His example. Jesus is Grace Incarnate (Rom. 5:15, 17) in the kingdom of Grace.

> "For the grace of God that brings salvation has appeared to all men" (Titus 2:11).

All of God's attributes are defined as: grace. Living by grace… is how we satisfy God's requirements of righteousness, goodness and holiness to enter into – and stay in – God's presence. Grace enables us to enter into His presence – by grace upon us and grace within us – whereby more grace is given to rest and abide with Him.

> "For you were once darkness, but now you are light in the Lord. Walk as children of light ^{9} (for ***the fruit of the Spirit is*** *in* all goodness, righteousness, and truth), ^{10} finding out what is acceptable to the Lord" (Eph. 5:8-10).

Noah Found Grace

> "But Noah found grace in the eyes of the Lord" (Gen. 6:8)

The law of first occurrence examines the first time a word is mentioned in the scriptures (which is not a law but a spiritual principal to help explain how the kingdom of God operates). In this instance, grace (*chen*-2580) means: favor. Grace (*chen*) occurs 69x in the Old Testament (*charis*-5485) and 156x in the New. "Grace indicates favor on the part of the giver and thanks of the part of the receiver."[62] Grace is a character attribute of God – which He attributes to those who walk according to His principles – such as Noah – and Moses.

Moses Found Grace

> "Then Moses said to the LORD, "See, You say to me, 'Bring up this people.' But You have not let me know whom You will send with me. Yet You have said, 'I know you by name, and you have also found **grace** in My sight.' ^{13} Now therefore, I pray, if I have found **grace** in Your sight, show me now Your way, that I may know You and that I may find

---

[62] Strong's Concordance.

grace in Your sight. And consider that this nation *is* Your people." ¹⁴ And He said, ***My Presence will go with you, and I will give you rest.*** " ¹⁵ Then he said to Him, "If Your Presence does not go *with us,* do not bring us up from here. ¹⁶ For how then will it be known that Your people and I have found **grace** in Your sight, except You go with us? So we shall be separate, Your people and I, from all the people who *are* upon the face of the earth." ¹⁷ So the LORD said to Moses, "I will also do this thing that you have spoken; for you have found **grace** in My sight, and I know you by name." ¹⁸ And he said, "Please, show me Your glory." ¹⁹ Then He said, "I will make all My goodness pass before you, and I will proclaim the name of the LORD before you. I will be **gracious** to whom I will be **gracious**, and I will have compassion on whom I will have compassion" (Ex. 33:12-18)

God's grace enables us to enter into God's presence, enables us to stay in His presence, and enables His grace to go with us. Consider how the Israelites moved through the wilderness; when the pillar of cloud and fire moved, they moved – and when it stopped, they stopped (Ex. 13:21). The same is true when we walk according to the Spirit – when the Spirit moves, we move – and when the Spirit hovers, we hover. As worshippers, we should always be ready and willing to hover during Sunday church service when the presence of the Lord is made manifest in the midst of us during worship. This represents the best we have to offer God – in spirit and in truth – when we reverence His presence.[63]

Greater Grace Found You

---

[63] Spiritual discernment is needed because the enemy can counterfeit the glory of God's presence using various means such as smoke machines, synthesizers, flashing lights and other electronic vibrations. Here is a hint: the man show will intervene with human words to manipulate emotions with humanistic appeals to enter into God's presence. When the Spirit does it, a holy hush is often sensed, whereby human coaching is unnecessary.

KINGDOMS

When anyone is called and commissioned by God to accomplish a task that is mission critical to establishing the kingdom of heaven on earth – grace is bestowed. Therefore, greater works will require greater grace!

> "Most assuredly, I say to you, he who believes in Me, the works that I do he will do also; and ***greater works than these he will do***, because I go to My Father" (John 14:12).

> "And with great power the apostles gave witness to the resurrection of the Lord Jesus. ***And great grace was upon them all***" (Acts 4:33).

This character attribute is applied to the Holy Spirit as well, who is called the Spirit of Christ, who was sent by the Lord to enable us to continue in-and-with the ministry of Jesus Christ.

> "Of how much worse punishment, do you suppose, will he be thought worthy who has trampled the Son of God underfoot, counted the blood of the covenant by which he was sanctified a common thing, and insulted the ***Spirit of grace***" (Heb. 10:29).

The Kingdom of Grace is reliant entirely upon God to effect His plan and influence the affairs of man. Words are optional. Worlds are conditional. Works are insufficient. Grace is all in all. Wonder and awe are byproducts of God's grace in action… through Whom the worlds were created (Heb. 1:2). From beginning to end… everything is a miraculous work of God's grace!

Truth, love, power, favor, blessing and honor are all attributes of God's grace and character.

When we examine all instances when the word grace appears, we might be surprised. The Apostle Paul's epistles (which contain 88 of 125 NKJV mentions translated as: grace, excluding 7x in

Hebrews) sends a very clear signal to those studying the scriptures: Paul – the minister of grace (Eph. 3:7, 8) – is teaching us about the gospel of grace. If I can effectively communicate one principle to everyone reading these words, it would be: live according to the doctrine of grace. The doctrine of grace is superior to the doctrine of sin, which was established through an Old Covenant as a type and shadow to make propitiation and atonement for sin through the sacrificial death of an animal that merely postponed the penalty of man's sin; blood was shed to allow the penalty to "pass over" until Christ reset the timeline of salvation whereby – all people are saved by grace – through faith in Jesus, the Lamb of God.

> "For by grace you have been saved through faith, and that not of yourselves; it is the gift of God" (Eph. 2:8).

> "Therefore it is of faith that it might be according to grace" (Rom. 4:16)... "through whom also we have access by faith into this grace in which we stand, and rejoice in hope of the glory of God" (Rom. 5:2).

God's grace builds us up and enables us to stand. When you falter, cling to God's truth and God's grace and allow Him to reposition you and strengthen you to stand in His presence.

> "So now, brethren, I commend you to God and to the word of His grace, which is able to build you up and give you an inheritance among all those who are sanctified" (Acts 20:32).

Sanctification by grace – is part of the salvation process. When you encounter suffering for the sake of the gospel (or any reason for that matter), it is important for followers of Jesus to understand – God is in you. God's presence goes with you! Cling to grace and God will help you through whatever you are going through.

This world will come against you and cause you to suffer because it is demonically influenced by Satan to persecute you and obliterate your existence; sometimes testing and trials come from

God to proof us in preparation for eternity in order to get more grace and truth into us. Regardless of how suffering comes to us, God's grace is sufficient to strengthen us in our time of need.

> "But may the God of all grace, who called us to His eternal glory by Christ Jesus, after you have suffered a while, perfect, establish, strengthen, and settle you" (1 Pet. 5:10).

> "Let us therefore come boldly to the throne of grace, that we may obtain mercy and find grace to help in time of need" (Heb. 4:16).

Why is this message of suffering such a prevalent topic in this book? Because – suffering from a biblical perspective is silent from the pulpit of man, and a time is coming when only grace and truth will be able to strengthen us. For example, when believers come under attack – their first impression is to withdraw and pull back. In fact, I've talked to many believers who tell me when they encounter any push-back, they withdraw from it as one means of identifying God's will and staying in God's perfect will. That is utterly preposterous! All believers of Jesus will come under attack, but disciples who follow Jesus will press forward because they know they are advancing the kingdom! "The kingdom suffers violence" – violent men are coming against the kingdom (Matt. 11:12)… and they also war against sons and daughters of the kingdom.

> "You therefore, my son, **be strong in the grace that is in Christ Jesus**. [2] And the things that you have heard from me among many witnesses, commit these to faithful men who will be able to teach others also. [3] **You therefore must endure hardship as a good soldier of Jesus Christ**. [4] No one engaged in warfare entangles himself with the affairs of this life, that he may please him who enlisted him as a soldier" (2 Tim. 1-4).

Two kingdoms are at war and you were enlisted as a soldier for battle! Do not retreat! Do not give up – and do not give in to the pattern of this demonic world. You were sent into enemy territory to advance the kingdom of heaven with the truth of the gospel. How dare we interject human wisdom to interpret suffering as something contrary to the will of God! Such a person has yet to undergo the new birth and the transformation that results from a renewed mind.

> "And do not be conformed to this world, but be transformed by the renewing of your mind, that you may prove what *is* that good and acceptable and perfect will of God" (Rom. 12:2).

This is the primary difference between sheep and goats. Sheep know the truth and they are able to walk with godly understanding to discern the good and acceptable and perfect will of God.

Sheep never stay in the same place very long (I'm not talking against being planted by the Lord in a particular geographic place – I'm talking about the territory of your heart that constantly needs to be changed and renewed). Sheep move when the Shepherd moves, but goats stay in the same place, overgraze – and eat dirt. You are – what you eat. You become – what you believe – so I admonish you stop watching TV shows and listening to music that contradicts God's truth.

Walk by grace – according to God truth.

***Believe it – until you become it*!**

Grace is a spiritual attribute provided by God to live a life that is pleasing to God and accomplishes the will of God through His saints.

- "***Grace to you and peace*** from God our Father and the Lord Jesus Christ" (Rom. 1:7)

- *"**Grace, mercy, and peace will be with you** from God the Father and from the Lord Jesus Christ, the Son of the Father, **in truth and love**"* (2 John 1:3).
- *"**Grace and peace be multiplied to you** in the knowledge of God and of Jesus our Lord"* (2 Pet. 1:2)

Allow grace and truth to be multiplied to you!!! Since the kingdom of God operates according to faith (which we manifest through our spirit), then we must perceive this truth: grace is on the front-end to initiate faith and on the back-end to activate and implement faith.

From beginning to end… it's all grace, through faith… and God gets the glory.

- The grace of God predestined us, purposed us, positioned us, prepared us and proofs us
- The grace of God pursued us when we drifted away from the presence of God
- The grace of God enables us to remain in His presence – and enter His rest
- The grace of God reveals to us – our true identity in Christ

What grace makes available – faith makes possible!

God's grace makes God's grace gifts available – by the Spirit of grace – to build, establish and advance the Kingdom of Grace – through faith. Grace is not dispensed to accomplish selfish agendas. However, grace with power is poured out liberally to advance the kingdom of God.

- "But by the grace of God I am what I am, and His grace toward me was not in vain; but I labored more abundantly than they all, yet not I, but the grace of God which was with me" (1 Cor. 15:10)

- "… of which I became a minister according to the gift of the grace of God given to me by the effective working of His power" (Eph. 3: 7)
- "Having then gifts differing according to the grace that is given to us, let us use them: if prophecy, let us prophesy in proportion to our faith" (Rom. 12:6)
- "But to each one of us grace was given according to the measure of Christ's gift" (Eph. 4:7)
- "As each one has received a gift, minister it to one another, as good stewards of the manifold grace of God" (1 Pet. 4:10)

Grace is a gift from God – that enables us to imitate Jesus – and worship God – apart from works. Grace and truth came through Jesus Christ" (John 1:17) so that grace and truth might be revealed through us – according to grace – which happens when we walk in love – according to truth.

Grace – In Christ

In order for us to operate in the spirit according to grace, we need to be "in Christ." Truly, Christ is dwelling in us, but in order for us to live according to grace, we must do this positionally "in Christ" in order to drink freely from the well of Grace. Christ in you – is our hope of glory in life eternal – yet you "being found in Christ" – creates a mysterious oneness with Christ that identifies you as a new creation (creature) that previously did not exist apart from faith. We get our identity and our commission from Christ – when we are found in Christ!

> "Yet indeed I also count all things loss for the excellence of the knowledge of Christ Jesus my Lord, for whom I have suffered the loss of all things, and count them as rubbish, that I may gain Christ [9] and ***be found in Him***, not having my own righteousness, which *is* from the law, but that which *is* through faith ***in Christ***, the righteousness which is from God by faith" (Phil. 3:8, 9).

When you are found in Christ – as someone belonging to Him – you are united in oneness of the Spirit – according to grace.

- "And the grace of our Lord was exceedingly abundant, with faith and love which are *in Christ Jesus*" (1 Tim. 1:14) "… who has saved us and called us with a holy calling, not according to our works, but according to His own purpose and grace which was given to us *in Christ Jesus* before time began" (2 Tim. 1:19)
- "For by grace you have been saved through faith, and that not of yourselves; it is the gift of God, [9] not of works, lest anyone should boast. [10] For we are His workmanship, created *in Christ Jesus* for good works, which God prepared beforehand that we should walk in them" (Eph. 2:9, 20)

"You therefore, my son [and daughter], be strong in the grace that is in Christ Jesus" 2 Tim. 2:1).

God's grace is all sufficient to uphold us and sustain us in the Kingdom of Grace.

"And He said to me, "My **grace** is sufficient for you, for My strength is made perfect in weakness." Therefore most gladly I will rather boast in my *weakness*, that the **power** of Christ may rest upon me" (2 Cor. 12:9; (*italics* by the author).

"For the Lord God is a sun and shield; ***the Lord will give grace and glory***; no good thing will He withhold from those who walk uprightly" (Psa. 84:11)

"… but **grow in the grace** and knowledge of our Lord and Savior Jesus Christ. To Him *be* the glory both now and forever: (2 Pet. 3:18).

Final Salutation on Grace:

> "The grace of the Lord Jesus Christ, and the love of God, and the communion of the Holy Spirit be with you all. Amen" (2 Cor. 13:14).

How important is grace? The final sentence in the Bible sums it up:

> "The grace of our Lord Jesus Christ be with you all. Amen" (Rev. 22:21).

Kingdom of Truth

> Jesus said: "For this cause I was born, and for this cause I have come into the world, that I should bear witness to the truth. *Everyone who is of the truth hears My voice*" (John 18:37). Pilate replied: "What is truth?" (John 18:38)

This is the ultimate question which philosophers, poets, scientists, mathematicians and all leaders (governmental and spiritual) have been seeking the answer to since time began: what is truth?

Jesus tells us a very important part of His earthly mission is to testify to the truth – and He sent the Holy Spirit to testify of Himself:[64]

> "But when the Helper comes, whom I shall send to you from the Father, *the Spirit of truth* who proceeds from the Father, He will testify of Me" (John 15:26).

One of the many names for the Holy Spirit is "the Spirit of truth" who guides us up to and into the truth. In order for us to perceive and comprehend the kingdom of Truth, we must also recognize Jesus as the Truth.

Truth is not an opinion – Truth is a Person!

> Jesus said: "I am the way, the truth, and the life. No one comes to the Father except through Me (John 14:6).

In order to hear the truth, you must be able to hear His voice. Jesus said (twice):

---

[64] Angels in heaven have the testimony of Jesus – and they are considered our brethren. (Rev. 19:10)

"My sheep hear My voice, and I know them, and they follow Me" (John 10:27).

"Everyone who is of the truth hears My voice" (John 18:37)

If you truly comprehend that it is Jesus who speaks to you, then revelation truth has become manifest in you – because Jesus is the Truth. And truly, it is the Lord Jesus and/or the Holy Spirit who speaks to us, and for this reason, we should be very suspect by all claims to the contrary.

Based upon these three scriptures and integrating them into one continuous thought, believers in Jesus will:

1. Hear the Voice of Truth
2. Follow the Shepherd of truth
3. Live according to the truth

When a person claims to be a follower of Jesus, all three of these points *must* be operational in their spiritual life (or walking in that direction which results in hearing the truth – and believing it). Many people rely on other spiritual leaders to listen for them, but that was never the Lord's intent. Jesus wants all of His followers to hear His voice – and follow Him.

Simply stated: if you cannot hear His voice, then you are not one of His sheep!

If you claim to be a follower of Jesus, but you cannot hear His voice – you are a goat! Jesus said His sheep hear His voice. Therefore, do all you can do to hear His voice because it comes with a promise: "And I give them eternal life" (John 10:28).

Furthermore, goats are by nature – stubborn! They will not listen to the Spirit of Truth, they are unable to discern truth… and they do not desire to walk in the truth.

In fact (taking this one step further): if we want to live and move and have our being as children of God, then we must align ourselves with the truth of God and not the wisdom of men.

> "Then Jesus said to those Jews who believed Him, "If you abide in My word, you are My disciples indeed. [32] And you shall know the truth, and the truth shall make you free" (John 8:31, 32).

Pay close attention: these Jews believed in Jesus... but they had one primary problem: they did not understand the message of truth Jesus taught (v.43).

Step #1: become followers of Jesus and listen to the Voice of truth. Herein a great many believers have been led astray by following goats pretending to be shepherds of the Way wherein the flock has been taught many things that are inconsistent with God's truth within the word of God (i.e. the Bible). Disciples of Jesus – follow Jesus – and only Jesus.

Jesus is Truth Incarnate – in the Kingdom of Truth.

Jesus taught us what our heavenly Father seeks: worshippers in spirit and in truth. These represent two dimensions of the Spirit's sanctifying work in us to change us into the type of creation the Father seeks: worshippers in spirit... and worshippers in truth.

> "God is Spirit, and those who worship Him must worship in spirit and truth" (John 4:24).

Can you have one without the other? Sadly, yes. I've witnessed some crazy happenings within the church of mystical, sensational kookiness that wants to operate in the realm of the Spirit by entering into bizarre behavior – and I've experienced messages from the pulpit trying to explain the realm of Christ from a human (man-based) perspective with lunatic asylum logic. God is Spirit. And likewise:

"Jesus is Lord" (Phil. 2:11)… and "The Lord is the Spirit" (2 Cor. 3:17). Meditate on that!

Do not underestimate the great significance of that statement aligned with this next statement: everything on earth, including everything we are and everything we have been called to be and to perform – originates in the One who created us on purpose for His purpose: Jesus! Jesus (*ktizo*-2936) fabricated us to conform to the Manufacturer's original specifications for His intended use, which is: we are image bearers sent to establish the kingdom of heaven on earth. Failing to produce this product renders the fabricated object – worthless, tasteless salt.

> "He [Jesus] is the image of the invisible God, the firstborn [4416] over all creation. [16] For by Him all things were created that are in heaven and that are on earth, visible and invisible, whether thrones or dominions or principalities or powers. All things were created through Him and for Him. [17] And He is before all things, and in Him all things consist. [18] And He is the head of the body, the church, who is the beginning, the firstborn from the dead, that in all things He may have the preeminence" (Col. 1:15-18).

Truth is oftentimes inconvenient. Jesus is the preeminence (*proteuo*-4409-first in order of importance, and *prototokos*-4416-first begotten) over all creation. Jesus Himself produced creation, thus He is accurately declared "Creator" – "by [whom] all things were created." Does this conflict with the truth your tradition teaches? (See also: Gen. 1:27; Isa. 41:20; 43:7; 44:24; John 1:1-5; Eph. 3:9; Col. 3:10; Heb. 1:2, 10; Rev. 4:1. Other scriptures include: 2 Cor. 4:4; John 1:18; 17:5; Phil. 2:5-7; Heb. 2:10). Research this truth for yourself and see Truth from God's perspective.

This earth belongs to the Creator, Jesus Christ, and this is why the earth and the generations of man (the host of earth) have been under attack since time began. The prince of darkness hates everything associated with Jesus... and that includes you! You've been under attack since you were begotten.

> "He has made everything beautiful in its time. Also He has put eternity in their hearts, except that ***no one can find out the work that God does from beginning to end***" (Eccl. 3:11).

People have been seeking after wonders and watching for signs from heaven to help them comprehend the times and season... which are nearly fulfilled. We train our telescopes on large meteors and develop mass-casualty scenarios in case one hits us – or if some idiot pushes the red button of mutual self-destruction. Somehow, intuitively, even non-believers know there is an impending end to all this chaos and madness, just as animals instinctively sense catastrophe and flee the impending disaster. Yet humans go about their business blithely drinking and celebrating, and consulting mediums and false prophets to discern the end without any care to what awaits them on the other side. Fools! Truth be known: there will come a day when all this ends. We can count on it because God's truth declares it. And then the regeneration begins! But what are we to do while we wait for it to happen? A: Be about the Master's business... and don't worry. Even the meteor belongs to Jesus.

God's plan for this planet is on schedule – and everything happens for a reason.

Whose plan are you living according to: God's – or yours?

Know the truth – walk in the truth – and preach the kingdom of truth.

Walk by grace – live by grace – and preach the kingdom of grace.

Allow the grace and truth of Jesus Christ – to flow through you. Amen!

It's All about Jesus – and God gets the glory!

Kingdom of Love

> "God is Spirit" (John 4:24)
> "God is love" (1 John 4:8)

Love! No attribute other than grace best defines the kingdom of God. Spirit is an attribute of *what God is*. Love is an attribute of *who He is* as one aspect of His Divine character.

God is – I AM

Love is supreme. Love desires the best for others. Love sees the best in others. Love is patient and kind. Love is longsuffering. Love does not create an offense nor does it hold onto an offense by others. Love forgives liberally. Love is heavenly. Love is divine.

> "God is Spirit, and those who worship Him must worship in spirit and truth" (John 4:24).

God is Spirit. And the fruit of the Spirit is love. Therefore, love – is an attribute of who we are as an element of what we are: spiritual beings created by God as a likeness of Him. Love is "the golden thread" woven throughout the kingdom of God that unifies all of God's messages to us – and for us (individually and corporately).

If you have not love, you have not God – is not a verse found in the scriptures. God is all in all and God is everywhere, so having love or having God is not the answer – but doing love – is!

> "He who does not love does not know God, for God is love" (1 John 4:8).

If you do not love, you know not God. We must "do" love. It is impossible to claim a relationship with God with any hope of life eternal in His kingdom without having and doing love. Learning to love is perhaps the first step in this life – by grace – in order to pass the test. And yes, this life is one giant test – to test us and proof us in preparation for eternity. If you want to pass the test, then begin with question #1: "Did you learn to love?"

How many times did Jesus say: "I love you"? This exact phrase is not found even when Jesus speaks about the Father. However, Jesus taught us many times and demonstrated to us the message of love through all His actions – an infinite number of times.

- "A new commandment I give to you, that you love one another; as I have loved you, that you also love one another" (John 13:34)
- "This is My commandment, that you love one another as I have loved you" (John 15:12)
- "These things I command you, that you love one another" (John 15:17)
- "By this all will know that you are My disciples, if you have love for one another" (John 13:35)

Love for one another – is the pattern language of God's kingdom. Love one another… for such is the kingdom of God.

> "Beloved, let us love one another, *for love is of God*; and everyone who loves is born of God and knows God" (1 John 4:7).

Through faith, you were born again through the washing of regeneration, which means you were born of God – to know God and love God. Biblical love will always have God as its first, best and highest affection. We must understand – love is born of God – as coming of/from God – and anyone who loves is therefore born of God – by God. It's a package deal.

> Jesus said: "And you shall love the Lord your God with all your heart, with all your soul, with all your mind, and with all your strength.' This is the first [*and great*] commandment" (Mark 12:30; [*added*] from Matt. 22:38).

This is the first and great commandment... and the second is like it:

> "And the second, like it, is this: 'You shall love your neighbor as yourself.' There is no other commandment greater than these" (Mark 12:31).

Jesus is Lord. Jesus is God. God Himself said to love the Lord your God – and to love your neighbor – is the greatest commandment in the entire universe! Think about the magnitude of that statement! This command is supreme! This command is absolute! This command is matchless! There is no virtue or law or axiom in the entire universe even remotely equal to the implementation of this godly command. The kingdom of heaven – is established by love!

> "For this is the message that you heard from the beginning, that we should love one another" (1 John 3:11).

You cannot belong to God unless you have love for your brothers, sisters, parents and neighbors. Stated somewhat differently: God cannot abide in you – if you do not have love for others! Love for God and your neighbor – is a package deal! God "dwells" (*meno*) temporarily in everyone because God is everywhere, but what God wants is to "abide permanently" (*mone*) in you – and this new creation within you through the new birth allows God's love to be perfected in you.

> "No one has seen God at any time. ***If we love one another, God abides in us***, and His love has been perfected in us" (1 John 4:12).

Love is not an emotion (initially). Love is (foremost) an act of your will. Love is a value-based decision made in your mind according to your will that results in an actionable and emotional response from your heart. You made "a love thought" in your mind – then your mind created "a love program" and planted that program in your heart – and then your heart responds to (acts upon) it. Love – is an act of your will. You **make** a decision to love – and then you **create** a loving act based upon that decision to love. Beloved, we are like God in this regard: we are able to make and create things that did not previously exist. To love – is divine!

"Your soul has two components: mind and heart. The mind of your soul does one thing and it does it really well: ***it thinks to produce thoughts.*** That's all it does! It gathers and accumulates tons a data and then assembles these ideas within the mind in order to produce one thing: a thought. It thinks, thinks, thinks, thinks, thinks – to produce a thought – which it plants as a seed in your heart. Thoughts of doubt, understanding, love, fear, forgiveness and goodness are all products of the mind – to will – and then your mind sends these thoughts to your heart – to act."[65]

> "… for it is God who works in you both to will and to do [act] for His good pleasure" (Phil. 2:13).

To will and to act – is the soul operating in "mind and heart" oneness. God wants us to do this according to righteousness, goodness and truth – and He is working "in us" to accomplish this – so we operate according to "His thoughts and His ways" (Isa. 55:8) – according to His likeness and Manufacturer's specifications (Eph. 2:10).

Made, created and formed according to His likeness (Gen. 1:26-28; 2:7) – is how we were made, created and formed by God who "thought" us into existence – and this is precisely the same manner by which we were designed to function – which explains why we operate this way: we operate according to Manufacturer's specifications. ***We think things into existence – and the greatest of these is love*** (1 Cor. 13:13).

Think on these things. Meditate on these things. Think love into existence. Meditate on love.

---

[65] Excerpt from "The Renewed Mind" from Chapter 1: "What is the Mind?"

> "Meditate on these things; give yourself entirely to them, that your progress may be evident to all" (1 Tim. 4:15; see also Phil. 4:8).

Love – as an act of our will – defines us and testifies on our behalf "Who" our spiritual Father is.

God is good. God is love. Love (*agape*-26; in a social or moral sense; from the root *agan* means: much).[66] Love (*agape*) represents: the highest good. Love desires the greatest good and the highest good for everyone regardless of who they are – and that includes your enemies.

> Jesus said: "You have heard that it was said, 'You shall love your neighbor and hate your enemy.' [44] But I say to you, *love your enemies*, bless those who curse you, do good to those who hate you, and pray for those who spitefully use you and persecute you" (Matt. 5:43, 44).

This type of love is not worldly. This type of love is divine – it is heavenly – it is supernatural – and it defines those who are aligned with God's kingdom to establish the kingdom of heaven on earth. This type of love is rooted in self-sacrifice to benefit others for their greater good – and this godly attitude toward others (and future brethren in Christ) is the definition of meekness: considering the needs of others ahead of self. Love – born of God – makes this happen.

Love is not self serving. Love is able to sacrifice personal benefit for the well-being of others.

God is good. All things work together for good – for God's good – and you are God's workmanship created in Christ – for good works! (Eph. 2:10) God created you as His instrument – as God's handiwork – to think love into existence – and act on it.

---

[66] Strong's Concordance.

Meditate on that!

Gateways of Love

If you are walking along a path the Lord established for you yet you seem alone and forgotten, beloved – let me encourage you – you are on the godly, narrow path! Be strong! Stay sweet! Stay on the pathway called: love. You are a gateway of God's love in a corrupt world. Many generations of faithful men and women plowed ahead and endured many tribulations to contend for "your" faith and salvation in Christ Jesus. Love was paid forward – for your benefit.

Love born of God for the sake of the gospel – is ultimately for the benefit of others:

> "Therefore I [Paul] endure all things for the sake of the elect, that they also may obtain the salvation which is in Christ Jesus with eternal glory" (2 Tim. 2:10).

Love is what binds us together – and makes us one. The lack of love for one another is what divides us. Whenever there is division – the loveless, hate-filled hand of the enemy is nearby.

> "For where two or three are gathered together in My name, I am there in the midst of them" (Matt. 18:20).

Whenever any two people can agree – and come together in unity – is a miraculous moment. There are around 7 billion people on this planet and we are all very different from one another, yet "the one thing" that unifies us is "oneness in God." Can you tell me how God makes us one? For most of my Christian life, I have said: faith in Christ Jesus. Faith is able to make us one body composed of many members, but something more provocative and profound is essential "through faith" to make us one: it's God's glory!

> "And the glory which You gave Me I have given them, that they may be one just as We are one" (John 17:22).

God sent Himself as a Son to manifest the glory of the Son as the glory of the Father (Luke 9:29; John 17:1-5). The Son manifested the glory of the Father – because Jesus is the Father who sent Himself as a Son to teach us how to be sons and daughters of the Father – and to live as disciples of Jesus – thereby loving one another through the bond of peace (Eph. 4:3).

> "And now, O Father, glorify Me together with Yourself, with the glory which I had with You before the world was" (John 17:5).

Revelation truth should cause the reset button in our mind to stop – ponder – and reconfigure.

The Son is One with the Father – always and eternally – and through faith in Jesus – you are one with the Father also – who predestined you since before the foundation of the world as sons and daughters (Eph. 1:4, 5) – according to grace. Your comprehension of your true spiritual identity just increased far beyond human reason or intellect. You've always been regarded as sons and daughters of adoption, but sin blinded you from perceiving this truth, yet now you know the truth about your true identity... and now you need to embrace it with the power made available by the Spirit through a renewed mind... to live according to the Spirit!

Jesus demonstrated His love in word and action without using the ubiquitous phase: "I love you." Preach the same gospel Jesus taught... and sometimes... use words.

> "Greater love has no one than this, than to lay down one's life for his friends" (John 15:13).

Love is sacrificial. Love desires the best for others. Love sees the best in others. Love will sacrifice self for the benefit of others. Love came to earth and became a sacrificial offering to set us free from the penalty of sin and bondage to sin by empowering us by His Spirit to live apart from sin with divine power to avoid sin. The Holy Spirit dwelling in us does not make us sinless – but He empowers us so we sin less.

Jesus was hung upon a cross – attached by only three nails, but His love is what held Him there. His incredible love for you and me – to set us free from captivity in darkness – was the single greatest sacrificial act by anyone on this planet.

> "I have been crucified with Christ; it is no longer I who live, but Christ lives in me; and the life which I now live in the flesh I live by faith in the Son of God, who loved me and gave Himself for me" (Gal. 2:20)

How many times did Jesus die for mankind? Only once! But in this one moment, Jesus not only died for us – He died "as" us: "I have been crucified *with* Christ."

> "Or do you not know that as many of us as were baptized into Christ Jesus were baptized into His death?" (Rom. 6:3)

There is an aspect of this life which we consider "ours" that we must sacrificially yield to Jesus unto death so that a new man can be birthed by the Spirit to walk in newness of life. We must surrender the sin-corrupted water-born life before we can embrace the Spirit-born life that Jesus offers. During this transition from self to "sacrificial offering" (Rom. 12:2), our thought patterns must also embrace a new paradigm of thought that loves others as our high calling in Christ in the kingdom of love. Love one another!

Consider the message by Jesus to Peter:

> "So when they had eaten breakfast, Jesus said to Simon Peter, "Simon, *son* of Jonah, do you love Me more than these?" He said to Him, "Yes, Lord; You know that I love You." He said to him, "Feed My lambs." ¹⁶ He said to him again a second time, "Simon, *son* of Jonah, do you love Me?" He said to Him, "Yes, Lord; You know that I love You." He said to him, "Tend My sheep." ¹⁷ He said to him the third time, "Simon, *son* of Jonah, do you love Me?" Peter was grieved because He said to him the third time, "Do you love Me?" And he said to Him, "Lord, You know all things; You know that I love You." Jesus said to him, "Feed My sheep" (John 21:15-17).

Loving Jesus – in grace and truth – is manifested by our love for one another. Since you love Jesus – feed His sheep. It's a package deal. Love is the single most defining attribute of God's character. Love is "the" defining attribute of the Lord's disciples. God's Spirit in you – will empower your renewed mind to produce love for others – or else God's Spirit is not in you.

> "For God has not given us a spirit of fear, but of power and of love and of a sound mind" (2 Tim. 1:7).

"The 'sound' mind '*sophronismos*' (4995) means "discipline; literally, this word means saving (*sozo*) the mind (*phren*) through admonishing and calling to soundness of mind and to <u>self-control</u>."[67] Knowing the truth is not enough; being trained in righteousness to live according to the truth as a disciple will result in a sound mind that is obedient to God – and therefore this mind will exercise self control."[68]

---

[67] Strong's Concordance.
[68] Excerpt from "The Renewed Mind" chapter 6: The Sound Mind.

Discipline for the mind (sophronismos) will produce (mathetes-3101) disciples for the Lord.

The Spirit within us initiates the renewing of our mind – with truth – to produce a sound mind. Our spiritual transformation from death to life and fear to faith does not begin with power to operate a sound mind to produce love; the transformation process by the Spirit of truth begins with – truth! God's truth empowers us to walk in obedience as disciples. God's truth in us enables us think love into existence. Once God's love is operational in us, then power is released through us as gateways of love to establish the kingdom of love – in the midst of darkness. So I ask: why were you created? You were created by Love as an extension (manifestation) of His love to be an instrument of God's love. The Spirit of God in you – makes this happen!

> "Do you not know that you are the temple of God and that the Spirit of God dwells in you?" (1 Cor. 3:16).

Beloved, love is the reason why! The answer to a thousand "whats and whys" – is "love."

> "Since you have purified your souls in obeying the truth through the Spirit in sincere love of the brethren, love one another fervently with a pure heart" (1 Pet. 1:22).

Grow in grace. Grow in love. Abound in grace. Abound in love. Abide in love. Amen!

> "***If we love one another, God abides in us***, and His love has been perfected in us" (1 John 4:12).

> "God is love, and he who abides in love abides in God, and God in him" (1 John 4:16).

> "And this commandment we have from Him: that he who loves God must love his brother also" (1

John 4:21).

How we manifest love toward one another can be diverse in application, yet the result remains the same: to care for others with Godly affection – and desiring the greatest good for others – is love born of God. Love is the fruit of God's Spirit being operational within us (singular in nature, yet diverse in application).

> "But ***the fruit*** [singular] ***of the Spirit is*** love, joy, peace, longsuffering, kindness, goodness, faithfulness, [23] gentleness, self-control. Against such there is no law" (Gal. 5:22, 23).

> "For you were once darkness, but now you are light in the Lord. Walk as children of light [9] (for ***the fruit of the Spirit is*** *in* all goodness, righteousness, and truth), [10] finding out what is acceptable to the Lord" (Eph. 5:8-10).

The fruit of the Spirit – which is love (singular) – is IN all goodness, righteousness and truth. Is it possible to love others according to the Spirit apart from goodness, righteousness and truth? No it's not. It's all interconnected in the kingdom of love. And for this reason, many in this world have sought to redefine goodness and righteousness according to their own standard by inventing an alternate, illegitimate truth to support their reprobate, fleshly definition of love. What standards are you using to define your world? Is it based upon God's truth?

> "Love suffers long and is kind; love does not envy; love does not parade itself, is not puffed up" (1 Cor. 13:4).

Let's go back and reconsider the word "self control" in Gal. 5:23. "Temperance" in the King James Version is a much better translation for '*egkrateia*-1466' rather than "self-control" in the NKJV because… "self-control is contradictory. If one has control of self, the Spirit's ministry is needless. The various powers bestowed by God upon man are capable of abuse; the right use demands the controlling power of the will under the operation of the Spirit of God."[69]

This, my friends, is a perfect illustration of man's will (the mind) under the supervision and influence of the Spirit to walk in obedience with a sound (right) mind. The Spirit renews our mind with truth which enables us to align our will with God's good and perfect will to conduct our affairs with a right mind to walk in goodness, righteousness and truth. Love – as an attribute of God – is a product of God's goodness, righteousness and truth.

The power of man's will to produce love – is a power bestowed upon him by God. By thoughts of our will, we think love into existence. Therefore, love is yet another type of power. Here are five types of power identified in the New Testament:

- *Kratos* (2904) "means might, relative and manifested power – chiefly of God"
- *Dunamis* (1411) "expresses power, natural ability, general and inherent"
- *Energeia* (1753) "denotes working power in exercise, operational power"
- *Exousia* (1849) "is primarily liberty in action, then authority – either as delegated power or as unrestrained, arbitrary power"
- *Iscus* (2479) "expresses strength, power, (especially physical) as an endowment"[70]

The operational power of love is manifested at many levels in a multiplicity of applications, which is why I consider love – the sixth power. Love is a divine power made available through the Spirit – in the mind of our spirit – to establish order in the midst of chaos – and affection in the midst of hate. "Where there is hatred, let me sow love." (Prayer of St. Francis)

---

[69] Strong's Concordance.
[70] Excerpt from "The Renewed Mind" chapter 6.

What you believe – creates the world you live in. If you consider love from an end-user perspective, having and getting love will never be enough. When you live out of love from a kingdom perspective, as a gateway of love connected to the Source of love, you will never be able to give it all away – even if you lived ten lifetimes. This is how the kingdom of paradox operates: "It is in giving that we receive." (Prayer of St. Francis) Love is the reason why!

Love conquers all. Love is supreme. Love without limits or restrictions. Love is the one attribute that defines those who are members of God's spiritual family.

> "In this the children of God and the children of the devil are manifest: **Whoever does not practice righteousness is not of God, nor is he who does not love his brother**" (1 John 3:10).

Beloved, love must be implemented as God intended based upon His goodness, His righteousness and His truth. Many counterfeit messages have already gone out into the world to corrupt weak and feeble minds to pervert the meaning of righteousness and truth, and even the inherent meaning of goodness has fallen victim to demonic influence.

> "Woe to those who call evil good, and good evil;
> who put darkness for light, and light for darkness;
> who put bitter for sweet, and sweet for bitter!" (Isa. 5:20)

What does God say about good and evil? They are oftentimes the product of our words: "Death and life are in the power of the tongue" (Prob. 18:21) as outcomes from those things in our heart.

> "See, I have set before you today life and good, death and evil" (Deut. 30:15).

> "Let love be without hypocrisy. Abhor [hate] what
> is evil. Cling to what is good" (Rom. 12:9).

The culture of this hypocritical world has switched the terminology to support a godless existence that does not need God except by invocation to get votes during an election, to manipulate a reduction in judicial judgment, to escape one dysfunction in exchange for another, or to give the appearance of religious piety. Godly love will be without hypocrisy!

The kingdom of darkness promotes love based on what you get – but the kingdom of love encourages you to give without benefit of reciprocity: i.e. giving without getting anything in return.

What this world calls "love" is merely a "temporary love" until a better offer comes along. Love is not something based upon personal preferences, like choosing Coke over Pepsi – or steak over chicken. Love is divine. Love is a Godly attribute according to His principles of goodness, righteousness and truth… against which no law can supersede, replace or diminish. When you operate according to love – as God intended – then no other standard applies. Love is supreme!

If you were expecting a chapter on love based upon the worldly romance novel version of love, well… all I can say is… you're reading the wrongs books. Get out of the world – drop the "L" – and get into the Word. Our mindset has been corrupted and polluted by the pattern of this world to such a great degree that it is nearly impossible to find love or goodness or righteousness or truth. There is only one possible scenario wherein mankind returns to the basic premise of love – and that's by returning through repentance to the Promise of Love Himself: Jesus Christ.

> "For God so loved the world that He gave His only
> begotten Son, that whoever believes in Him should
> not perish but have everlasting life" (John 3:16.).

What message about love would be complete without this precious pearl of truth? Rarely have I used this scripture because it is overused and oftentimes falsely misinterpreted to imply: since God loves everyone – He will save everyone from the Pit of Hell. Not so! Loving Jesus and salvation from the Pit – are a package deal. Love is mutual – love is reciprocal – love is not one-sided, nor is it self-centered. Love of God enables oneness with God... based upon God's truth.

> "We love Him [Jesus] because He first loved us" (1 John 4:19).

Faith in Jesus – according to truth – radiates love for Jesus – to walk in the truth – which enables us to escape the dragnet of fear and doubt that keeps us enslaved in darkness and rebellion. Faith is one thing devils and demons do not possess whereby they remain ensnared in the fowler's net. Faith in Jesus is the grace by which we are saved from destruction... which also sets us free: A) to walk in liberty and love to set other captives free and B) to walk in dominion authority with power to establish the kingdom of heaven on earth. God's story of loving us and dwelling among us – begins and ends with King Jesus! Jesus is:

"King of kings and Lord of lords" (Rev. 19:16)

Jesus personified God. Jesus personified Love. Jesus personified Glory. Jesus personified Grace and Truth. Jesus is the source of all life – because Jesus is the Life.

> Jesus said: "**I am** the way, the truth, and **the life**. No one comes to the Father except through Me" (John 14:6).

This next statement is not meant as some great mystery revealed: all roads lead to Jesus. Whatever path you're on to seek and find whatever answer you're looking for – ultimately leads to Jesus. King Jesus is the only answer you'll ever need because He is the lover of your soul. Jesus is love – and Jesus is the only One who can fill the hole in your soul – because Jesus is the One who created you that way. Why would Jesus create us in such a way that we are dependent upon Him? Perhaps a better way to say this is: we cannot exist apart from Him. How is this even possible? Because "in Him" all things are held together (consist; Col. 1:17). Focus on Jesus. "Apart from Jesus – you can do nothing" (John 15:5). Apart from Jesus – you are nothing. And the second one is like it: without love – you are nothing.

> "Though I speak with the tongues of men and of angels, but have not love, I have become sounding brass or a clanging cymbal. ^{2} And though I have the gift of prophecy, and understand all mysteries and all knowledge, and though I have all faith, so that I could remove mountains, **but have not love, I am nothing**. ^{3} And though I bestow all my goods to feed the poor, and though I give my body to be burned, but have not love, it profits me nothing. ^{4} Love suffers long and is kind; love does not envy; love does not parade itself, is not puffed up; ^{5} does not behave rudely, does not seek its own, is not provoked, thinks no evil; ^{6} does not rejoice in iniquity, but rejoices in the truth; ^{7} bears all things, believes all things, hopes all things, endures all things. ^{8} Love never fails" (1 Cor. 13:1-8).

In oneness with Jesus – the unity of the Spirit is maintained – in the bond of peace.

> "I, therefore, the prisoner of the Lord, beseech you to walk worthy of the calling with which you were called, ^{2} with all lowliness and gentleness, with longsuffering, **bearing with one another in love, ^{3} endeavoring to keep the unity of the Spirit in the bond of peace**. ^{4} There is one body and one Spirit, just as you were called in one hope of your calling; ^{5} one Lord, one faith, one baptism; ^{6} one God and Father of all, who is above all, and through all, and in you all" (Eph. 4:1-6).

> "Therefore if there is any consolation in Christ, ***if any comfort of love***, if any fellowship of the Spirit, if any affection and mercy, [2] fulfill my joy by being like-minded, ***having the same love, being of one accord***, of one mind. [3] Let nothing be done through selfish ambition or conceit, but in lowliness of mind let each esteem others better than himself" (Phil. 2:1-3).

Do you see the recurring theme in these scriptures? Love appears with and corresponds to oneness. Love makes us one – in the unity of the Spirit. Unity of the Spirit – makes us one with God. The glory that Jesus gave us – makes us one with God. Oneness with the Spirit – is paramount!

The kingdom of love – is also the kingdom of oneness.

There is one God and Father – who is above all and through all – and in you all! This is the message I've been teaching for many years: God is with you – God is in you – God is for you – and God is "in you all." The Father has been dwelling in you since the beginning. You were never alone. God is everywhere. The Father is in everyone. And it is for this reason we are all without excuse: we've all heard the Spirit of the Father speaking truth to us, but we've also heard and listened to the voice of rebellion that deceived us and lead us astray... causing us to believe many lies and seek after many schemes.

> "Truly, this only I have found: that God made man upright, but they have sought out many schemes" (Eccl. 7:29).

The Voice of Love that whispers to us was never intended to compete against the banging drums the enemy uses to confuse and disorient us. Noise is one of their primary weapons; silence and stillness before the Lord in prayer and meditation is how we overcome noise – and abide with God. Resting in God's peace is about abiding in His loving presence and dwelling intimately with

Him – which the enemy tries to prevent in order to keep us separated from Him. The kingdom of darkness does not deceive you because they want you on their side – they only want to keep you apart from Jesus and the Father's love – to dwell in captivity without hope or love.

The battle between light and darkness – is for your soul – either for salvation or destruction.

Because the Father is in you and He is with you, the enemy begins their diabolical lie with a contradictory thought: you must earn the Father's love through good works. Once you've failed in doing well, the lies of the enemy flow like cascading messages causing fear, doubt and confusion to undercut the basis of God's love for you – which is based upon: trust in God.

> "Trust in the LORD with all your heart, and lean not on your own understanding; [6] in all your ways acknowledge Him, and He shall direct your paths" (Prov. 3:5, 6).

Love and trust are two legs of a stool called INTIMACY and the third leg is called: reverence.

Acknowledge Him. Call to remembrance all that God is – and all He has done for you.

Jesus sent Himself as a Son and died for you in order to teach you how to live according to love. You cannot be saved apart from abiding in God's love or without loving others with God's love. You cannot have salvation with life eternal in Paradise unless you comply with the terms of God's covenantal agreement for everyone: repent – and believe Jesus is Lord and Christ. No one comes to the Father except through faith in the Son: Jesus Christ. Faith, in this regard, is not what you believe; faith is living according to what you believe. If you believe it but don't live it, it cannot be credited to you as faith… for "even demons believe… and tremble" (James 2:19).

> "Now faith is the substance of things hoped for, the evidence of things not seen. ² *For by it the elders obtained a good testimony* (Heb. 11:1, 2).

Faith is not what you believe. Faith is doing what you believe is truth. Faith is living according to truth – and Jesus is the Truth! People believe a lot of crazy things even within the church, but that does not mean those things are truth – nor can it be considered faith. It merely implies those people believe those things are truth based upon their opinion. What you believe must be compared to God's truth contained in God's Word, the Bible, and must be in agreement with God's message. Truth is never contradicted to justify an opinion. Truth is never minimized to accommodate sinful behavior. Truth does not need to be defined or defended. Let truth out – and the Spirit of truth will defend Herself.

Why is truth such an integral part of the kingdom of love? Because it is! Faith is based upon truth. Hope is based upon truth. Love is based upon truth.

> "And now abide faith, hope, love, these three; but the greatest of these is love" (1 Cor. 13:13).

Faith is built upon God's truth. Truth is communicated to us by the Spirit of truth. Therefore, the Spirit of God is the origin of truth and the certainty of faith resulting in our salvation.

> "Now hope does not disappoint, because the love of God has been poured out in our hearts by the Holy Spirit who was given to us" (Rom. 5:5).

Love cannot be known or implemented unless reason (being of right mind) has been restored to the snarled mind of man. This is the ministry of the Holy Spirit: to fill our hearts with love (Rom. 5:5), to renew our mind with truth (Rom. 12:2), and operate in soundness of mind with logic and reason (Luke 8:35).

> "For this is the love of God, that we keep His commandments" (1 John 5:3).

Eternal glory in Paradise is where we're all headed. However, Jesus used many examples to describe this future dwelling place – in present tense! Jesus never said the kingdom of heaven is going to be like; Jesus said "The kingdom of heaven is like" 11 times in story after story to communicate and illustrate the golden thread of love woven between the pages of HisStory (sic) to redeem His creation – which includes you and me – and how the kingdom of heaven operates.

Love is present tense. Love is perfect. The kingdom of love is being implemented by us – in present tense – now! Now go…and love one another…

> "And as you go, preach, saying, '***The kingdom of heaven is at hand***' " (Matt. 10:7).
>
> ***It's all about Love – and God gets the glory! Amen.***

Kingdom of Joy

The race does not belong to the swift. The race belongs to the mighty. The joy of the Lord is my strength. Joy – is one way we have victory over our adversary. Joy triumphs over all adversity with rejoicing!

> "Do not sorrow, for the joy of the Lord is your strength" (Neh. 8:10).

Joy is one of the attributes of God's kingdom that confirms His reality is operational within you. This was one of the first things I noticed about Jesus people: they had joy... and they walked in love. Joy with love creates a supernatural attraction for people dwelling in darkness which causes them to walk toward these missing elements in their chaotic life. Intuitively, they know joy brings wholeness and healing to broken hearts... and the joy within disciples of Jesus acts like a spiritual magnet that is able to melt cast iron hearts.

Happiness is not the same as joy.

Things will never make you happy. Happiness comes from a joyful heart. Happiness is oftentimes an emotional response (the product) to an event happening <u>to</u> you, but joy is based upon a deeper reality <u>within</u> you. Happiness is based on circumstances; joy is based upon God's truth, goodness and divine favor for you. Joy, peace and contentment are produced when you know the God of all love, joy, peace, contentment and truth – and you put your trust in Him. These attributes represent the highest good in God's kingdom.

Joy wells up within us whereby rejoicing is spiritually released through us. Humans do this... because God does this... because God created us in His image as a likeness of Him.

> "And I will make an everlasting covenant with them, that I will not turn away from doing them

good; but I will put My fear in their hearts so that they will not depart from Me. [41] ***Yes, I will rejoice over them to do them good***, and I will assuredly plant them in this land, *with all My heart and with all My soul*" (Jer. 32:41).

You have a heart and soul because the Lord has a heart and soul. Allow this truth to liberate you: He created you to become another likeness and representation of who He is… and He rejoices over <u>you</u> to do you good! Why does He do this? Because God is good! And because God is good, He created you good and upright – to imitate Him, to do good, and to rejoice.

- We were created very good (Gen. 1:30)
- We were made upright (Eccl. 7:9)
- We are the precious thoughts of God (Psa. 40:15; 139:17)
- We are fearfully and wonderfully made (Psa. 139:14)

God rejoices over you! Not many people perceive that God rejoices over them because we focus more on our failure rather than the truth He planted within us, but we need to comprehend this revelation: when we trust in the Lord… God is enthroned <u>in</u> the praises of His people (Psa. 22:3).

> "The Lord your God in your midst, The Mighty One, will save; ***He will rejoice over you with gladness***, He will quiet you with His love, ***He will rejoice over you with singing***" (Zeph. 3:17).

Jesus sings over you! Why haven't I ever heard a sermon about that! When others do well (in a worldly sense), our natural response is to congratulate them, compliment their achievement, urge them on and rejoice over them (this response is similar to fans rejoicing after a game-winning touchdown or homerun). Our spiritual response is no different – on earth as it is in heaven. When we joyfully rejoice in God's goodness – we give glory to God – and all the host of heaven and earth break into one giant happy-dance.

> "Let the heavens rejoice, and let the earth be glad; and let them say among the nations, "The Lord reigns" (1 Chron. 16:31).

When we obediently do what the Lord asks of us, He raises His hand in witness to bless us. The Hebrew word "bless" (*barak*-1288) also means "to salute." Before God formed any person, the Lord pronounced a blessing over us (Gen. 1:26-28) to be fruitful and multiply – not only in regard to children but also in respect to man accomplishing God's plan to redeem the earth. To be blessed also means to be praised by God! ***God blessed us – God praises us – and God rejoices over us with singing!*** This concept is so amazing to grasp! God "crowned us with glory and honor" (Psa. 8) to accomplish the monumental tasks for which we were created whereby He blessed us with glory and honor. Can you imagine God being so proud of you that He would salute you? Beloved, God blessed you before you were even sent here in order to ensure your success! You are greatly blessed and highly favored! God gave us authority with power to have dominion over the earth. What God has blessed – He also empowers!

Think about that for a moment: what God has blessed – He also empowers.

Any time we believe the lie of the enemy to accept a reality different than what the Lord prescribed – represents a failure to understand the purpose for which God created us – as His workmanship created in Christ Jesus for good works (Eph. 2:10).

> "For we are His workmanship, ***created in Christ Jesus for good works, which God prepared beforehand*** that we should walk in them" (Eph. 2:10).

You were created on purpose for His purpose. The Lord's hand blesses you and salutes you!

> "The Lord your God will make you abound in all the work of your hand, in the fruit of your body, in the increase of your livestock, and in the produce of your land for good. ***For the Lord will again rejoice over you for good*** as He rejoiced over your fathers" (Deut. 30:9).

Not only does the Lord rejoice over you, but angels rejoice also.

> Jesus said: "Likewise, I say to you, there is joy in the presence of the angels of God over one sinner who repents" (Luke 15:10).

The terms "joy" and "rejoicing" are the same exact terms regardless if done by God, angels in heaven… or mankind.

> "Praise Him, all His angels; Praise Him, all His hosts!" (Psa. 148:2)

> "Rejoice in the Lord always. Again I will say, rejoice!" (Phil. 4:4)

The Greek word "blessed" (*eulogeo*-2127) is a compound of two words: (*eu*-2095-good) and (*logos*-3056-word; the expression of thought) and literally means: "to speak well of; to praise, to celebrate with praises."[71] God celebrates over you with praises! Regardless of what this world thinks of you or declares over you, your Father in heaven rejoices over you with praise! He speaks well of you and He has blessed you with every spiritual blessing in order to accomplish His purposes which He reveals in you – and then accomplishes through you.

> "Blessed be the God and Father of our Lord Jesus Christ, who has blessed us with every spiritual blessing in the heavenly places in Christ" (Eph. 1:3).

---

[71] Strong's Concordance.

Substitute the word "empowered" for the word "blessed" (above) and see this from God's perspective. Every spiritual blessing (*eulogia*-2129) from which we get the word "eulogy" as "an excellent commendation"[72] are good words that bestow honor and praise on someone (by God in this instance). God blesses us with good words – and we can repeat this process unto others.

God commissioned us with authority and power to have dominion on earth in His name – and then He blessed us and empowered us to accomplish the individual task appointed unto us.

The pattern God established for every saint is quite simple: when we enter His gates with thanksgiving, we are allowed to enter His courts with praise. Close your eyes to envision yourself passing though His gates with thanksgiving… and when you open your eyes you are in His court of praise. Praise opens the heart of the Divine through which blessings flow in both directions. God pronounced a blessing over you – to be a blessing unto Him.

> "Enter into His gates with thanksgiving, and into His courts with praise. Be thankful to Him, and bless His name" (Psa. 100:4).

This level of joy with thankfulness and praise is not natural; it is supernatural – as something born of the Spirit and accomplished in our spirit by the Spirit.

Allow me to put this chapter in context, which was given to me by the Spirit and after all other chapters had been written. While this is not unusual (because the Lord is always adding one more thing to chapters, books, and your book of life as well), this chapter is being written (present tense) after experiencing a rejection by my pastor. To be blunt: I didn't fit the organizational pattern for his church. My ministry to teach and disciple was negated, and I've been kicked to the curb because my lifestyle as an unorthodox (i.e. indigent) disciple does not include many relationships outside of

---

[72] IBID.

church (and painfully… very few within church either). If you are struggling for relevancy in ministry or life in general, then allow me to encourage you: joy comes in the morning. Every morning represents another opportunity to allow the joy of the Lord to disinfect any bitterness, resentment, offense, unforgiveness, and feelings of worthlessness, insignificance, inferiority and insecurity from having any lasting impact in your life by what other people think and say about you. God is in control! The only thing that matters is: what does God say about you?[73]

You are chosen. Not forsaken. You are loved. You are His beloved. You are significant.

As the song goes: "I am who You say that I am!"

> "Your words were found, and I ate them, and Your word was to me the joy and rejoicing of my heart; for I am called by Your name, O Lord God of hosts" (Jer. 15:16).

If you are going through hell on earth, then I commend you – to rejoice – and again I say rejoice! "Blessed (empowered) are the poor in spirit, for theirs is the kingdom of heaven" (Matt. 5:3). If you are able to rejoice and be glad and praise Him and continue to be thankful regardless of your circumstances, then you're walking in victory… and the Lord will bless you to walk in supernatural joy. This is how we fight our battles: by worshipping Him and offering praise with thanksgiving despite the hellish existence we experience. We fight joyfully from a position of victory as we contend for victory in an all consuming battle in which the enemy attacks you with everything in its arsenal of doubt and despair to create fear and hopelessness. How does the enemy do this? By telling you a lie! The enemy will accuse you and say: you aren't this or that; you aren't who God says you are; you are less than dirt and lower than pond scum; you're a failure; you're an addict; you've got a history; you forfeited your destiny; your failure is irredeemable; you aren't saved. So I ask – have you ever thought

---

[73] This topic will be discussed in book #10: The Renewed Mind, Chapter 4.

this thought: why would God choose you and use you? Beloved, I tell you: that was not your thought! The enemy keeps speaking that lie to you because you keep believing it, but once you embrace what God says about you – that He has blessed you and rejoices over you with the new name He has given you – then you will operate from a position of victory – from faith – to accomplish much for the kingdom of heaven. The Lord blessed us so we can accomplish our earthly mission: to have dominion as His agents of redemption – and be fruitful.

> "And you became followers of us and of the Lord, having received the word in much affliction, with joy of the Holy Spirit" (1 Thess. 1:6)

Within two weeks after that experience with my pastor, another traumatic event happened: the engine in my minivan (my tiny RV home) blew up. As I was meditating on this message of joy to persevere and get through this new event, wave after wave of demonic attack (by the spirit of depression) came against me for several weeks. Multiple times an hour and multiple times per day this spirit overwhelmed my mind with thoughts of despair and failure. I was brokenhearted and grief stricken; I was emotionally wrecked with incredibly deep sorrow for two weeks. Beloved, the race does not belong to the swift – the race belongs to those who put the fullness of their trust in Jesus their Deliverer. Focus on Jesus. If you are following Jesus and you're expecting an emotional high with euphoric bliss, happiness, goose-bumps, tingling and Holy Spirit ecstasy, then someone forgot to tell you about the cataclysmic demonic battle that surrounds you… whereby you are attacked more frequently by the enemy for faithfulness to Jesus as His disciple – yet less so for faithlessness in wishy-washy, mediocre, complacent Christianity.

This is one of the hardest messages I've ever written – about joy in the midst of deep sorrow. Allow the Lord to help you through it. That's why Jesus is your Deliverer!

If you are valuable to the kingdom of God – then you are vulnerable to enemy attack. Consider this: the Jewish Temple resides in Jerusalem. Jerusalem has been attacked 26 times.[74] The enemy attacked Jerusalem and it attacks you and me for the same reason: you are God's holy temple. You are God's holy possession. You are precious to God (Lam. 4:2; Jer. 25:34; Isa. 43:4; Psa. 40:15; 139:17; 1 Pet. 1:7).

> "Or do you not know that your body is the temple of the Holy Spirit who is in you, whom you have from God, and *you are not your own*?" (1 Cor. 6:19)

Where does an enemy attack a walled city? At the gateways! What is man's gateway: the heart! What is the gatekeeper for man's heart? The mind! The first place the enemy will attack is your mind, so make sure you've put on the helmet of salvation (Eph. 6:17). Once the mind has been conquered by truth (or lies) – the heart will follow – either for good (or evil). This is why we must allow our mind to be conquered by God's truth… and then renewed by the Spirit of truth.

Consider Job… an upright man unlike any other, yet God allowed Satan to sift him. Job knew he had not raised his hand against God and he also knew he was righteous before God, and wave after wave of accusation by his three friends could not convince him otherwise. Then his wife turned against him. Job remained resolute in his joy-with-sorrow devotion to God despite an invisible hand of justice turned against him. Job persevered!

> "Behold, happy *is* the man whom God corrects; therefore do not despise the chastening of the Almighty. [18] For He bruises, but He binds up; He

---

[74] Source: Biblestudy.org. This number does not include current attacks. Additionally: "During its long history, Jerusalem has been attacked 52 times, captured and recaptured 44 times, besieged 23 times, and destroyed twice. The oldest part of the city was settled in the 4th millennium BCE, making Jerusalem one of the oldest cities in the world." Source: Wikipedia.

> wounds, but His hands make whole. ¹⁹ He shall deliver you in six troubles, yes, in seven no evil shall touch you" (Job 5:17-19).

Such is the sanctifying of our soul by the Spirit of the Lord. So I encourage you: stand your ground! Be strong and courageous! God dwells in you. You are God's temple!

> "You are of God, little children, and have overcome them, because ***He who is in you is greater than he who is in the world***" (1 John 4:4).

Sometimes, the battles we encounter are meant to strengthen us – so we can encourage others to stay focused on Jesus and be steadfast and faithful in the commission He gave them. That history lesson from my life was meant to encourage others going through similar circumstances. So I commend you… to trust in the Lord… always and again! And again I say, trust and rejoice!

Sometimes our brokenness – is in preparation for breakthrough!

God takes our test – and it becomes our testimony! Our mess – becomes our message!

God is love. God is peace. God is joy. Jesus is God – which means Jesus is joy. The joy within you is because Jesus (abiding in you) is the joy of your salvation (John 17:13). Jesus rejoices over you and Jesus planted the fullness of Himself – which includes joy – within you! Your joy to overcome everything is based upon the King of Joy's presence within you.

> "And He [Jesus] said to me [Paul], "My grace is sufficient for you, for My strength [miraculous power] is made perfect in weakness" (2 Cor. 12:9).

Beloved, I tell you my story (in the midst of a chapter titled "joy") to comprehend God's power of joy within you to sustain you in the midst of the enemy's continuous battle against you to accomplish one thing: obliterate you. The enemy hates you because you are God's beloved. Believe God's truth! Hold tightly to it! Reject the lie! Trust Jesus! God loves you! I write this message having passed the test! By grace – I overcame the enemy – I withstood the enemy's onslaught dozens of times before – and there will be more tests and attacks in the future. So I admonish you: stay in the loving presence of Jesus during these times… and He will strengthen you. Jesus is your Joy! Let Jesus wrap you in His love for you… as you melt in His presence.

> "Yet I will rejoice in the Lord, I will joy in the God of my salvation" (Hab. 3:18).

Joy comes from rejoicing – and worship (which is one of our offensive weapons) causes the enemy to scatter. If you are being overwhelmed by the enemy, then I command you: worship King Jesus! Sing joyfully to the Lord. The King of Joy abides within you. Alleluia!

- "Oh come, let us sing to the Lord! Let us shout joyfully to the Rock of our salvation" (Psa. 95:1)
- "Shout joyfully to the Lord, all the earth; break forth in song, rejoice, and sing praises" (Psa. 98:4)
- "With trumpets and the sound of a horn; shout joyfully before the Lord, the King" (Psa. 98:6)
- "Make a joyful shout to the Lord, all you lands!" (Psa. 100:1)
- "Praise the Lord! Oh, give thanks to the Lord, for He is good! For His mercy endures forever" (Psa. 106:1)
- "***The humble also shall increase their joy in the Lord***, and the poor among men shall rejoice in the Holy One of Israel" (Isa. 29:19)

This entire book is about kingdoms – including the future kingdom you will inherit, so read this next scripture very carefully:

> ***"Blessed are the poor in spirit,***
> ***For theirs is the kingdom of heaven" (Matt. 5:3)***

What God has blessed – He also empowers! Re-read the Beatitudes (Matt. 5) and insert the word "empowered" every time you see the word "blessed."

> "Blessed are you when they revile and persecute you, and say all kinds of evil against you falsely for My sake. ¹² **Rejoice and be exceedingly glad**, for great is your reward in heaven, for so they persecuted the prophets who were before you" (Matt. 5:11, 12).

Types Of Supernatural Joy

Let's examine several NT words before we see some incredible examples of joy and rejoicing in the scriptures. For starters, the word joy (*chara*-5479) originates from rejoice (*chairo*-5463).[75] The joy we have comes from the rejoicing we received when God rejoiced over us! Amen!

- Joy – (*chara*-5479; from 5463) "cheerfulness; joy; calm delight; on the occasion of joy or the cause of joy" and is translated: joy 51x; gladness 3x (Phil.2:29; Acts12:14; Mark 4:16); joyful 1x; joyous 1x; joyfulness 1x; joyfully+*3326* 1x; greatly 1x
- Rejoice – (*chairo*-5463) to be cheerful, calmly happy; be glad
- Rejoice – (*sugchairo*-4796) to rejoice in or rejoice with (twice by Jesus; Luke 15:6, 9)
- Rejoiced – (*agalliao*-21) exuberant joy, to jump for joy (once by Jesus; John 8:56)

The Parable of the Prodigal Son (Luke 15) is one of the most famous of all parables by Jesus which is perhaps better named: The Expectant Father. This father had two sons, but one took his inheritance and wasted it on prodigal living. The son came to his senses one day and decided to return home and seek forgiveness,

---

[75] All terms from Strong's Concordance

and this is the part of the story that amazes me: the father saw his son's head appearing on the horizon because… he never stopped looking for him to appear even after much time had passed. God never takes His eyes off His children!

> "But when he was still a great way off, his father saw him and had compassion, and ran and fell on his neck and kissed him. [21] And the son said to him, 'Father, I have sinned against heaven and in your sight, and am no longer worthy to be called your son.' [22] "But the father said to his servants, 'Bring out the best robe and put it on him, and put a ring on his hand and sandals on his feet. [23] And bring the fatted calf here and kill it, **and let us eat and be merry**; [24] for this my son was dead and is alive again; he was lost and is found.' **And they began to be merry**" (Luke 15:20-24)

This is how your heavenly Father longs for you with rejoicing over you. This is how your Father celebrates and is "merry" because of you. Merry (*euphraino*-2165) means: to put in a good frame of mind; translated rejoice (6x).[76] Put yourself in the same position of this father for this lost son and you will experience a joy which words are unable to express; this type of exuberant joy is best expressed with a kiss and tears of gladness! God is for us. God loves us. God rejoices over us. We are His offspring. And God waits patiently and expectantly for your head to appear on the horizon to kiss you and hug you every time you drift from His presence. The marvelous love the Father has for us exceeds all expectations!

> "Behold what manner of love the Father has bestowed on us, that we should be called children of God! Therefore the world does not know us, because it did not know Him" (1 John 3:1).

---

[76] Strong's Concordance.

Rhoda at the Door (Acts 12:14). Peter was miraculously released from prison by angels and he immediately went to Mary's house. When Rhoda answered the knocks at the door, she was overwhelmed with such joyful glee that she forgot to open it. Exuberant joy sometimes makes us do incredibly stupid and impulsive things. Wouldn't it be great if we all acted this way?

Unorthodox Swimming (John 21:1-14). After Jesus rose from the grave, He appeared to over 500 people. During one visit, the Lord appeared on the shore where the disciples fished all night yet caught nothing. Then a Voice from the shore told them to cast their nets on the other side of the boat whereby they caught 153 fish. I like to go fishing and I usually get skunked, but when I catch more than one – it's a good day – but when I catch five or more, it is an astounding fishing trip with a story that grows every time I tell it. For these disciples, their nets were filled to the full, and then John knew the Voice was Jesus. "Therefore that disciple whom Jesus loved said to Peter, "It is the Lord!" Now when Simon Peter heard that it was the Lord, he put on his outer garment (for he had removed it), and plunged into the sea" (John 21:7). Peter did the exact opposite of swimming protocol: take off all outer garments (or as many as acceptable). When we are confronted by the nearness of Jesus, our joy makes us do impulsively stupid things.

If you've done something embarrassing or impulsive under the influence of joy, then all I can say is: stand in line... because I've done it too (but take heart because your story wasn't written down for generations of believers to read over and over again). Move on. God knows your heart. And He still smiles in cheerful glee when He remembers it.

David Danced Recklessly (2 Sam. 6:14). David entered into a unique form of worship that others perceived as scandalous and provocative, but David wasn't doing it to impress others... nor was he limited by their attitudes toward him. David focused on only one thing: the presence of the Lord in his midst! When your worship rises to this level of intensity, intimacy and devotion to your Lord, you will experience the atmosphere of heaven under an open heaven... and great will your gladness and joy of heart be. Your joyful response to the Lord's presence will cause "leaping and whirling before the LORD" just like David – with no regard for what others think.

We are living under an open heaven – now! Imagine heaven touching you. Imagine encountering the presence of God during prayer and meditation. Touching heaven – changing earth – is what our mission on earth is all about. Would you like to experience Jesus like this? If yes, then allow your soul to dwell in stillness and listen attentively for His still small voice.

> "He will rejoice over you with gladness, **He will quiet you with His love**, He will rejoice over you with singing" (Zeph. 3:17).

Joyful Seeds (Mark 4:16). In the Parable of the Sower, the word of God is received joyfully by stony-hearted people, but their faith is shallow-rooted by not understanding the truth. When hardships come, joy disappears and they stumble. Worldly joy is preached from the pulpit more often than truth because worldly joy is more contagious than the flu, but worldly joy is merely an emotional fix – and there are plenty of pills available to artificially produce this type of joy (as well as combat its close cousin: depression). Life on this planet was originally purposed to be joyful based upon your relationship with Jesus. You've gotta dig deep to find the Rock (which involves removing stones from your own heart), so don't give up when the going gets tough. Dependency on anything (including emotional fixes) must seek a deeper level of joy, but no one can enter into joy apart from understanding and trusting God's plan for your life... which includes suffering... which God allows to sanctify us and strengthen us in preparation for "tribulation or persecution for the words' sake."

The Pearl of Great Price (Matt. 13:45). A certain man – because of his great joy – went and sold everything to purchase a field that contained a priceless pearl. Once you thoroughly comprehend this revelatory truth – that the King of Heaven and Heaven are a package deal – you will copy this man whereby a wellspring of joy will rise up within you to shout joyfully to the God of your salvation. This man was willing to do anything to acquire this wellspring of never-ending joy. In contrast, the man with great wealth went away sad (Mark 10:21) when the Lord told him to sell everything and give to the poor. Choice is what separates goats from sheep, so I say: obey the Lord when you hear His voice!

> "His lord said to him, 'Well done, good and faithful servant; you have been faithful over a few things, I will make you ruler over many things. Enter into the joy of your lord" (Matt. 25:23).

We shout joyfully now as we escape temporary to walk in eternity, yet when the Dayspring comes and we appear before Him as faithful servants without compromise or complacency, an even greater exuberance will be experienced by us as we enter the joy of our Lord!

Joyful Disciples

> "Then the seventy returned with joy, saying, "Lord, even the demons are subject to us in Your name" (Luke 10:17).

Imagine this scene for a moment. The disciples returned from casting out demons and healing the sick and they shared stories amongst themselves. Do you think they did this with muffled speech… or with much exuberant excitement? I imagine them bouncing wildly with only gravity restraining them to the land over which they hovered. Can you sense the raised tenor of their voices and the heightened inflection of words infused with emotion and the dramatic expressions on their faces with hands waiving wildly yet somehow failing through insufficient powerless words to convey the miraculous deeds they were able to perform – as mere mortals under the Lord's authority. They transcended passive obedience into exuberant rejoicing.

That level of joy may seem scary, but it should be normal for the believer.

> "Nevertheless do not rejoice in this, that the spirits are subject to you, but rather rejoice because your names are written in heaven" (Luke 10:20).

If your walk of faith has not encountered this level of fire and animated expression which magnifies the Lord according to what He accomplished through you, then I say to you: find a church where this expression is normal and sense the shift in the atmosphere. It is intoxicating. It is exuberant. It is other-worldly. It is supernatural (what I call "spirit normal").

> "For unclean spirits, crying with a loud voice, came out of many who were possessed; and many who were paralyzed and lame were healed. ⁸ **And there was great joy in that city**" (Acts 8:7, 8).

There are unique expressions of joy found throughout the Bible. It's as if an unknown supernatural power is released from an invisible reservoir deep within us that causes us to sing and jump for joy. When this much joy is encountered, which happens often to the bride during the marriage ceremony… or when someone is released from prison, some people cry for joy. Something miraculous and mysterious rises up from within our spirit to escape the confines of our humanity that sends our soul into euphoric bliss. These extreme emotional responses are something I think angels in heaven find most curious as they observe us.

> "For as a young man marries a virgin, so shall your sons marry you; and as the bridegroom rejoices over the bride, so shall your God rejoice over you" (Isa. 62:5).

There is joy with gladness, there is joy with great gladness, and there is also exceedingly great joy. When our internal response to external factors reaches the intersection of hopeful expectancy and liberating truth causing our reality to emotionally boil over with spontaneity, exuberant joy is inevitable. I felt this with the birth of my first son... whereby an uncontainable joy released a joyful shout the entire neighborhood heard. The continuance of my family name now had a successor; my joy was complete!

The Wisdom of Three Joyful Men

> "When they saw the star, they rejoiced with exceedingly great joy" (Matt. 2:10)

Consider the facts of this story. Three kings from far away countries left home and family to pay homage to a new King. This journey likely took several years – as Jesus was a young Child (not a baby) when they arrived (Matt. 2:9). These three kings knew the significance of this star and at great expense they took a very long journey with much expectancy in finding Him. Do you think they were passive in their demeanor when they found Jesus? Absolutely not! ***They rejoiced with exceedingly great joy***!!! Perhaps you can imagine the great celebration by which they rejoiced after finding the One they searched for. Truly I say: wise men still seek Him.

> "The king shall have joy in Your strength, O Lord; and in Your salvation how greatly shall he rejoice" (Psa. 21:1).

Whenever you find what you've been looking for, much joy is expressed, but when length of time *with tribulation* is added onto the hope for which you patiently wait, something marvelous bursts within you once you attain that for which you hoped. How long are you willing to wait for a precious promise or prophecy to be fulfilled? How much are you willing to endure? Beloved, I promise you this: the longer you wait upon the Lord's promises, the greater your joy will be! Contend against time and never lose faith while waiting with patient endurance. Heavenly joy enables us and empowers us to faithfully contend even in the midst of cataclysmic failure and rejection. Heavenly joy is not an emotion than can be taken from you or suppressed by people or circumstances. The joy of the Lord is new every morning. I know this experientially! I listen to hear His voice every morning – and abide in His joy continuously.

> "Then I will go to the altar of God, to God my exceeding joy; and on the harp I will praise You, O God, my God" (Psa. 43:4).

Abraham Rejoiced (John 8:56). When Jesus was being confronted by the religious elite and accused of having a demon, Jesus said: "Your father Abraham rejoiced to see My day, and he saw it and was glad." The word "rejoiced" (*agalliao*-21) means: to exuberantly jump for joy! Can you envision Abraham, the father of faith, jumping joyfully because the Word became flesh? Jesus appeared to Abraham three times (Gen. 12:7; 17:1; 18:1) and I can only image his joyful exuberance when the ancient Promise was now manifested for all to see.

> "… he [Abraham] waited for the city which has foundations, whose builder and maker is God" (Heb. 11:10).

Abraham rejoiced to see Jesus in the day He visited him because he recognized Jesus as Lord. But those religious leaders could not perceive Jesus as Lord "that Day" because of too much toxic theology and many burdensome doctrines; they wanted the Messiah to come as a conquering King to establish His kingdom – and not according to the manner of a servant. So I ask… how do you perceive Jesus? What are you looking for and are hoping to find? What are your expectations? Do you have some preconceived idea what Jesus will look like and what He will do when He manifests Himself? Truly, Jesus appeared at least 30 times in the Old Testament (called Theophanies; read book #3: Image), He appeared at least 15 times after He rose from the grave, and there is nothing preventing Jesus from appearing as many times as He wants – however He wants – whenever He wants – to whomever He wants. Jesus said He will come again in glory and we all wait expectantly for that Day… but He never said He wouldn't visit us between now and then. Focus on Who Jesus Is –

and not what others say about Him!

Now let's get to the heart of the matter: does Jesus abide in your heart? By faith, we say He does (Eph. 3:18). Does Jesus abide in the heart of all persons according to faith? The answer is: yes. So in this sense, Jesus has manifested Himself millions of times. Not only do you represent Him – but you also re-present Him to those willing to receive Him. So I ask: why do you treat your brother or sister in Christ with contempt? Why do you show such disregard for those who are in need or in deep despair or in poverty or struggling with addiction? Why do you turn away or cross the street to avoid eye contact with them? Is this how you treat Jesus who abides in them? How we treat one another is how we treat Jesus right now! And this is how we will be judged:

> "And the King will answer and say to them, 'Assuredly, I say to you, inasmuch as you did it to one of the least of these My brethren, you did it to Me" (Matt. 25:40).

The Woman at the Well (John 4:6-42). Put yourself in the position of this woman getting water from the well. Many of you know the character of this woman getting water during a time of day in which no one gets water. Jesus knew her past, the people in her town were familiar with her sexual history, but when Jesus shows up – a paradigm shift happens in her life. He revealed His identity to her – and in her glee she left her water pot and went quickly into the city to share an incredible story ("come and see Jesus" 4:29) which enabled two things to occur: A) Jesus planted Himself in that place several days, and B) the whole city came to faith. Wow indeed!

When Jesus shows up, it may seem like a chance encounter, but from God's perspective – it was well choreographed. Everything God does is designed to redeem and save. God designed you as His image bearer and partner – to redeem and save. So I ask: do you get excited about God's redemption and His plan of salvation to save souls? We need to be more mindful of the things of God and focus more time on doing the will of the Father. The good news is: your history does not need to get in the way of your destiny. God knows all about your brokenness, your failures, your history, and your baggage because God has been dwelling within you the entire time. Consider this: He is there because He loves you with a never-ending love. All those times you've stumbled through life – are the times He's carried you! Beloved – you've never been alone on this journey. Embrace the God who is always near at hand!

> "Am I a God near at hand," says the LORD, "And not a God afar off? [24] Can anyone hide himself in secret places, so I shall not see him?" says the LORD; "Do I not fill heaven and earth?" says the LORD" (Jer. 23:23, 24).
>
> "See that you do not refuse Him who speaks" (Heb. 12:25).

Only One Returned With Thanks (Luke 17:11-17). Imagine for a moment you have an outwardly apparent disease that everyone can see… and you've been shunned by everyone because of it. Consider, now, the story of ten lepers and the shameful humiliation they felt – not just being shunned – but also being ostracized because Judaic Law prevented anyone from associating with them. And then… along comes Jesus. All ten lepers were healed, so I ask: do you think they went away glumly and told no one – or do you think they presented themselves and their miraculous healing to everyone who rejected them so they might be reunited with friends and loved ones. I tell you, they left the presence of Jesus with great joy – yet only one returned to give thanks and reverence. Of these ten persons, which one do you most likely identify with? When was the last time you rejoiced exuberantly because of the blessing Jesus blessed over you? We most often bless Jesus and thank Him when we get good things, so how grateful are you for your eternal salvation? How grateful are you for what you have? When was the last time you told Him how grateful you are? Truly, I say, you will never be grateful for what you want… until you are grateful for what you have. The abundance of things does not make a person rich. Gratefulness to Jesus with thanksgiving puts you in proper alignment to experience the joy of your salvation. This alone makes one wealthy in the kingdom of Christ.

According to Jewish Law, if you touched a leper, you became unclean. According to grace, when Jesus touches you and you experience His presence – you become clean. This is how the kingdom of Christ is supposed to operate – according to grace! Lord Jesus, we need more grace!

Grace removes guilt, mercy removes misery.[77]

Joy and Biblical Suffering

> "Therefore you now have sorrow; but I will see you again and your heart will rejoice, and your joy no one will take from you" (John 16:22). "Until now you have asked nothing in My name. Ask, and you will receive, that your joy may be full" (John 16:24).

Saints, we've prayed many prayers over many years. Most of these prayers are for things we want. Now start praying for things Jesus wants... like more disciples to build His church. Some of us have been on the front line interceding for the church and have come under demonic attack and have even felt the arrows of the enemy; some of us have wrestled with devils. My suggestion now is to pray into His kingdom and ask Jesus for spiritual gifts (wisdom, understanding, revelation, and revival) to establish the kingdom of heaven on earth – through you. Take the joy of the Lord seriously and stop chasing glory clouds to experience an emotional high in the glory of His presence. You host His presence within you, so take His message of love to your friends, your family, your neighbors, your co-workers, and all saints and fellow worshippers – and go all in! Stop chasing after

---

[77] Strong's Concordance; word study on grace (*charis*-5485).

manifestations of God's glory – and go boldly in advance to become a new expression of His manifest presence to create a new glory cloud. You were sent here to take back what the enemy stole, redeem it, occupy, defend it and then advance the kingdom of heaven in the midst of darkness. Repent from having a foxhole mentality. Maranatha – Come Lord Jesus – happens when you get off the sofa and start walking in the joy of the Lord to shift the atmosphere around you. If you are sad with feelings of despair, take a prescription called: thankfulness. If you are struggling with depression, then overdose on a medicine called: JOY. If you are overcome with feelings of suicide, then twirl with glee with Jesus who abides in you. You are not alone!!! Jesus is in you and He is with you!!! Jesus knows what you are going through, but you cannot keep living with Jesus as your co-pilot. You're sitting in the wrong seat, so move over and put Jesus in the Pilot's seat.

> Jesus told us: "These things I have spoken to you, that My joy may remain in you, and that your joy may be full" (John 15:11)

When we have joy, we must share it with others. True biblical contentment understands – God can do whatever He wants with His things – and that includes you! Everything belongs to Him! God never promised us happiness. God never promised us rose gardens or smooth roads. God never promised us life without pain or suffering, yet many of us have heard and embraced the wisdom of this world by well-meaning saints who say: God does not want you to suffer. How unbiblical! What an unkind and merciless thing to say to someone knee-deep in travail, as if you are greater than Jesus Himself who suffered on your behalf. That is a sales pitch from the health-and-wealth gospel of self-centered narcissistic man. Consider the larger perspective from this scripture:

> "And from the days of John the Baptist until now the kingdom of heaven suffers violence, and the violent take it by force" (Matt. 11:12).

Literally: and the violent enter violently! The kingdom of heaven has been under attack by violent men aligned with darkness in rebellious opposition to God. The kingdom of this world is violently opposed to the kingdom of heaven – and those who usher in God's kingdom will be violently opposed by demonic forces which they cannot see. What the pre-tribulation church needs most of all is a biblical understanding of suffering – and why "all things" (i.e. suffering) mysteriously relates to joy (Rom. 8:28). Here again, the kingdom of paradox enables us to perceive how the kingdom of God operates – as power manifested through weakness – as joy manifested through suffering – as leaders manifested as servants – as poor who inherit the kingdom of heaven. If you are being persecuted – rejoice and be exceedingly glad. "All things work together for good"... and great is your reward in heaven!

- Jesus said: "Rejoice and be exceedingly glad, for great is your reward in heaven, for so they persecuted the prophets who were before you" (Matt. 5:12)
- "... but rejoice to the extent that you partake of Christ's sufferings, that when His glory is revealed, you may also be glad with exceeding joy" (1 Pet. 4:13)

Sometimes suffering (*pathema*-3804-to undergo hardship or pain; affliction) is done to purge something from us – and sometimes it happens to perfect something in us. Sometimes it happens because you serve Jesus as Lord and King – and sometimes it happens when you advance His kingdom. There may be a reason... even if the reason remains a mystery. For example: there is no earthly reason why Jesus had to suffer because He did absolutely nothing wrong. Nonetheless, Jesus endured suffering – for your benefit and mine:

> "... let us run with endurance the race that is set before us, [2] looking unto Jesus, the author and finisher of *our* faith, who ***for the joy that was set before Him endured the cross, despising the shame***, and has sat down at the right hand of the throne of God" (Heb. 12:1b, 2).

We profess great boasts in the Lord on Sunday to demonstrate how blessed we are – as some indication God has proved us worthy of His outpouring or blessing – but how many of us would be willing to suffer harm to benefit another person? We talk about imitating Jesus and loving others just as Jesus loved, but how many of us would forfeit our life for another person?

> "Greater love has no one than this, than to lay down one's life for his friends" (John 15:13).

The kingdom of love and the kingdom of joy have one thing in common: they are parts of a kingdom of peace that suffers violence… yet another paradox. What did any prophet do that warranted man's wrath? All they did was tell the truth. Why did Ezekiel have to lay on his left side 390 days, then 40 days on his right side and cook his food using animal excrement? Because he purposed in himself to always say "Yes" to God whenever God asked him to do something for the kingdom! Once you realize your importance to the kingdom may result in your life being required of you or some privileges or benefits being withheld from you, you quickly understand the reason why few hear the Lord call them: disciple. Many heard the call, and they count the cost – yet decided to withdraw because the cost was too great. And for this reason biblical pain and biblical suffering are rarely mentioned from the pulpit of man. It's an inconvenient truth.

Enduring suffering for the sake of the gospel – is ultimately for the benefit of others:

> "Therefore I [Paul] endure all things ***for the sake of the elect***, that they also may obtain the salvation which is in Christ Jesus with eternal glory" (2 Tim. 2:10).

The Apostle Paul endured suffering for your benefit… to make up for what was lacking in the affliction of Christ. [78]

> "*I now rejoice in my sufferings for you*, and fill up in my flesh what is lacking in the afflictions of Christ, for the sake of His body, which is the church" (Col. 1:24).

Paul endured suffering and affliction for "your" benefit; he endured rejection for "your" benefit; and he endured persecution for "your" benefit. Paul embraced the life of a disciple as a sojourner in the wilderness for the sake of your soul and the souls of others as an exceedingly excellent minister of the gospel who received an excellent testimony. Think about that the next time you read one of his mighty epistles! What are you willing to endure, suffer, surrender, or forfeit as a minister worthy of God's calling – to advance the kingdom of God?

Jesus endured much suffering for you. As a disciple of Jesus, should you expect anything less?

> "He is despised and rejected by men, a Man of sorrows and acquainted with grief. And we hid, as it were, our faces from Him; He was despised, and we did not esteem Him. [4] Surely He has borne our griefs and carried our sorrows; yet we esteemed Him stricken, smitten by God, and afflicted. [5] But He was wounded for our transgressions, He was bruised for our iniquities; the chastisement for our peace was upon Him, and by His stripes we are healed. [6] All we like sheep have gone astray; we have turned, every one, to his own way; and the LORD has laid on Him the iniquity of us all. [7] He was oppressed and He was afflicted, yet He opened not His mouth; He was led as a lamb to the

---

[78] It is hard to imagine any affliction beyond what Jesus experienced, yet Paul knows what he speaks. Many of his epistles were written while in prison. So I encourage you - even in prison, goodness happens.

slaughter, and as a sheep before its shearers is silent, so He opened not His mouth. [8] He was taken from prison and from judgment, and who will declare His generation? For He was cut off from the land of the living; for the transgressions of My people He was stricken. [9] And they made His grave with the wicked—but with the rich at His death, because He had done no violence, nor was any deceit in His mouth. [10] Yet it pleased the LORD to bruise Him; He has put Him to grief. When You make His soul an offering for sin, He shall see His seed, He shall prolong His days, and the pleasure of the LORD shall prosper in His hand" (Isa. 53:3-10).

Consider what the Apostle Paul sacrificed and suffered for your benefit:

"Are they ministers of Christ?—I speak as a fool—I am more: in labors more abundant, in stripes above measure, in prisons more frequently, ***in deaths often***. [24] From the Jews five times I received forty stripes minus one. [25] Three times I was beaten with rods; once I was stoned; three times I was shipwrecked; a night and a day I have been in the deep; [26] in journeys often, in perils of waters, in perils of robbers, in perils of my own countrymen, in perils of the Gentiles, in perils in the city, in perils in the wilderness, in perils in the sea, in perils among false brethren; [27] in weariness and toil, in sleeplessness often, in hunger and thirst, in fastings often, in cold and nakedness – [28] besides the other things, what comes upon me daily: my deep concern for all the churches.[29] Who is weak, and I am not weak? Who is made to stumble, and I do not burn with indignation? [30] ***If I must boast, I will boast in the things which concern my infirmity***" (2 Cor. 11:23-30).

Consider all the generations that have gone before you who

contended for the faith and endured much tribulation, persecution and suffering in order for the gospel of grace to be preached to you! How dare we *not* consider their sacrifice part of the joy we currently enjoy – and how dare we consider ourselves better than Christ Himself who suffered for us? How dare we insulate ourselves from suffering and persecution rather than advance the gospel of Christ!

> "And we labor, working with our own hands. Being reviled, we bless; being persecuted, we endure" (1 Cor. 4:12).

The point I'm trying to make is this: a biblical understanding of suffering (not self martyrdom) should be expected and can be endured with divine assistance from the Holy Spirit because the spiritual benefit of others hangs in the balance. Disciples of Jesus understand this.

Sacrifice and suffering for the cause of Christ – is for the sake of others! Your spiritual maturity in Christ must be willing to embrace biblical suffering as exemplified by Paul and many prophets as well to help others attain salvation and contend for the same promise…

> "… so that we ourselves boast of you among the churches of God for your patience and faith in all your persecutions and tribulations that you endure" (2 Thess. 1:4).

Consider all the giants of faith and what was written about them in the Book of Faith (Hebrews 11); most of us want the glorious first half of this message describing great leaders of the faith, but no one wants the suffering servant second half (***bold italics***):

> "And what more shall I say? For the time would fail me to tell of Gideon and Barak and Samson and Jephthah, also *of* David and Samuel and the prophets: [33] who through faith subdued kingdoms,

worked righteousness, obtained promises, stopped the mouths of lions, [34] quenched the violence of fire, escaped the edge of the sword, out of weakness were made strong, became valiant in battle, turned to flight the armies of the aliens. [35] Women received their dead raised to life again. ***Others were tortured, not accepting deliverance, that they might obtain a better resurrection.*** [36] ***Still others had trial of mockings and scourgings, yes, and of chains and imprisonment.*** [37] ***They were stoned, they were sawn in two, were tempted, were slain with the sword. They wandered about in sheepskins and goatskins, being destitute, afflicted, tormented—*** [38] ***of whom the world was not worthy. They wandered in deserts and mountains, in dens and caves of the earth.*** [39] And all these, having obtained a good testimony through faith, did not receive the promise, [40] God having provided something better for us, that they should not be made perfect apart from us" (Heb. 11:32-40).

The perfecting of your faith and mine – builds upon the faith and testimonies of others – to perfect one another through faith in preparation for the promise yet to be revealed – in us.

What is "the better resurrection" the writer of Hebrews mentioned? The first resurrection for martyrs (Rev. 20:5) – who will rule and reign with Christ for a millennium! None of us are getting off earth alive (Heb. 9:27), but know this: ***when*** you return and ***how*** you are recompensed is predicated upon ***what*** you accomplished or suffered in this life – ***for the sake of Christ Jesus***.

> "But recall the former days in which, after you were illuminated, you endured a great struggle with sufferings: [33] partly while you were made a spectacle both by reproaches and tribulations, and partly while you became companions of those who were so treated" (Heb. 10:32, 33).

This message is contrary to human understanding. Suffering alongside companions contradicts worldly wisdom (except in the military). It works against all the things we've been taught to believe in the church, and yet – the evidence is overwhelming! If you are suffering for the sake of Christ, don't try to figure it out. Endure it! Bless those who curse you. Suffering for the cause of Christ is biblical. In fact, many disciples I've observed who've endured great suffering have also received the most intense dreams, visions, revelations and supernatural encounters with God than typical believers. God's most precious flowers are produced in the pressure-cooker called: crucible – the testing of faith. Most of us want to experience the great testimonies of others, but most refuse to embrace what those giants of faith went through and endured to encounter the experience. So, if you are encountering deep sorrow, suffering, rejection, persecution, then do it biblically – and endure it patiently! Give thanks – in all circumstances!

***What seems to break you – may be God setting you up for breakthrough*!!!**

***Your test – becomes your testimony*!!!**

***Your setback – may be a divine setup*!!!**

Enduring suffering as a disciple for the sake of Christ produces soldiers worthy of battle:

> "You therefore must endure hardship as a good soldier of Jesus Christ" (2 Tim. 2:3).

> "But when you do good and suffer, if you take it patiently, this is commendable before God" (1 Pet. 2:20b).

When you do good... and suffer... this is commendable... if you take it patiently. So I ask: do you really want to be a disciple of Jesus Christ? If yes, then count the cost! If you are suffering according to biblical suffering, then do it joyfully – keep your eyes focused on Jesus – understand the purpose – perceive how others will benefit from it – patiently endure with much perseverance – and you will obtain a good testimony.

> "My brethren, **count it all joy when you fall into various trials**, [3] knowing that the testing of your faith produces patience. [4] But let patience have its perfect work, that you may be perfect and complete, lacking nothing" (James 1:2-4).

Job understood "God gives and He takes away" – because that's His right as God Almighty, yet Job struggled to understand why horribly bad things were happening to him. Did Job do anything to cause his suffering? No! Did anyone come to comfort and console him? No one, not even his wife! He lost all his possessions, his children and even his health, so if you think you've got it bad, consider what Job endured. Job was thoroughly crushed and broken.

Now look at this story from God's perspective so you may see the larger plan of God unfolding in Job's life – and perhaps in your life as well:

> "Then the Lord said to Satan, "Have you considered My servant Job, that there is none like him on the earth, a blameless and upright man, one who fears God and shuns evil? And still he holds fast to his integrity, although you incited Me against him, to destroy him without cause" (Job 2:3).

The Lord was bragging about Job to Satan. What an amazing testimony to have! Job learned biblical suffering – by the things he suffered – yet in all this he maintained his righteousness before God and did not bring an accusation against Him. If you are going through difficult circumstances, consider this: your life may be on display – as well. Let God brag on you!

> "Oh, that my grief were fully weighed, and my calamity laid with it on the scales! [3] For then it

> would be heavier than the sand of the sea—therefore my words have been rash. ⁴ For the arrows of the Almighty are within me; my spirit drinks in their poison; the terrors of God are arrayed against me" (Job 6:2-4).

> "For destruction from God is a terror to me, and because of His magnificence I cannot endure" (Job 31:23).

Not only did the Lord allow Job's suffering to happen by the hand of Satan, it also appears the Lord afflicted Job as well. Job experienced suffering on a scale few of us can imagine. Yet Job endured... and his patient endurance became his eternal testimony among the saints.

> "Indeed we count them blessed who endure. You have heard of the perseverance of Job and seen the end intended by the Lord—that the Lord is very compassionate and merciful" (James 5:11).

If you are under attack – it's because you're valuable to God's kingdom. If you're human – you will come under attack because Satan hates all humans with vengeful anger because God created you as His image bearer; his violent rage will not be quenched until all humans are obliterated for this reason: you are an image bearer sent as a light into his kingdom of darkness. Look carefully at this next scripture and see the much larger picture regarding your life:

> "And the Lord said, "Simon, Simon! Indeed, Satan has asked for you, that he may sift you as wheat. ³² ***But I have prayed for you, that your faith should not fail***; and when you have returned to Me, strengthen your brethren." ³³ But he said to Him, "Lord, I am ready to go with You, both to prison and to death" (Luke 22:31-33).

The Apostle Peter came under attack by Satan for this purpose: to sift his faith. The same is true for you and me: the sifting of our faith sanctifies us and perfects our character. This is one of the most important points of this book: you are under demonic attack to prevent a spiritual regime change from darkness to light. Satan will come against you to:

> A) sift your faith and weaken your resolve to stand strong in the truth
> B) diminish your capability to walk in the truth in unity with your brethren
> C) hinder your growth in grace and truth to become a disciple with authority and miraculous power
> D) destroy your testimony and steal your destiny as a fellow soldier for Christ, and
> E) hinder your worship to magnify the Lord of Heaven and Earth to thwart God's purpose on earth that is being revealed in you: the kingdom of heaven made manifest through you.

Satan accomplishes his agenda by confronting truth through lies followed by doubt, deception, unbelief, confusion and fear, so be wary of his tactics. Be strong and courageous. Know the truth! Stand strong in the Lord and the strength of His might!

If you're going through hell……. don't stop!

Endure! Press through! Fight the good fight – and keep going!

You need to see one more thing from the scripture above: Satan knew exactly who Jesus was (he asked His permission to sift Peter just like Satan asked God to sift Job). If you are being sifted right now, take comfort in this: A) Satan knows who you are, and B) Jesus knows you are strong enough to endure it and persevere. ***Rejoice and be glad in this*** – because your identity has become known in the heavenly realm. So, then, the phrase: "God never gives us more than we can handle" is wrong on two counts: 1) God allows it (does not give it), and 2) sometimes He allows more than you can handle to help you understand who you really are… so you realize just how strong you really are.

If you are being sifted, then Satan had to ask permission to sift you beforehand – which means – Satan knows just how valuable you are to God's kingdom. And so does Jesus. ***Rejoice and be glad because of this***! The person that needs to comprehend this truth most of all – is the same person who doubts in unbelief. So I say: walk in the truth! The Lord of Glory abides in you – and He fights this battle with you! Jesus already won the battle. You are part of God's clean-up crew to take back and redeem earth (Rom. 8:19)! You fight from a position of victory – for victory! Fight for your destiny – in Christ! "Fight the good fight of faith" (1 Tim. 6:12) and let future generations know how valiantly you contended for the Lord in battle – through much testing and travail. Let the evidence of faith be found – upon you. Walk the path of a disciple – and embrace biblical suffering as a badge of honor.

> "So now, brethren, I commend you to God and to
> the word of His grace, which is able to build you up
> and give you an inheritance among all those who
> are sanctified" (Acts 20:32).

Consider this word from the Lord that was received by the prophet Isaiah:

> "For a mere moment I have forsaken you,
> But with great mercies I will gather you.
> ^{8} With a little wrath I hid My face from you
> for a moment;
> ***But with everlasting kindness***
> ***I will have mercy on you***,"
> Says the LORD, your Redeemer" (Isa. 54:7, 8).

Our affliction is for a moment – but His mercy is everlasting! Grace makes this happen.

Job understood suffering, affliction and adversity from a biblical perspective:

> ***"Shall we indeed accept good from God, and shall we not accept adversity?"*** (Job 2:10)

Jeremiah understood suffering from a biblical perspective:

> "And do you seek great things for yourself? Do not seek them; for behold, I will bring adversity on all flesh," says the Lord. "But I will give your life to you as a prize in all places, wherever you go." ' " (Jer. 45:5).

Likewise, the Psalmist understood biblical suffering:

> "For His anger is but for a moment, ***His favor is for life***; weeping may endure for a night, but joy comes in the morning" (Psa. 30:5).

Now, perhaps, this scripture makes sense in light of the momentary tribulations we endure:

> "Precious in the sight of the Lord is the death of His saints" (Psa. 116:15).

God had a very reason for reducing the number of years that man suffers on earth from 950 to 120... its called mercy (Gen. 6:3). Life expectancy was cut short for our benefit. God created us as weak and dependent creatures; He knows that we are dust. Yet even in this, the Lord who walks alongside us and dwells with us – is great, mighty and magnificent! In our weakness and suffering, His grace is sufficient and His power is perfected – in us – to enable us to endure and persevere – as a testimony against His enemies.

Suffering enables you to become – God's testimony! God rejoices over you! God delights Himself – in you!

> "He shall pray to God, ***and He will delight in him***, he shall see His face with joy, for He restores to man His righteousness" (Job 33:26).

KINGDOMS

Let your triumph over various trials become God's testimony!

Jesus is God and King, yet He came to earth as a Suffering Servant. Beloved, we are no different than Christ; we are suffering servants during this season of eternity.

What testimony can be accredited to you? Greater love and devotion for Jesus enables His disciples to go "all in" regardless of any personal cost. The message I keep teaching is: what are you willing to exchange in this life that will benefit your soul in eternity? What you sacrifice or suffer in this life – will be recompensed (paid back and multiplied) in Paradise.

As the song goes: "Sometimes the trials in this life – are mercies in disguise."

Since we are expected to endure trials, suffering, sadness and sorrow as we walk by faith, some may ask: what's the point of faith? The point of faith is not trying to avoid negative things, but to trust God and His mercy to get you through it. Everyone will encounter these things. Life is not about avoiding the rain… but learning to dance in it. Faith – is learning how to live by grace.

> "Let us therefore come boldly to the throne of grace, that we may obtain mercy and find grace to help in time of need" (Heb. 4:16).
>
> "But may the God of all grace, who called us to His eternal glory by Christ Jesus, after you have suffered a while, perfect, establish, strengthen, and settle you" (1 Pet. 5:10).

Whatever you focus on – gets bigger. Don't focus on suffering or self or evil when it comes against you. Focus on Jesus and magnify Him.

Joseph, son of Isaac, understood suffering from a biblical perspective. His brothers conspired to kill him and then sold him into slavery, yet despite all the woe he encountered, he maintained a heavenly perspective: "you meant evil against me; but God meant it for good." There is a heavenly reason why we suffer affliction: we are part of God's plan to save many souls alive!

> "But as for you, you meant evil against me; but God meant it for good, in order to bring it about as it is this day, ***to save many people alive***" (Gen. 50:20).

Don't give Satan or evil people any credit when bad things happen to you. Stop playing the "sin game" to disparage others when bad things happen to them. Ultimately – God means it for good!

> Jesus said: "But I say to you, love your enemies, bless those who curse you, do good to those who hate you, and pray for those who spitefully use you and persecute you" (Matt. 5:44).

Beloved, stay focused on Jesus. Give God the credit and the glory in all things – even when evil things happen to you! Rejoicing in all things – robs evil of the glory we give it by worrying or focusing on it.

Meditate on this truth: "Repay no one evil for evil" (Rom. 12:17). ***Repay evil with good***! Turn the other cheek. Bless those who curse you and spitefully use you. Shift the atmosphere with love and grace… and produce a worthy testimony. Patiently endure adversity and affliction – and receive recompense from the Lord in the New Earth.

Job understood the deeper truth of suffering: trust the Lord!

> "Though He slay me, yet will I trust Him. Even so, I will defend my own ways before Him" (Job 13:15).

The deeper lesson of suffering is to lay hold of God's mercy as you trust Him with your life. A disciple of Jesus will never bring an accusation against the Lord or lift up a hand in protest against Him. You are His! You belong to the Lord (not the other way around).

God is more interested in your character than your comfort. He cares more about His kingdom than yours, and He is infinitely more concerned about souls than stuff. The knowledge of this deep truth should help us see why everything visible is temporary... in order to prepare our character for eternity.

"The Lord's message is two-fold: 1) truth can be put into us, but that may not effectively change us if there are things (thought patterns) in us that prevent us from embracing God's truth and advancing into maturity – which only come out of us through suffering; and 2) suffering from a biblical point of view will be rewarded in eternity. Suffering, it seems, is for <u>our</u> benefit."[79]

Suffering allows God to get more out of us, so He can put more into us... and reward us later.

Suffering for the cause of Christ... in honorable! Be a soldier of great valor!

What an odd closure to a chapter titled: the kingdom of joy. The kingdom of joy... suffers sorrow. The kingdom of joy... suffers persecution. The kingdom of joy... suffers violence.

Joy and sorrow are a package deal. Life and death are a package deal. Good and evil are a package deal. Health and illness are a package deal. Pain and suffering in this life are a package deal. You cannot have one without the other – in the kingdom of paradox! The good news of the gospel is: Jesus will help you through it! His Spirit dwells with our spirit to strengthen us and encourage us to endure and persevere with faith. In the end, when you hold onto Jesus with everything that lies within you – you will discover another package deal: The King of Heaven and the Kingdom of Heaven.

This was a very difficult word to process and compose – even for me. Beloved, I am able to comprehend this truth as someone going

---

[79] Excerpt from "The Renewed Mind" chapter 5.

through travail right now – after contending against much for the past six years – waiting patiently, by grace, writing passionately, through faith, without a full-time job or house – living in poverty – in tents and vehicles as I endure patiently for the Lord to release provision through odd jobs to meet my meager $6,200/year need – that I might learn to trust Him for everything – and in everything – fear Him with great reverence and awe as well. With great assurance, I say: everything I currently endure (including the hurt and pain) enables me to write these words with conviction to communicate the truth of this message – from personal experience. I've written these words – for your benefit! My pain and suffering – is for your benefit! But this message did not begin with that perspective. My initial focus was on self with some self pity for all the problems I've encountered – because of this reason: I took my eyes off Jesus. Now that my focus is properly redirected onto the Joy of my Salvation – my Lord and my Deliverer, I am now able to endure more for your sake – and for the sake of the gospel (much like the Apostle Paul himself).

Any adversity we encounter – is intended by God strengthen us – for the benefit of others.

- ***Sacrifice and suffering for the cause of Christ – is for the benefit of others!***
- ***Love and mercy – is for the benefit of others!***
- ***Forgiveness – is for the benefit of others!***

The patience of Job is considered his most admirable quality, but I'd rather have his perseverance! The message of Job is: bad things are allowed to happen to us. Even Job questioned why bad things were happening to him. That's normal. We all do it. The problem with Job and the rest of us is – we've been asking the wrong question. We should be asking: "Who will help me through it?" The Person who helps us is also the Person who defines us, who protects us and leads us through the valley of the shadow of death. Trust the Lord. Trust Jesus. Focus on Jesus. Abide with Jesus. When we abide with Jesus, we are able to endure and overcome "all things" the kingdom of darkness throws at us…

including death itself!

Job prayed to God for answers, but all he heard was silence. There will be dark nights of the soul when we cry out to the Lord for assistance yet hear nothing; some disciples have experienced years like this, but they never wavered in the hope they would hear His voice again. Why is that? Because they know He was and is alongside them the entire time. When this happens to you – do not despair. Jesus never leaves us or forsakes us. We never encounter suffering alone – when we are joined to the Lord.

Embrace suffering from a biblical perspective – and allow God to make you one of His testimonies – so He can bless you, salute you and celebrate with praises over you!

"Now to Him who is able to keep you from stumbling,
and to present you
faultless before the presence of His glory
with exceeding joy" (Jude 1:24).

It's all about Jesus – and God gets the glory! Forever and ever, Amen!

Kingdom of Rest

> "Heaven is My throne, and earth is My footstool.
> What house will you build for Me? says the Lord,
> Or what is the place of My rest" (Acts 7:49).

There's a lot of talk these days about Shekinah Glory as a supreme manifestation of God's glory; however, Shekinah Glory is less about glory... and more about abiding intimately with the Lord.

"Rest" is what happens when we enter into His presence and abide in oneness with Him... where His glory dwells!

Entering into the Lord's rest and abiding in His presence and are related to each other – which becomes paramount for us to comprehend. The scripture below identifies two types of rest: physical (*anapauo*) and spiritual (*anapausis*). This theme will reoccur throughout this teaching.

> "Come to Me, all you who labor and are heavy laden, and I will give you rest [*anapauo;* intermission]. Take My yoke upon you and learn from Me, for I am gentle and lowly in heart, and you will find rest [*anapausis*; refreshment] for your souls" (Matt. 11:28, 29).

- *Anapausis* (G372) *an-ap-ow-sis*, means: cessation, refreshment, rest (from *anapauo*-373, to refresh and recover strength; by implication: recreation). "Christ's rest is not a rest from work, but in work, not the rest of inactivity, but of the harmonious working of all the faculties and affections – of will, heart, imagination, conscience – because each has found in God the ideal sphere for its satisfaction and development." [80]

---

[80] All terms and definitions from Strong's Concordance.

Now let's examine two words which are used to convey the essence of spiritual rest. *Shakan* "dwelt, abode" is comparatively similar to the Greek *mone* "dwell, abide" (John 14:23).

> "Now the glory of the Lord rested [*shakan*; abided, dwelled] on Mount Sinai" (Ex. 24:16)

> "Jesus answered and said to him, 'If anyone loves Me, he will keep My word; and My Father will love him, and We will come to him and make Our home [*mone*; abode; a permanent abiding place] with him'" (John 14:23).

- *Shakan* (H7931) *shaw-khan*, through the idea of lodging; to reside or permanently stay; – dwell (92x), abide (8x), remain (7x), inhabit (4x), rest (3x); *shakan* (the root word for Shekinah) is akin to '*shakab*-7901' – to lie down, rest, sexual connection (intimacy)

The kingdom of rest is based upon a relationship wherein intimacy is expressed when two dwell together… as two becoming one. Deep abiding relationships are established upon love and trust – and the result is intimacy. This is what God desires with everyone – without exception. The Church refers to this as having "a personal relationship with Jesus" yet somehow… knowing about Jesus (factually) is not the definition of intimacy. Jesus is the lover of our soul, yet somehow we fail to perceive Him as our Beloved.

> "I opened for my beloved, but my beloved had turned away and was gone. My heart leaped up when he spoke. I sought him, but I could not find him; I called him, but he gave me no answer" (Song of Solomon 5:6)

Intimacy involves trust which is a factor of reverence, honor, and respect; and we see these ideas woven within the first three commandments. Intimacy also involves love which is a factor of devotion, affection, and loyalty which are interwoven alongside trust. These descriptions, though, are not all inclusive. The divine relationship that God desires with each of us is quite simple: A) love Him, B) trust Him, and C) don't let anything get between you and Lord... or His Sabbath time with you (Command #4).

Proximity is not intimacy. The Lord wants to have an intimate personal encounter with all people wherever they may be. If you cannot remember having this encounter with Jesus or remember the last time you heard His voice, then perhaps it's time to sit still and get alone with Jesus so you can hear His voice. Let me put it to you like this: if you claim to have a relationship with your wife but you never had a two-way conversation with her... would a relationship exist? No! So I ask: what was the last thing Jesus said to you? See what I mean?

The message from heaven is: God is with us and desires to tabernacle with us. How close we get is up to us. That, my friend, is the litmus test of your real relationship with Jesus. Jesus said:

> "***My sheep hear My voice***, and I know them, and they follow Me" (John 10:27).

Consider all the times Jesus went to pray. Jesus lived in oneness with the Father (John 10:30), so He didn't need to pray this way... but He lived this way in order to teach us how to live and pray. If you want to get intimate with the Father, then you've gotta act like the Son and find quiet places to get still and commune with God. For ministers reading this message, it is imperative for you to follow Christ's example and also for church leadership to understand as well because you must help facilitate this for those ministers who have a responsibility for you... and the flock.

The Lord chose Israel as one nation among many as His special people; however, in the Exodus example – instead of Israelites coming up (spiritually) and drawing near to God's presence where He rested (which they refused; Ex. 24:16), God came down and tabernacled (dwelt) among them (Ex. 25:8). Some say the Israelites did not refuse to come up the mountain – they were forbidden by God, which is true – so why would God forbid it if that's what He wants? Well, the Lord instructed Moses to prevent the people from coming up because of their heart condition: He will not allow anyone to enter His presence without reverencing Him first. Before you do anything on God's behalf, reverence Him – first!

Time after time, the Israelites saw God's mighty deeds on their behalf, yet they did not reverence Him. They complained about everything! They brought many accusations against God (and against His servant, Moses) because they did not trust Him as their Provider and Deliverer even though God proved Himself time and time again. They saw the power of God part the Red Sea and destroy an entire army, yet they did not fear Him when they acted recklessly and rebelliously toward Him. Adam feared God (Gen. 3:10); Noah feared God (Gen. 6:22); Abraham feared God (Gen. 22:12); Jacob feared God (Gen. 28:17)… and the Israelites feared God as well (Ex. 14:31). They feared… but they did not reverence the Lord. Big mistake!

When Moses approached the burning bush, he did so out of curiosity as an ordinary man. When he got closer, the Lord told him to take off his sandals because he was about to enter the Lord's presence. God is holy. And this is how every person must approach God – with reverence, awe, honor, respect… and in holy fear with a clear conscience.

> "Draw near to God and He will draw near to you. Cleanse your hands, you sinners; and purify your hearts, you double-minded" (James 4:8).

> "Walk prudently when you go to the house of God; and draw near to hear rather than to give the sacrifice of fools, for they do not know that they do evil" (Eccl. 5:1).

This is imperative: anyone desiring to enter into God's presence – must do so in holy fear with a clean conscience. This principle of the kingdom occurs over and over: you can seek the Lord as a seeker willing to draw near and be sanctified, but you cannot enter the Lord's presence with an unclean heart or spiritual imperfection (sin, guilt, iniquity, impurity, transgression). In an extreme way of communicating this point, Israelite Priests were not permitted to serve if they had physical blemishes (Lev. 21: 16, 27), and we, likewise, are not permitted to draw near to the altar if we have unforgiveness toward our brother (Matt. 5:24). The Lord wants us to draw near, but coming "up" into His presence – is based upon our heart condition and our relationship with Him (Ex. 19:10-13).

> Jesus said: "Therefore you shall be perfect, just as your Father in heaven is perfect" (Matt. 5:48).

This is the gold standard. The word "perfect" (*teleios*-5046) means: "complete; mature; one who is *teleios* has attained the moral end for which he was intended, namely to be a man in Christ."[81] Mature saints understand... immorality is not an option.

> "... but as He who called you is holy, you also be holy in all your conduct" (1 Pet. 1:15).

The cleaner you are... the closer you'll get. God does not expect us to be perfect (as the world defines perfection because we are imperfect people), but He desires us to be holy, blameless and mature in faith when we come before Him. Living in this manner is difficult, yet He rewards those who are diligent.

> "But without faith it is impossible to please Him, for he who comes to God must believe that He is, and that He is a rewarder of those who diligently seek Him" (Heb. 11:6).

What, then, is our primary aim in attaining faith? Loving God, trusting God... and dwelling in His presence. Intimacy is the result!

---

[81] Strong's Concordance.

> "But it is good for me to draw near to God; I have put my trust in the Lord God, that I may declare all Your works" (Psa. 73:28).

The Shekinah glory of God's manifest presence rested on Mount Sinai (Ex. 24:16), but the Lord (Jesus) prevented irreverent and disrespectful people from drawing near to Him.

> "And the LORD said to Moses, "Go down and warn the people, lest they break through to gaze at the LORD, and many of them perish. [22] Also **let the priests who come near the LORD** consecrate themselves, lest the LORD break out against them" (Ex. 19:21, 22).

God wanted Israelite leaders to come before Him, hear His voice, and experience His manifest presence, but Moses got in the way by countermanding the Lord's request by throwing another "but" at the Lord (Ex. 19:23). Sometimes even good leaders (like Moses) can get between the Lord and His people.

The glory of the Lord "rested" on Mount Sinai, and this is the type of rest He invites everyone to enter into: His manifest presence! Therefore – draw near – but do so in reverential fear.

Connect these concepts: A) the Lord's rest implies – intimacy; B) Jesus gave us His glory to make us one (John 17:21); C) Shekinah implies – intimacy in His manifest presence; and when we connect these concepts: D) Shekinah glory is intimacy with God – in His presence – that produces oneness with Him! Rest and glory is about manifesting God's oneness for God's glory.

And the two… become one! Marriage is the shadow and the substance of what God desires… and we are the bride! (Matt. 25:1)

Church leadership would do well to study this interplay between Moses and God. God wants all leaders to experience His presence because – once they know God experientially and perhaps intimately as well – then they are able to teach others about it so they may begin this journey on their own. This is the message of the kingdom: make disciples so they may disciple others.

So I ask: do you think it's better to be honored and revered... or feared? Which one do you think God prefers? Revere God... honor the King... and fear not!

> "Fear not, for I am with you; be not dismayed, for I am your God. I will strengthen you, Yes, I will help you, I will uphold you with My righteous right hand" (Isa. 41:10).

"Fear not" – appears many times in scripture as words to encourage us: "I will strengthen you" (Isa. 41:10); "I will help you" (Isa. 41:13, 14); "I have redeemed you" (Isa. 43:1); "I am with you" (Isa. 43:5); "whom I have chosen" (Isa. 44:2); "Peace to you; be strong, yes, be strong" (Dan. 10:19); "Be glad and rejoice" (Joel 2:21); "your King is coming" (John 12:15). When Jesus walked on water and appeared to the disciples, He said: "I am, do not be afraid" (John 6:20). When Jesus appeared after rising from the dead, He said to His disciples: "Peace to you" (Luke 24:36). Jesus also appeared to John the revelator:

> "And when I saw Him, I fell at His feet as dead. But He laid His right hand on me, saying to me, "***Do not be afraid***; I am the First and the Last. [18] I *am* He who lives, and was dead, and behold, I am alive forevermore" (Rev. 1:17, 18).

Our God is not a God who terrorizes. Our God makes peace with those who are peaceable and makes war with those who are rebellious. This is why He says of Israel:

> "So I swore in My wrath, 'They shall not enter My rest'" (Heb. 3:11; Psa. 95:11).

> "And Moses said to the people, "Do not fear; for God has come to test you, and that His fear may be

before you, so that you may not sin" (Ex. 20:20).

"The fear of the Lord" is not the fear of something or someone where terror results; Godly fear implies having a reverential respect and awe for His position, authority and power to do as He pleases. "Even the winds and the seas obey Him" (Matt. 8:27).

> "And do not fear those who kill the body but cannot kill the soul. But rather fear Him [Jesus] who is able to destroy both soul and body in hell" (Matt. 10:28).

Sadly, rather than accepting the Lord's invitation by drawing near to the Lord to rest and abide with Him, the Jews preferred to listen to the voice of Moses rather than God, and thus – He gave them ordinances that were too burdensome to carry and obediently follow. As a result, they lost their liberty of the spirit to dwell freely wherein more time was spent following rules and religious ordinances rather than seeking the Lord and abiding in His presence. God's gift of free will – allows us to make unwise choices.

Jesus demonstrated to us the pattern for mankind: host God's presence and operate in oneness with Him. Examples of "rest" the Lord desires with us – are found throughout scripture.

> "Now it happened as they went that He entered a certain village; and a certain woman named Martha welcomed Him into her house. [39] And she had a sister called Mary, who also sat at Jesus' feet and heard His word. [40] But Martha was distracted with much serving, and she approached Him and said, "Lord, do You not care that my sister has left me to serve alone? Therefore tell her to help me." [41] And Jesus answered and said to her, "Martha, Martha, you are worried and troubled about many things. [42] But one thing is needed, and Mary has chosen that good part, which will not be taken away from her" (Luke 10:38-42).

The Lord of Rest – wants us to know Him and be known by Him.

The Lord of Rest tells us "one thing is needed" above all else – intimacy with Him. Mary chose the good part – the higher calling in serving Her Lord and Master – by dwelling in His presence. God is not telling us to choose one over the other; we must learn to do both. But the "one thing" that is needed above all else – is "intimacy" with Him.

We must spend time hosting His presence. Serving as host for others "in the name of Jesus" is not a substitute. Do not misconstrue hospitality (as a spiritual gift, which is the hosting and taking care of others) – with worldly hospitality which is overly concerned and consumed by the busyness of daily affairs and affections. Both are important, yet from God's perspective... one is the "good part."

Charitable good works is not a substitute for hosting God's presence either, nor should physical inattention suffer on the sideline of spiritual affections. Harmonious oneness is the ultimate aim in Christian hospitality (we must host His presence – and – serve others out of that presence).

We were designed by God as earthen tabernacles to host His presence. We are earthly temples to host the indwelling Holy Spirit (1 Cor. 6:19; Ezek. 36:27; John 14:17).

> "Do you not know that you are the temple of God and that the Spirit of God dwells in you?" (1 Cor. 3:16).

This is "what" you really are! You are a tabernacle for the One True Living God!

> "But Solomon built Him a house" (Acts 7:47).

"But... Solomon" (said by Stephen before he was stoned to death) is a contrarian statement to what God had intended because the

Temple was not 'the house' the Lord wanted David or Solomon to build (2 Sam. 7:5), nor is God even interested in us building "houses made with human hands" because these temples become physical gateways that get used by us and becomes our focus... which clouds our ability to perceive the "spiritual heart" within us... is a spiritual gateway within the "house of man" that God uses to fulfill His purposes on earth – through men.

> "However, the Most High does not dwell in temples made with hands, as the prophet says: [49] 'Heaven is My throne, and earth is My footstool. **What house will you build for Me? says the LORD, or what is the place of My rest**? [50] Has My hand not made all these things?' [51] "You stiff-necked and uncircumcised in heart and ears! You always resist the Holy Spirit; as your fathers did, so do you" (Acts 7:48-51).

The Lord's place of rest... i.e. His permanent abiding dwelling place... is in our heart.

> ***God does not dwell in temples made with human hands.***
> ***God dwells in temples that have human hands!***

Home – is where your heart is!

What have buildings got to do with any of this?

Mone and Meno

House is a term which is very specific and similarly vague as well. We oftentimes consider houses as permanent dwelling places; however, within the context of time... earthly houses begin as permanent yet become temporary through age while spiritual abodes which begin as temporary rooms become permanent through faith.   Here are the Greek and Hebrew terms for house associated with Acts 7:49 (above) and its corresponding verse in Isa. 66:1:

- (*bayith*-H1004) "as a noun denotes a fixed, established structure made from some kind of material as a permanent dwelling place."[82] The first biblical occurrence is found in Gen. 6:14 which offers us a glimpse into the spiritual application of this word: "Make yourself an ark of gopherwood; make rooms [*bayith*] in the ark, and cover it inside and outside with pitch." Rooms in the ark represent a type and shadow of the permanent dwelling place (room or receptacle) the Lord wants us to construct in our heart-house. Those dwelling with the Lord abiding in them become part of a spiritual family or household.
- (*oikos*-G3624) "a house, a dwelling, by implication: a family"[83] Different terms are used in John 14:2 to describe the Father's house (*oikia*-3614-a residence) and the dwelling place (*mone*-3438-abode) where "They" make an abode in our heart-house, yet despite these subtle differences, the terminology all points back to the original intent: the Lord's purpose according to faith is for us to establish a <u>permanent</u> dwelling place or room within our earthen vessel (i.e. a heart-house) for the Lord to abide – eternally!

There is an interesting correlation between two terms Jesus used in John 14 to teach truth with understanding regarding the kingdom of God: '*mone*' (3438) and '*meno*' (3306). '*Mone*' is a permanent abode and '*meno*' is a temporary dwelling place, which is similar in meaning to '*katoikio*' (2730) as a quasi-permanent place to dwell while temporarily living '*kata*' (2596-down) on earth (Eph. 3:17) i.e. dwelling in the Father's '*oikia*' *house* under His '*oikos*' *estate*.

"The translation and meaning of these words can oftentimes be confused. Many things which are considered permanent dwelling places upon the earth, such houses and buildings, are actually temporary structures upon the earth at this present time. Much of

---

[82] Strong's Concordance.
[83] IBID.

what we consider permanent is actually only a type and shadow of the true spiritual reality that surrounds us (Col. 2:16-18)."[84]

- Jesus said: "Do you not believe that I am in the Father, and the Father in Me? The words that I speak to you I do not speak on My own authority; but the Father who dwells [*meno*] in Me does the works" (John 14:10)
- "... the Spirit of truth, whom the world cannot receive, because it neither sees Him nor knows Him; but you know Him, for He dwells [*meno*] with you and will be in you" (John 14:17)
- "These things I have spoken to you while being present [*meno*] with you" (John 14:25).

Isn't this interesting: the Father dwelled temporarily in Jesus (John 14:10)? The Lord is always with us – and yet temporarily dwells in us. This may seem like a contradiction, but it isn't because – the flesh profits nothing. The earth suit is merely a temporary tabernacle while the heart-house is a permanent *mone*! The most marvelous dichotomy of living spiritually is: even the Spirit dwells temporarily (*meno*) **with us** (in earthen vessels; physical) yet abides permanently (*mone*) **in us** (in heart-houses not made with humans hands; spiritual).

Which one is the greater? Go ask Mary. She knows!

As earthly tabernacles for Jesus, His grace abides in us as He sojourns with us. Carefully read these words spoken to the Apostle Paul by the Lord Himself.[85]

> "And He [the Lord] said to me, "My grace is sufficient for you, for My strength is made perfect in weakness [*astheneia*]." Therefore most gladly I will rather boast in my ~~infirmities~~ [weaknesses –

---

[84] Excerpt from "Dominion" section titled "Mone and Meno" in Chapter 10: The Kingdom of God.
[85] The next seven sections are excerpts copied from "Commission" section titled: "The Flesh Is Weak."

astheneia], that the power of Christ may rest upon [1981] me" (2 Cor. 12:9).

"My strength is made perfect in weakness" is literally: My *dunamis* (miraculous power) in *astheneia* weakness (i.e. within the body of flesh) is *perfected* (*teleioo*-5048; divine character consummated and completely accomplished in us according to grace wherein Christ's character has been fully and perfectly formed in us).

Man's greatest obstacle to perceiving the heavenly reality that surrounds us and exists within us – is the weakness imposed by the earth suit which was formed upon us... which also sanctifies us.

"Rest upon" in this instance is the word '*episkenoo*-1981' which means: "to spread a tabernacle over; to tent upon; to cover" (from '*skenoo*-4637' "to occupy (as a mansion)" and from "*skenos*-4636; a hut or *temporary residence*), i.e. (figuratively, it speaks of) the human body (as the **abode** of the spirit... and used metaphorically of the body as the **tabernacle** of the soul, 2 Cor. 5:1, 4)."[86] Strong's stated it perfectly!

> "For we know that if our earthly house, this tent [4636-temporary tabernacle], is destroyed, we have a building from God, a house not made with hands, eternal in the heavens. ² For in this we groan, earnestly desiring to be clothed with our habitation which is *from* [*ex*; from-out-of] heaven" (2 Cor. 5:1, 2).

Our body is the tabernacle of the soul.
And our body is the abode of the spirit where the Lord abides
(John 14:23).

---

[86] Strong's Concordance.

The word '*mone*' (abode) which was spoken by Jesus in John 14:2; "In my Father's house are many (*mone*) abodes" (also translated "*mansions*") are literally: many dwelling places.

Our soul is "the expression" of who we are, and our body and spirit are manifest expressions of what we are, who we are and what purpose God commissioned us to fulfill. Think of your spiritual and physical construction as three gloves, with your spirit inflated within you and your body formed upon you... functioning as a tabernacle for the soul and spirit.

The problem presented thus far is: how do we transition from physical reality into spiritual identity? Jesus told us: that which is flesh – is temporary, but that which is spirit – is eternal.

> "That which is born of the flesh is flesh, and that which is born of the Spirit is spirit. ⁷ Do not marvel that I said to you, 'You must be born again'" (John 3:6, 7).

In order to know "what and who" you really are, it is imperative to be born again whereby the Spirit of God begins renewing your mind to help you perceive your dual identity from a spiritual perspective. Logic, reason and intellect are unable to grasp the realm of the spirit which God formed within you (Zech. 12:1). Faith is the means whereby we let go of worldly things, thoughts, ideas and opinions – to seek the Lord – and put our trust in God to guide us and teach us heavenly truth.

> "You **must be** born again" (John 3:7).

> "And no one puts new wine into old wineskins; or else the new wine bursts the wineskins, the wine is spilled, and the wineskins are ruined. But new wine **must be** put into new wineskins" (Mark 2:22).

We (you and me) **must be** born again (literally, born anew from above) by the Holy Spirit for this purpose: to become tabernacles and holy habitations for the Lord of glory to abide within us – thus enabling us to become gateways of greater grace, greater works and greater glory flowing through us. Our outward bodies never changed (though some miraculous healings have occurred), but the true and permanent change within us – where the Lord abides within the spiritual heart of our soul – is what carries forward into eternity.

The undiscovered territory the Lord of Glory conquers... is the heart of your soul.

This "born again" message occurs numerous times in my books because it is highly important: you must be born again. From Jesus' perspective – "must" is non-negotiable! We were all born of water into this world, but we must be born again by the Spirit if we want to enter Paradise.

The water-born man must die before the Spirit-born man can be born. (Luke 9:24)

There are multitudes with "religious faith" who profess belief in Jesus as the Son of God, but this does not constitute saving faith with guaranteed entrance into heaven (which Jesus never promised); it merely means you avoid torment in the Pit of Hell. Unless you've been born anew, you cannot enter Paradise where worshippers worship King Jesus in spirit and in truth – who have already yielded their sovereignty and learned to live lovingly and obediently under the Lordship of Jesus.

However, if you have faith but have not been born again, there is another place where you shall reside in eternity called: Outer Darkness. It's better than Hell... but it isn't Paradise. Preachers have been selling heaven for 2,000 years as one of two places we go after we die, but they cannot explain what Outer Darkness is because it doesn't fit their heaven-only narrative.

Let me explain: Jesus never promised us heaven, the apostles never preached it and our Creeds don't teach it. Jesus promised us life eternal... in Paradise... which is the New Earth after the regeneration. After a person's body dies, their soul continues in a state of existence and goes to one of four temporary holding places for the dead:

1. Hades (the temporary holding place for persons with faith; Rev. 1:18)
2. Death (the temporary holding place for persons without faith; Rev. 1:18)
3. The Sea (which ceases to exist in the regeneration; Rev. 21:1)
4. Under the Altar in Heaven (for those martyred on account of faith, who come alive again to rule and reign with Jesus for a millennium; this is the first resurrection; Rev. 20:4)

Hades and Death are not Hell (Hell is the absence of God).[87] The dead waiting in Death are not judged because they rejected faith in Jesus – and have counted themselves unworthy of judgment. The dead waiting under the Altar have already been acquitted on account of faith. The rest of the dead are raised up, then judged by Jesus and then sent to one of two places: the resurrection of condemnation or the resurrection of life (John 5:29). Those raised in the resurrection of life will spend eternity with Jesus with life eternal in Paradise, but they are very few in number.[88]

> "Then one said to Him, "Lord, are there few who are saved?" And He [Jesus] said to them, [24] "Strive to enter through the narrow gate, for many, I say to you, will seek to enter and will not be able" (Luke 13:23, 24).

Those raised in the resurrection of condemnation are many and they, likewise, will receive life eternal in a place called Outer Darkness. Why are so few saved? Simple: because they refused to seek the Lord, obey His voice, know Him as King and

---

[87] Read "HERE – The Kingdom Of Heaven Is" by the author (Chapter 6) to learn more.
[88] Jesus' own words differ dramatically from messages from the pulpit – and eulogies spoken over the dead.

acknowledge Jesus as Lord of their life! Jesus wants to have an intimate personal relationship with us – whereby we know Him and are known by Him – whereby we've declared our steadfast obedience and allegiance to Him as Lord, Master and King. How you live now is the way you shall continue to live in eternity. Only His sheep that follow Him will dwell in Paradise; goats will dwell in Outer Darkness.

> "Not everyone who says to Me, 'Lord, Lord,' shall enter the kingdom of heaven, but he who does the will of My Father in heaven. ^{22} Many will say to Me in that day, 'Lord, Lord, have we not prophesied in Your name, cast out demons in Your name, and done many wonders in Your name?' ^{23} And then I will declare to them, '*I never knew you*; depart from Me, you who practice lawlessness!'" (Matt. 7:21-23).

"Knowing Jesus" means having an intimate personal relationship with Him – which becomes the litmus test of attaining life eternal with Him.

> "My sheep hear My voice, and *I know them*, and they follow Me" (John 10:27).

Our entrance into life eternal in Paradise is based upon Jesus knowing us. Period! Intimacy is what the Lord of Rest desires! Paradise is for the sheep of His pasture! Even if you are known as a "friend of Jesus" or "A King's Kid" – labels and titles do not tip the scales in your favor. Some who are known as "sons of the kingdom" will be cast into Outer Darkness. Understand the message – and have ears to hear!

- "But the sons of the kingdom will be cast out into outer darkness. There will be weeping and gnashing of teeth" (Matt. 8:12)

- "But when the king came in to see the guests, he saw a man there who did not have on a wedding garment. ¹² So he said to him, 'Friend, how did you come in here without a wedding garment?' And he was speechless. ¹³ Then the king said to the servants, 'Bind him hand and foot, take him away, and cast him into outer darkness; there will be weeping and gnashing of teeth.' ¹⁴ "*For many are called, but few are chosen*" (Matt. 22:11-14)

- "For to everyone who has, more will be given, and he will have abundance; but from him who does not have, even what he has will be taken away. ³⁰ And cast the unprofitable servant into the outer darkness. There will be weeping and gnashing of teeth" (Matt. 25: 29, 30)

Outer Darkness – is the place reserved for hypocrites, wicked, lazy, abominable and unprofitable servants, and unfaithful stewards where eternal torment following judgment occurs (Matt. 8:12; 22:13; 25:30; Jude 13).

This message does not come as delicately as many may have hoped – but which would you rather know: God's truth or the preacher's sermon? Strive to enter the narrow gate.

> "For the LORD is our Judge, the LORD is our
> Lawgiver, the LORD is our King" (Isa. 33:22).

We've listened to many sermons about "glory" and "the glory cloud" as well, but many chase after clouds rather than having an intimate encounter with Jesus where His glory dwells. Revival begins – in the power of one! Why chase a glory cloud… when you can initiate one through intimacy with Jesus? Seek His righteousness… enter His rest… then all these things will be added unto you. ***Shekinah – starts with you!***

Souls with faith shall remain captives in earthen vessels until our end-of-days, then our soul waits temporarily in Hades for Judgment and Resurrection (Rev. 1:18), but until that day comes –

our hope is Christ! This is why the new birth is mission critical for believers to comprehend!

> "I will give you a new heart and put a new spirit within you; I will take the heart of stone out of your flesh and give you a heart of flesh. ^{27} I will put My Spirit within you and cause you to walk in My statutes, and you will keep My judgments and do them" (Ezek. 36:26, 27).

In the new birth, we are given a new heart, a new spirit, and the indwelling Holy Spirit… to help us continue in faithful obedience to Christ (despite trials and tribulations) and continue the original plan we were sent to accomplish on earth: have dominion. The only thing that is <u>not</u> made new in the new birth is the mind of your soul. The sanctification of your soul through the renewing of your mind (Rom. 12:1, 2)… is your responsibility!

> "Set your mind on things above, not on things on the earth" (Col. 3:2).

"These bodies are houses with an inner tabernacle (the most holy place). These bodies do not belong to us (1 Cor. 6:20); they were loaned to us in order for God to see what we put in them (our storehouse), what we produce through them (for His glory) and, most importantly… if we will establish a permanent inner room for the Lord to abide within us. If a permanent dwelling place (abode) for the Lord has not been established, then our godless house is expendable."[89]

Jesus came to abide in us and tabernacle with us… to be – not just one **with us** – but *one **in us***!

> "Or do you not know that your body is the temple of the Holy Spirit *who is* in you, whom you have

---

[89] IBID. Excerpt from "Commission" section titled: Living Tabernacles for the Divine."

from God, and you are not your own? [20] For you were bought at a price; therefore glorify God ***in your body and in your spirit, which are God's***" (1 Cor. 6:19, 20).

Jesus wants to abide in and dwell with us, so Jesus went beyond the limits of an architectural sanctuary to abide within earthly vessels in human sanctuaries called: the hearts of men. Jesus wants to inhabit our earthly form and dwell with us; Jesus wants to reside in us as we rest in Him. How marvelously awesome is this divine relationship we have "in/with" Jesus Christ!

Magnificent temples have been constructed all over the world as an expression of worship within created things, and yet, these are merely types and shadows of the true temple – the tabernacle of the heart – the abode of the spirit – where men can worship the Lord their God, freely, day and night, through gateway-hearts filled with joyous love, affection and adoration. The kingdom of heaven is neither up nor down…

…the journey is in!

A sojourner and a servant dwell temporarily in a '*meno*' (body as a temporary dwelling place), but a son or daughter abides permanently in a '*mone*' (heart-home "with" the Lord; John 14:23).

Shekinah Glory

Shekinah (or the Aramaic *shekinot*) is used to describe when God would "settle in" or "dwell with" His people. This is the ideal that God desires for His people: a permanent rest where His glory dwells in us – and also a physical place where others can draw near to Him and enter His presence. God's rest has two components: He desires intimacy with His people (as we host His presence in us) – as they reside in the place of His choosing (where others can likewise draw near to Him).

When we abide in Him and He abides in us, we enter His rest – which can also be interpreted to mean: we are resting in the intermission phase of our salvation between two acts of a play called: temporary and eternity. If we are not resting in His presence, then our souls are not being refreshed. If we are still working, then we have neither entered nor comprehended the meaning of His rest.

In the Parable of the Pearl of Great Price, a man sold everything in order to purchase the field with the pearl. The Pearl (Jesus) and the field (the place of His presence where His glory dwells) are a package deal; you cannot have the field (Paradise) without the King of Heaven (Jesus).

This word has two parts: we must understand why Jesus desires intimacy with us… and understand why He wants to manifest (plant) His Shekinah presence in geographic places. So I challenge you: what type of field is your church plowing in preparation for revival?

Azusa Street, Brownsville, Toronto, and many other places became known for the Lord's glory and presence in particular places. People plowed for years in prayer contending for the Spirit's release… and revival happened. Mount Sinai is an example where revival didn't happen simply because the people didn't want to listen to His voice and "enter into intimacy."

The Lord wants to manifest Himself and His glory in certain places for revival, but first… we must understand who Jesus is. Read "IMAGE" to understand more of what I'm saying. The third great awakening is going to be a "Jesus Only" movement. Therefore, it is incumbent upon us to understand who Jesus is – and partner with Him to initiate revival in our communities and reformation in His church that hosts His presence and allows the Holy Spirit to operate unencumbered by the man show.

For years I've observed this: the Lord visits churches and begins "kicking tires" in preparation for worldwide revival to seek and find those who faithfully worship Him in spirit and in truth. We see this imagery clearly in the letter written "to the angel" of the church of the Laodiceans:

> "Behold, I stand at the door and knock. If anyone hears My voice and opens the door, I will come into Him and dine with Him, and he with Me" (Rev. 3:20).

"This letter was written to the lukewarm, complacent, ambivalent, fatty, wealthy, lethargic church. These church members have lost their fire and have forsaken their "first love" (personal relationship) with Christ, who is now standing *outside* this door – knocking. When Christ first came to us, He called us by name with the coo of a loving whisper in our ear, but now these professed followers of Christ have shut Him out of their life; they have lost their zeal, their passion, their intimacy and, most of all, their joy. Do you see this knocking by Jesus as gentle tapping to invite them back or as the striking of the door with jealous rebuke to wake them up? And this is why many of my writings to the institutional church are stern; condemnational, no, but critical, yes! I write what I'm told to write. It is time for the bride to awaken from her slumber and answer the door – and that time is now!"[90]

If your church is being tested, then it is being proofed beforehand. So get ready; the Lord is going to put fresh air in your tires for rapid acceleration into greater grace, greater works and greater glory. The church age is over; the kingdom age has begun.

> "But the hour is coming, and now is, when the true worshipers will worship the Father in spirit and truth; for the Father is seeking such to worship Him. [24] God is Spirit, and those who worship Him must worship in spirit and truth" (John 4:23, 24).

The Lord is seeking worshippers – in spirit and truth – as tabernacle/dwelling places of His presence who: A) love Him in

---

[90] Excerpt from "Listen" section titled: "Riding A Dead Horse."

quiet, prayerful, intimate rest; B) and serve Him as intercessors like Him; and C) worship Him with reckless abandon as David did before the ark of the Lord (2 Sam. 6:14). God is glorified in these expressions.

Too often I've seen the opposite occur in church. When God gets silent, two things happen: A) the music gets louder and theatrics more rambunctious; and B) the spirit of control prevents the Holy Spirit from guiding worship.

The current church model is broken! "We keep creating new programs, imagine new ways to improve the church experience, change the music and tempo, preach about paradigm shifts, invigorate the message with entertainment words and theatrics to titillate the ears of the listeners, and yet, we (the people) continue to thirst and hunger for the deeper things of God. We hunger for His presence… and O, how the Holy Spirit grieves when the man-show interrupts the prompting of the Spirit. The church has a heart condition which cannot be cured with superficial solutions and hyper-managed programmatic ideas. How many more ideas and imaginative programs are we going to keep throwing at the current church model?"[91]

In my own life I've learned: when God gets silent, it is then that I must match His invitation and become *'raphah'* – motionless in stillness (Psa. 46:10). Quiet moments of prayer, meditation, rest, and reverence early in the morning are keys to opening the heart of the Divine. I am always listening for the sound of His voice… and typically wait an hour or more every morning like this, sometimes waiting days anticipating His response, and sometimes years regarding messages of greatest importance. Don't rush it. Wait for it (Hab. 2:1-3). Even though it tarries… wait for it. Wait on The Lord. From experience I say: it's worth it!!! There's nothing on earth quite like it!

---

[91] Excerpt from "Listen" section titled: "What Is A Hardened Heart?"

The fear we experience with silence – is continued silence. When God doesn't speak, questions begin to arise in our mind, like: am I off spiritually? I can remember one instance the Lord told me He would speak on a particular issue the following day, so I waited and waited until sleep settled in without hearing anything. The next day, I asked Him what's up, and He said: He was testing me to see if I would raise my hand (make an accusation) against Him. Our God is faithful… and He spends much time teaching us how to be patient and faithful – like Him.

> "Truly my soul silently waits for God; from Him comes my salvation" (Psa. 62:1).

Back on point: "The ark of the covenant is where the presence of God resided in what was called the *shekinah* glory. The word *shekinah* and the word *mishkan* (tabernacle) both are derived from the same root word *shakan* which means: dwelling. Thus the tabernacle was the dwelling place of God's presence. The Aramaic word *shekinot* is found in the Talmud (Talmud Baba Kamma 92b) and is described *as a nest*. Thus this dwelling place was like a nest where a bird would nurture its young. The word *shekinah* is not even found in Scripture but the Jews applied this word because of the feminine ending. The Shekinah glory represents the feminine or nurturing, loving and caring nature of God."[92]

The idea of Shekinah being a nest where a bird nurtures its young – is the same imagery in the creation account of the Holy Spirit "hovering [*rachaph*] over the face of the waters" (Gen. 1:2) like a stork mothering her brood.

Rachaph (7363) *raw-khaf* means: to brood, by implication: to be relaxed. This word is uniquely juxtaposed with "darkness" in Gen. 1:2 for dramatic effect. When we consider the character of the earth as being void, chaotic and utterly destroyed on account of Satan's expulsion from heaven onto earth, this phraseology adds great clarity to the creation account; God's Spirit hovers and

---

[92] Source: chainbentorah.com.

creates a relaxed atmosphere in the midst of chaotic, evil darkness. The world was utterly destroyed, and in due process the sons of men will be utterly destroyed as well, yet we have this hope: the Spirit of God hovers over us. How awesome is this inexpressible and inexhaustible nurturing love that God has for us, that even while *we were yet to become sinners*, He provided a loving and merciful way of escape for us called: hear and follow Me.

Rachaph occurs only three times in scripture:

1. Gen. 1:2 – "The earth was without form, and void; and darkness *was* on the face of the deep. And the Spirit of God was hovering [*rachaph*] over the face of the waters."
2. Jer. 23:9 – "My heart within me is broken because of the prophets; all my bones shake [*rachaph*]. I am like a drunken man, and like a man whom wine has overcome, because of the LORD, and because of His holy words." This scripture must be known within the context of the entire message against false prophets and empty oracles: "Woe to the shepherds who destroy and scatter the sheep of My pasture!" says the LORD. ² Therefore thus says the LORD God of Israel against the shepherds who feed My people: "You have scattered My flock, driven them away, and not attended to them. Behold, I will attend to you for the evil of your doings," says the LORD. ³ "But I will gather the remnant of My flock out of all countries where I have driven them, and bring them back to their folds; and they shall be fruitful and increase. ⁴ I will set up shepherds over them who will feed them; and they shall fear no more, nor be dismayed, nor shall they be lacking," says the LORD" (Jer. 23:1-4; perhaps "all my bones *hover*" is a better translation).
3. Deut. 32:11 – "He found him in a desert land and in the wasteland, a howling wilderness;
He encircled him, He instructed him, He kept him as the apple of His eye. ¹¹ As an eagle stirs up its nest, hovers [*rachaph*] over its young, spreading out its wings, taking them up, carrying them on its wings"

Our God is Jehovah Raah – The Lord My Shepherd (Psa. 23:1); the God who nurtures.

The Kingdom of Rest is a tranquil Paradise wherein we maintain eternal intimacy with Jesus.

Jesus gave us His glory – so oneness happens.

> "And the glory which You gave Me I have given them, that they may be one just as We are one" (John 17:22).

"The whole point of life on earth – is to restore the oneness we had with the Father – as sons of God who were "daily in His presence" (Prov. 8:30) before we were sent to earth.

Glory – is about Oneness with the Father!!! United in oneness with the Father – with one heart and one mind – in oneness with the Spirit – is what our faith journey is all about!!!!!!"[93]

> **"But he who is joined [glued] to the Lord is one spirit with Him" (1 Cor. 6:17).**

The Kingdom of Rest abides within the Kingdom of Oneness.

Jesus is the Prince of Peace. If you are not resting in Him, then putting "Rest in Peace" on your tombstone epitaph is utterly meaningless. Our God "is not the God of the dead, but the God of the living" (Mark 12:27). God wants us to "rest" with Him right now; death of the body is merely an intermission. If Jesus abides in you – and you abide with Christ – then you will always be alive. Death has no power or mastery over you! Fear not! You are already living eternally – right now!

Enter into God's rest and cease striving through human effort. Jesus loves you! Let Jesus be God – in you, with you, to you, through you and for you. Allow Jesus to rule and rein in your

---

[93] Excerpt copied from the chapter titled: "Kingdom of the Spirit."

mortal body. Prepare a room in your heart for Him. Yield to Him by allowing Him to be the best expression of Himself that He chooses to reveal – in you and through you.

Relax… enter His rest… and purpose to do
the one thing Jesus desires most:
Abide with Him.
Be intimate with Him.
You are His beloved!
Does Jesus know you?
Be known like John… as the disciple whom Jesus loved.

The Lover of your Soul waits for you.

Kingdom of Oneness

Newness, through truth, change and oneness – is what our mission on earth is all about.

What is oneness? Is there a definition by which we may understand it? Not really. Many years ago I heard this message about "Mash Potato Love" which helps explain one aspect of oneness. There are nearly 7 billion people on earth and we are all very different people... much akin to many types of potatoes. If you cooked all those potatoes and mashed them in a pot, they would become – mashed potatoes. Their individual uniqueness can still be found in the oneness of many potatoes, but their individuality has taken on a new identity: ones mashed into oneness.

Here is an excellent example: before a symphony begins to play music, the conductor brings everyone to attention, a single note is played by one instrument, and then all other instruments play that same note to ensure their instrument is properly tuned. Every musician must change the tune of their individual instrument to match the preparatory note so they all perform in harmonious oneness.

Jesus is the Conductor... and the Spirit made sure this note has gone out (Rom. 10:18).

> "But he who is joined to the Lord is one spirit with Him" (1 Cor. 6:17).

This is what the Spirit of Christ has in mind for each of us: oneness until we are all seen as one and heard as one with the identity of the One – Jesus Christ.

> "For "who has known the mind of the Lord that he may instruct Him?" But we have the mind of Christ" (1 Cor. 2:16).

When our minds are renewed and transformed by the Spirit, we will operate with the mind of Christ. This is not some future promise in Paradise… this promise is present-active for today.

> "Let this mind be in you which was also in Christ Jesus" (Phil. 2:5).

This is not some great mystery to comprehend: when we think like Jesus – then we will act like Jesus. The Spirit accomplishes this in us – to the glory of the Father. By one Spirit, we are changed and renewed to think anew and operate in oneness. If there is division among us, then we have not listened to the Spirit and/or have not yielded to the Spirit who transforms us by renewing our mind… which is mission critical for all believers as they live as disciples of Jesus.

> "And do not be conformed to this world, but be transformed by the renewing of your mind, that you may prove what *is* that good and acceptable and perfect will of God" (Rom. 12:2).

If we (as members in a church) remain divided regarding "what *is* that good and acceptable and perfect will of God" (for the local church), then perhaps the new birth hasn't happened in us yet. We may have been baptized in water and the Spirit, but if we do not resemble Christ and operate according to His likeness with His Divine attributes – by grace – and establish His kingdom on earth, then perhaps the oneness condition never took hold because of: hardness in our heart.

The Spirit makes us one. If we are not one – in oneness with the Spirit – then allow the Spirit to change your way. Align yourself with the Spirit… who makes us one in Christ Jesus.

> "There is one body and one Spirit, just as you were called in one hope of your calling; [5] one Lord, one faith, one baptism; [6] *one God and Father of all, who is above all, and through all, **and in you all**'* (Eph. 4:4-6).

God is "in you all" (Eph. 4:6) and "the Spirit of God dwells in you" also (1 Cor. 3:16). There should never be an "us" or "them" in church; we should be "one" in the Spirit!

The Spirit of God in us – restores us in oneness with the Father.

> "For through Him we both have access by one Spirit to the Father" (Eph. 2:18).

"When the Son speaks on behalf of the Father, the Father is magnified by the Son – because they speak as One. When the Son does the will of the Father, the Son glorifies the Father and the Father is glorified in the Son – because they are One. When the Son rejoices in the Spirit, the Father is exalted by the Son – because they abide in Oneness, always and eternally."[94]

When you walk and talk like Jesus – you will be able to say what Jesus said: "I and the Father are One." I assure you: this is neither mystical nor heretical! Jesus came – as a Son – to teach us how to become adopted sons and daughters in the Father's spiritual kingdom. We must imitate Jesus. For this reason among many, Jesus sent the Holy Spirit: to make us one with the Father. When you live in oneness with the Father in "the *unity* of the Spirit" (Eph. 4:3) and "the *unity* of the faith" (Eph. 4:13), you are able to say: "I and the Father are one." The word *unity* '*henotes*-1775' means: oneness; unanimity. Grace initiates this change in us – and glory effects it.

> Jesus said: "And the glory which You [Father] gave Me I have given them, that they may be one just as We are one" (John 17:22).

Jesus gave us His glory for this reason: to make us one with the Father. The Spirit makes this happen! Meditate on that kingdom principle.

---

[94] Excerpt copied from "Image" section titled "If Jesus Did It – So Can We."

We need to define "glory" to better understand how it applies to oneness. The word glory 'doxa-1391' in its most basic sense means: "an opinion." Whatever you think is your opinion. Whatever God thinks is His opinion, and all God's thoughts are good and righteous and true. Our opinions (thoughts) need to align harmoniously with God's thoughts. When our thoughts imitate His thoughts, we give glory (good opinions) to God. When we exalt the goodness of God, and the righteousness of God, and the truth of God, we give glory (good opinions) to God!

This oneness mindset is able to shift paradigms and effect revolutionary change on earth.

- "***Be of the same mind toward one another***. Do not set your mind on high things, but associate with the humble. Do not be wise in your own opinion" (Ron. 12:16)
- "Now may the God of patience and comfort grant you to ***be like-minded toward one another***, according to Christ Jesus, ***that you may with one mind and one mouth glorify the God and Father of our Lord Jesus Christ***" (Rom. 15:5, 6)
- "Become complete. Be of good comfort, ***be of one mind, live in peace***; and the God of love and peace will be with you" (2 Cor. 13:11)
- "Only let your conduct be worthy of the gospel of Christ, so that whether I come and see you or am absent, I may hear of your affairs, that you ***stand fast in one spirit, with one mind*** striving together for the faith of the gospel" (Phil 1:27)
- "fulfill my joy by being like-minded, having the same love, ***being of one accord, of one mind***" (Phil. 2:2)

    "***Finally, all of you be of one mind, having compassion for one another; love as brothers, be tenderhearted, be courteous***" (1 Pet. 3:8)

When we operate as one mind with the mind of Christ, there will be no distinction between us.

The word "minded" is *'phroneo'* (G5426) – "to think, to exercise the mind; to be minded in a certain way;" "to be like-minded" according to Christ Jesus (Phil. 2:5; Rom. 15:5); "be of one mind" (Phil. 2:2; 2 Cor. 13:11) lit. "minding the one thing"… in one accord; "be of the same mind" (Phil 4:2); to be none otherwise minded (Gal. 5:10)." [95]

When our minds become "minded in a certain way – the way of Christ," we will all begin to look and sound like Jesus. Honestly – isn't that the whole point of faith: to reflect Jesus? We are His image bearers who were created according to His likeness to become little christs: i.e. Christians.

"When it comes so setting our mind on Christ, it implies we are being mindful to think in a certain way, which in this case, is on Christ – to become like (in the similitude of) Christ Jesus. We are setting the focus of our attention and the fullness of our affection on Christ in order to imitate the way and manner in which He thought and, likewise, lived. We are a nation, that is, a culture of people who have decided, through faith, to live according to certain principles and lifeways as disciples of Jesus Christ. The "one thing" that we have in common (*koinos*)… is to become like Christ Jesus."[96]

Koinonia (from *koinos*) implies – Christian fellowship – wherein all share this one thing in common with other believers: faith in Jesus as Lord of all.

> "Therefore if there *is* any consolation in Christ, if any comfort of love, ***if any fellowship of the Spirit***, if any affection and mercy, ² fulfill my joy ***by being like-minded, having the same love, being of one accord, of one mind***. ³ Let nothing be done through selfish ambition or conceit, but in lowliness of mind let each esteem others better than himself" (Phil. 2:1-3).

---

[95] Strong's Concordance.
[96] Excerpt from "Understand" section titled: "Thinking Like Jesus."

Esteeming others ahead of self (not better than) – is the definition of meekness. By injecting the translation "better than" we have attributed a worldly value irrespective of honor wherein some persons are better than while others must be less than… when in fact all are equal in the eyes of God. How do you esteem others? How do you value others? How do you honor others? How does your character and demeanor measure up to this standard?

The literal Greek is: ἀλλὰ (but) τῇ (-) ταπεινοφροσύνῃ (in humility) ἀλλήλους² (one another) ἡγούμενοι¹ (deeming) ὑπερέχοντας (surpassing) ἑαυτῶν (themselves). The word translated "better than" is (ὑπερέχοντας-*huperecho*-5242) from (*huper*-5228-over, above, more than) and (*echo*-2192-to hold) thus "to hold above as surpassing" (in this case, surpassing self) as perhaps a more accurate meaning… occurs five times in scripture of which three are found in Philippians:

- Better than himself – (Phil. 2:3) – (to hold above as surpassing self)
- Excellence – "I also count all things loss for the excellence [5242] of the knowledge of Christ Jesus my Lord, for whom I have suffered the loss of all things" (Phil 3:8)
- Surpass/Passeth – "Be anxious for nothing, but in everything by prayer and supplication, with thanksgiving, let your requests be made known to God; ⁷ and the peace of God, which surpasses [5242] all understanding, will guard your hearts and minds through Christ Jesus" (Phil. 4:7)
- The other two occurrences are Rom. 13:1 (higher; "Let every soul be subject to higher/superior authorities") and 1 Pet. 2:13 (supreme; "Therefore submit yourselves to every ordinance of man for the Lord's sake, whether to the king as supreme")

If the Spirit in us is the great Equalizer, than meekness is the principal delineator that sets us apart from the world and worldly standards.

Meekness (4235) is one of the character attributes exhibited by Jesus (translated 'gentle' Matt. 11:29; translated 'lowly' Matt. 21:5; NKJV) who taught us the greatest commandment: love God with all you've got – and love others ahead of selfish self-interests. "Gentleness or meekness is the opposite of self assertiveness and self interest. It stems from trust in God's goodness and control over the situation. The gentle person is not occupied with self at all. Thus, meekness toward evil people means knowing God is permitting the injuries they inflict."[97]

God is in control. Give all glory to God. God humbles the proud, yet exalts the humble.

Give God the Preeminence – and give neighbors preference – for such is the kingdom of God. Once we understand meekness and adopt this pattern for living, strife and contentions will cease. This is the way of the cross: exhibiting meekness in both vertical and horizontal (God and neighbor) alignments. The New Earth will be inhabited by saints who live according to meekness – with God – and in meekness with one another. How could it be otherwise?

> "Blessed are the meek, for they shall inherit the earth" (Matt. 5:5).

Meekness is not worldly. This attribute is heavenly. Meekness enables us to operate in oneness with one another without bias, malice or prejudice. A radical work of Grace is needed to initiate this process whereby we are returned to a prior operating system called: grace.

From beginning to end – it's all grace. The Spirit of Oneness makes this happen!

---

[97] Strong's Concordance. Word study on "meekness-*praios*-4235).

The One Thing[98]

As I was meditating on these things, I asked the Lord how we can all get on the same page and "be of one mind," and then I looked in the distance at a trucking company with a fleet of trucks. Then, this understanding came to me: they are all going in different directions with different loads for different purposes, but all are being coordinated by "the one thing" i.e. the dispatcher.

When the Spirit speaks, we are being guided and coordinated by Jesus, through the Spirit (our spiritual Dispatcher), who communicates words from Jesus to guide us and teach us in the way of Christ. When we listen to the Spirit, we are being guided by the One, to think and act like the Holy One, Jesus Christ, and to operate in oneness "through Him, with Him and in Him," in oneness with one another – according to pattern as exemplified by Christ Jesus. This is how we all must get on the same spiritual page: listen to the Spirit!

The Spirit!!! The Spirit!!! The Spirit!!! We are born anew by the Spirit, and are taught by the Spirit, and are being guided in truth by the Spirit of Christ so that we may become a manifest expression of Jesus upon the earth.... according to the Spirit of life in Christ Jesus.

> "But the Helper, the Holy Spirit, whom the Father will send in My name, He will teach you all things, and bring to your remembrance all things that I said to you" (John 14:26).

> "When He, the Spirit of truth, has come, He will guide you into all truth; for He will not speak on His own authority, but whatever He hears He will speak; and He will tell you things to come" (John 16:13).

---

[98] Entire section is an excerpt from "Understand" section titled: "The One Thing."

If you do not know what to say, then fear not, and listen for the voice of the Spirit...

> "For the Holy Spirit will teach you in that very hour what you ought to say." (Luke 12:12).

If you do not know what to do, then fear not, and listen to the voice of the Spirit...

> "For those who live according to the flesh set their minds on the things of the flesh, but those who live according to the Spirit, the things of the Spirit" (Rom. 8:5).

If you do not know what to think, then fear not, and listen to the voice of the Spirit...

> "For God has not given us a spirit of fear, but of power and of love and of a *sound* mind" (2 Tim. 1:7; (*sophronismos*-G4995) "a disciplined, self-controlled mind"[99]).

Listen to the Voice of Truth. He speaks the Words of Christ Jesus. Hear the Spirit's Voice. Do whatever it takes to Hear God's Voice. It starts by becoming – *raphah* – motionless in stillness.

Oneness is impossible apart from the Spirit – for the Spirit does not speak on His Own accord. The Spirit speaks what He hears from Jesus (John 16:13). Apart from the Spirit, we know nothing. Apart from Jesus, we are nothing.

> "But you have an anointing from the Holy One, and you know all things" (1 John 2:20).

What more could I possibly say to you in a manner that helps you understand? Well, my words are not what helps you understand, because that is the responsibility of the Inner Witness...

---

[99] Strong's Concordance.

The Inner Witness

> *"And it is the Spirit who bears witness, because the Spirit is truth"* (1 John 5:6).
> *"He who believes in the Son of God has the witness in himself"* (1 John 5:10).

The Holy Spirit is "the witness" alongside Jesus and the Spirit is also "the inner witness" dwelling within each one of us. The Spirit was given to each of us by God – so that we may always have access to the Father and God's truth through One Spirit (Eph. 2:18) through faith in Jesus Christ (Eph. 4:4). Oneness happens… when we listen to the Inner Witness Himself.

The hardest part about my faith journey was overcoming much toxic theology (I listened to a multitude of teachings and preachers). Our human condition eagerly believes what we are taught by other believers as "gospel truth" and then we planted these thoughts and opinions in our heart to grow a fruit precious in the sight of God called: faith. Thirty years I lived like this until a radical "grace awakening" happened: the Spirit invaded my reality. It took the Spirit two years to defrag my thought processes enough for me to become a student of the Word. I enrolled in Faith 101 and eagerly received tutoring by the Spirit. Then my faith was tested in the Spirit's next class: Trust 201. What I received I pass onto you for this reason: yield to the Spirit and allow Him to teach you and guide you in all truth. That's His primary function!

During this time, many thoughts (from the Spirit) kept popping into my mind when I read the scriptures and I wondered if the revelation I was receiving was actually – of the Spirit. Why did I doubt? Because the truth I received (from the Spirit) was incredible! It contradicted many foundational messages I was taught in all branches of church doctrine (Catholic, Protestant, Baptist, Pentecostal, etc.). So let me ask you: have you ever wondered why there are so many denominations (over 2,700)? Because they are not tuned into the One Voice! There may be errors in some of my messages, but none were intentional. The

Spirit of Truth is also the Spirit of Correction and the Spirit of Revelation. Trust the Spirit. I get corrected all the time. So will you. Walk in grace.

The revelation I was receiving had arisen to the point of potentially being church doctrine heresy, so I consulted those who were mature in the Spirit and they simply said: keep listening. One night during group intercessory prayer, I asked God (privately in my mind): "Where does my spirit end and where does Yours' begin?" And then I clearly heard His voice: "We are one." In an instant, my understanding changed. It was 2014 and I was only two years into this renewal process, and yet... the Spirit confirmed something of monumental importance: I was walking in the truth... according to grace.

So I ask: if you desire to become another likeness of Jesus on earth, then do what Jesus did: lay aside all covenants, sacraments, ordinances and legalistic obligations. Jesus did not disregard or violate any of these things I just mentioned; however, He understood the meaning of laying them aside as "less important" than "one thing."

What is the One thing? Oneness with God! When you come to know who Jesus is, then you will also come to know the Father – for they operate in Oneness. Jesus is the Father who sent Himself as a Son – to teach us how to become and live as sons and daughters of the Father.

Let's examine several "types and shadows" of living in oneness with God.

Communion

This word '*koinonia*-2842' translated "communion" four times (I Cor. 10:16 (3x); 2 Cor. 6:14; 13:14) also implies "Christian partnership and fellowship." The base of this word '*koinos*-2839' means: common (oftentimes with a negative connotation, as unclean or profane), which does not make sense until it is set in context with '*hagios*-40-holy' as things set apart for God and consecrated as holy unto Him. On earth, all people are *koinos* (common) until God calls them, visits them and "sets them apart" as *hagios* – as holy unto Him. This invitation is open to all, yet few accept. Having been consecrated, we are then sanctified as vessels and instruments made ready for the Masters' designated (predestined) use. All were predestined, yet even fewer accept. By virtue of God's influence, the common becomes uncommon and the profane becomes holy. Sacraments and ordinances cannot accomplish this; only the Spirit can. Communion is not based upon works or manmade efforts; communion is a function of grace as something done by God which man is woefully incapable of accomplishing by himself or of his own merit.

When communion is perceived in context between God and man, it can be viewed as two entering into an uncommon, holy oneness… thus, a holy partnership and covenant between two entities previously separated by sin (i.e. rebellion against God) become joined together. Faith in Jesus is the common denominator. Intimacy with honor and reverence should be experienced by this **common-union** (communion). From the perspective of communion as a church sacrament, that which is spiritual (unseen) becomes visual (physically experienced) to reveal what is happening within this covenantal moment: the wafer (representing Jesus) and the believer – become one.

Consider this spiritual mystery in natural terms: you are what you eat. In the natural – what you eat becomes you; in the spiritual – you become what you eat! In this moment, you are symbolically becoming what you eat – Christ Jesus. Isn't that the whole point of faith… to imitate Jesus and become another likeness of Him on earth? Jesus is the Bread of Life (John 6:35).[100] Take the bread and eat it. Visualize oneness with God while doing it.

---

[100] Jesus said: "I am the bread which came down from heaven" (John 6:41) referring to Manna during the Exodus (Ex. 16:4).

> "The cup of blessing which we bless, is it not the communion of the blood of Christ? The bread which we break, is it not the communion of the body of Christ? [17] For we, though many, are one bread and one body; for we all partake of that one bread" 1 Cor. 10:16, 17).

During communion, we become one body. For this reason we are admonished to examine ourselves before partaking communion lest we bring judgment upon us (and the one body) by refusing to wash our conscience beforehand through repentance. A little mold affects the loaf.

> "Therefore whoever eats this bread or drinks this cup of the Lord in an unworthy manner will be guilty of the body and blood of the Lord. [28] But let a man examine himself, and so let him eat of the bread and drink of the cup. [29] For he who eats and drinks in an unworthy manner eats and drinks judgment to himself, not discerning the Lord's body" (1 Cor. 11:27-29).

Don't put that which is Holy into an unholy vessel! Sanctify yourselves beforehand – and do not regard your covenant with the Lord as contemptible (made common or ordinary). Oneness is happening in this moment. When you hold the Lord in contempt, you will be held in contempt!

The body of Christ (wafer) has been interpreted by the institutional church to be Christ's body, but examine the words above closely: "We, though many, are one bread and one body." The Church is the body of Christ... with many members (Rom. 12:5; 1 Cor. 12:12; Eph. 4:12; 5:23). Communion is a eucharistic thanksgiving celebration wherein we should be joyfully exuberant and thankful for our redemption, salvation and the coming together of other likeminded souls who found their harmonious expression in the oneness of the One – through Jesus – the Bread of Life. The bread is blessed, broken, divided and given out to those with faith in Him whereby we – as many members – unite together in unbroken unity and oneness found only in Christ.

> "Now you are the body of Christ, and members individually" (1 Cor. 12:27).

Likewise, take the cup... "Do this in remembrance of Me. For as often as you eat this bread and drink this cup, you proclaim the Lord's death till He comes" (1 Cor. 11:23-26). The purpose is to do it – and keep doing it until He returns – and remember also what Jesus did for us – and why (because sheep need help remembering). Keep doing it – and remember the covenant He made with you. Don't forget.

Jesus is your Lord, your Salvation, your God and Master and King.

Take this same idea and transcend the physical into the spiritual: you are what you think! When you consume the truth of God, you will be changed, transformed and eventually conformed to the truth you believed. Thus, the mystical has become quite practical for teaching and edification. Thus, this is how we begin to operate with the mind of Christ (1 Cor. 2:16). In the spiritual realm, we become like the food we eat. So eat truth – consume truth in great quantities – and you will operate with the mind of Christ.

> "Let this mind be in you which was also in Christ Jesus" (Phil. 2:5).

When we live according to truth, we are no longer living as hostile enemies of God. We are now on the same side... as one called alongside many... becoming oneness in Him.

> "And He [Jesus] is before all things, and in Him [Christ] all things consist [are held together]" (Col. 1:17).

We began this journey "in Him [Christ] before the foundation of the world" (Eph. 1:4) and we've been invited to continue this journey – through faith. And even though we walk through the valley of the shadow of death where trials and tribulations wage war against the soul, the Lord will stay with us and carry us until we get to the other side. Oneness with Jesus – in unity with the Spirit as our seal of salvation – is our only guarantee of life eternal.

When we participate in communion on Sunday, we have much to reflect upon. If we, who are called according to His name and have made an abiding place for Christ in us – but have unconfessed sin or trespasses that we have committed (including omissions) – then we must call to mind these offenses and ask forgiveness before we even consider putting our hand forward to dip our bread into the communion cup of Christ in the likeness of Judas. When we agreed to enter into a covenant agreement with Christ (the cup of the New Covenant), the dividing wall of separation was removed and we entered into a "oneness relationship" with Christ. If you dip your wafer into the cup without seeking forgiveness and repentance, then you are dipping into the cup of judgment – and the Spirit of Grace will hold you in contempt!

Eating and drinking the body and blood of Jesus is a meaningless sacrament… unless our communion with Christ provokes us and compels us to become more like Jesus. If we partake of the Lord's Supper by eating His flesh and drinking His blood by celebrating Eucharist, yet refuse to become more like Him, then "what's" the point? Entering into oneness is the point of communion! Communion comes from the root word '*koinos*' (having in common) that results in '*koinonia*' (fellowship with God) and fellowship with those aligned with God through faith in Jesus Christ – and are becoming "one body" in oneness of the Spirit.

You are what you eat! You are what you think! You become… what you focus on!

Communion is an "entering into oneness." Jesus did not say, "I will come into you and then you will abide in Me." He said, "You will abide in Me and (then) I will abide in you."

Finally, those who enter in, and abide, must remain in Him, as a grafted branch to the vine – or else they are cast out as a branch that is withered – to be gathered and thrown into the fire. You cannot remain in Christ if you choose not to abide in the vine (Jesus). You are to enter into communion with Him, and abide in oneness with Him, because He is "the resurrection and the life" in you, but if you choose to build your home any other way than *with* Him, or for Him, then He will have no part of your kingdom building program in His kingdom. In this regard, the principle of "once saved, always saved" does not seem to hold water, now, does it?

> "Now she who is really a widow, and left alone, trusts in God and continues in supplications and prayers night and day. [6] *But she who lives in pleasure **is dead while she lives**"* (1 Tim. 5:5, 6).

People walk away from their covenant obligations to the Lord every day. "Dead while she lives" is a common condition in the church today, as one who was alive yet is "dead" even while she lives. Disciples must never subject the Lord to this indignation.

> "For it is impossible for those who were once enlightened, and have tasted the heavenly gift, and have become partakers of the Holy Spirit, [5] and have tasted the good word of God and the powers of the age to come, [6] if they fall away, to renew them again to repentance, since they crucify again for themselves the Son of God, and put Him to an open shame" (Heb. 5:4-6).

Consider their end. Consider your current state of affairs. Conviction is preferable to condemnation! Don't keep reading if you have accounts to settle with the Lord.

Once saved always saved – is salvation from the place called Death into the place called Hades, but don't stop there – continue through sanctification to rise above Outer Darkness and therefore enter Paradise.

Marriage - the covenant of "two becoming one"[101]

Just as communion is a covenant of oneness witnessed by the Lord, so also is marriage.

> "For this reason a man shall leave his father and mother and be joined to his wife, and the two shall become one flesh" (Matt. 19:5).

Here is another example of oneness made available by the covenant of marriage. This event restores the oneness of Adam (man), as two becoming one. The Hebrew word '*Adam*-120' (pronounced *aw-dawm*) means: man, mankind, people (from the word '*adam*-119' meaning: ruddy, reddish; to flush or turn rosy). The Lord God created the person "Adam" as male and female (both), then bifurcated (subdivided) from the man an element of himself (a rib) to fashion (build) a helper of/from him and for him... i.e. the woman. This is why "two become one flesh" in marriage makes "the original expression of man" one flesh again through the idea of creating "a new person" within the marriage covenant. The marriage covenant restores the divided "Adam" to his original condition in wholeness again – lacking nothing – in oneness.

> "... and the two shall become one flesh'; so then they are no longer two, but one flesh" (Mark 10:8).

This is very important to comprehend on the natural level when two individuals become one in marriage because – on a spiritual level – each of us needs to be united in marriage to Jesus. Jesus is our Husband. We are the bride. Once a disciple is married to Jesus, they have devoted themselves to this spiritual union despite whatever happens. This pledge of obedience by a disciple must never engage in sexual perversion or immorality because – you are disregarding your marriage covenant with Jesus. You are subjecting Him who dwells within you to the act itself. Anathema – means: you are cursed with a curse!

---

[101] Excerpt copied from "Make Disciples" (Book #11).

When a bridegroom invites a bride to become one with him, he must do so knowing the Lord is the Principal Witness of this covenant; the Lord is the third strand that unifies two individuals to become oneness in the Lord:

> "Though one may be overpowered by another, two can withstand him. And a threefold cord is not quickly broken" (Eccl. 4:12)

The cord is symbolic as "something" binding two things together… as one. Within the covenant of marriage, the Lord with His Spirit is that "Something" who also serves as Witness.

Sex between two individuals is symbolic and also emblematic of oneness because this union is the means whereby two divided people are able to become one and produce – another new creation called: children. The exponential implications of this covenant trace all the way back to our second dominion mandate: be fruitful and multiply (Gen. 1:28). Within the mystery of conception, oneness continues to be the recurring principle of God's kingdom: one… out of many… and many… out of One. The marriage covenant sets the highest standard of unity and oneness on earth because it all began in the presence of "The One" to facilitate the restoration of the kingdom of heaven on earth. Think back to the message of "rest" (which implies intimacy) as the type of "relationship in oneness" the Lord desires "with" His people.

Marriage must never be entered into lightly. Your marriage covenant with the Lord must never become complacent or common. Diligently honor the marriage vow.

Prayer with Thanksgiving

We often come before the Lord in prayer with a "list" of petitions for Divine intervention, but when was the last time you entered into prayer with praise and thanksgiving?

> "Enter into His gates with thanksgiving, and into
> His courts with praise. Be thankful to Him, and
> bless His name" (Psa. 100:4).

When we call to remembrance all the wonderful things God has done for us – with grateful hearts – we are rendering Glory (a good opinion) unto God for His lovingkindness. Too often we forget to "remember the testimony" concerning all the good things God has done for us. Take a moment to reflect on those things you're grateful for. Thank Him for the air you breathe and breath in your lungs. Thank Him for your heart that pumps life-blood through your veins. Thank Him for fingers and toes. Thank Him for all body parts and organs – even those which may not be working. Thank Him for eyes by which you are able to read these words and for ears to hear. Thank Him for the roof over your head and shoes on your feet. By now, some may have become discouraged because they lack functionality in some of these members (myself included), but I thank God for one thing above all broken members in my body: a sound mind and a willing heart that makes me one with the Father (1 Chron. 28:9). I focus not on what doesn't work or those members I've lost, but I rejoice nonetheless in His faithful promises to carry me in my weakness and sustain me until my end-of-days so that I may faithfully accomplish all that He commissioned me to do. Live by grace. Go thus, and do likewise.

> "For as the body is one and has many members, but
> all the members of that one body, being many, are
> one body, so also *is* Christ" (1 Cor. 2:12).

Our relationship from the perspective of oneness (individuals becoming one body) within the community of faith – is very powerful! Individually, praise with thanksgiving – opens the heart of the Divine – yet corporately, praise with thanksgiving initiates worship in the oneness of the One – under an open heaven – with angels in attendance. Hymns, choirs and organs are nice; praise and worship bands are nice; a-cappella worship initiated by the Spirit is awesome, yet hearing the sound of 300 voices in a room with only two hundred humans in attendance – is supernatural. Nothing anywhere on earth compares to this.

Thanksgiving acknowledges and is grateful for what you do have – not what you don't.

Praise rises up from hearts filled with thanksgiving to give credit, gratitude and adoration to God.

Thanksgiving and praise is what we offer to God; worship enables us to enter into oneness with the Spirit in the heavenly realm to exalt God – and give Him glory and honor.

Much of what I write about is merely preparing us – to do now – those very same things we will be doing eternally. My challenge to you is to operate now according to the pattern by which you will operate in the New Earth, for example:

> "And the nations of those who are saved shall walk in its light, and ***the kings of the earth bring their glory and honor into it***. [25] Its gates shall not be shut at all by day (there shall be no night there). [26] And they shall bring the glory and the honor of the nations into it" (Rev. 21:24-26).
>
> "And the name of the city from that day shall be: THE LORD IS THERE" (Ezek. 48:35).

Why wait for eternity... when you can live like an angel now. Worship the Lord in the beauty of His Majesty... now!

> ***"Give unto the Lord the glory due to His name; Worship the Lord in the beauty of holiness" (Psa. 29:2).***

Worship With Sacrifice

If what you do during worship is a requirement or an obligation, then no sacrifice is involved. Sacrifice involves going above and beyond that which was required of you. Go two miles when only one is requested. Thanksgiving with praise is mandatory in the house of God (as offerings), but when someone is able to offer praise and thanksgiving within the anguish of much adversity, brokenness and despair, I can assure you… heaven is listening! Sacrifices are being offered. God is close to the brokenhearted.

> "The Lord is near to those who have a broken heart, and saves such as have a contrite spirit" (Psa. 34:18).

> "The sacrifices of God are a broken spirit, a broken and a contrite heart— These, O God, You will not despise" (Psa. 51:17).

Truly, Jesus came to heal the brokenhearted (Isa. 61:1; Luke 4:18). In much the same way brokenness is able to yield praise – sacrifice is a component of worship. Something "unnatural" happens (or perhaps supernatural) in the moment when ordinary men take their eyes off self and off stuff and off circumstances in order to – focus on God – and enter in – to worship Him.

Worship always involves sacrifice, so when we worship the Lord, we should offer Him more than what is required; we should offer Him our best. Worship should always cost us something.

- "And Abraham [whom the Lord told to sacrifice his only son] said to his young men, "Stay here with the donkey; the lad and I will go yonder and worship, and we will come back to you" (Gen. 22:5)
- "This man went up from his city yearly to worship and sacrifice to the Lord of hosts in Shiloh" (1 Sam. 1:3)
- "But the Lord, who brought you up from the land of Egypt with great power and an outstretched arm, Him you shall fear, Him you shall worship, and to Him you shall offer sacrifice" (2 Kings 17:36)
- "Give to the Lord the glory due His name; bring an offering, and come before Him. Oh, worship the Lord in the beauty of holiness!" (1 Chron. 16:29)
- "Then King David said to Ornan, "No, but I will surely buy it for the full price, for I will not take what is yours for the

> Lord, nor offer burnt offerings with that which costs me nothing" (1 Chron. 21:24)

Ornan was willing to give King David his threshing floor, but David refused. He knew better because he understood this kingdom principle: worship involves sacrifice. This threshing floor later became the site the Temple.

> "Then Hezekiah commanded them to offer the burnt offering on the altar. And when the burnt offering began, the song of the LORD also began, with the trumpets and with the instruments of David king of Israel. ^{28} So all the assembly worshiped, the singers sang, and the trumpeters sounded; all this continued until the burnt offering was finished. ^{29} And when they had finished offering, the king and all who were present with him bowed and worshiped" (2 Chron. 29:27-29).

Worship is a sacrificial act that transcends obedience. Worshippers in spirit and in truth understand why worship involves love, adoration, exaltation – and reverential fear. The Lord is a God of love – a God of vengeance – a God of recompense – and a God of war!

Consider Job, the man of God like no other (Job 1:8). When catastrophic calamity came upon him, he worshipped the God who gives and takes away. So great was his distress that he was only able to "worship" God – once – during this entire ordeal. Some of you reading this know what Job was going through, as do I.

> "Then Job arose, tore his robe, and shaved his head; and he fell to the ground and worshiped" (Job 1:20)

When you get to the end of everything and there is nothing left to hang onto, then do what Job did. Follow his example – and worship God – and let God deliver you out of your distress. Job suffered, and then his friends offered sacrifices on his behalf (Job

42:8). Job suffered, and was eventually recompensed 200% by God for what he suffered through. Now then... be encouraged. Our struggle has been shortened. These light and momentary afflictions and "the sufferings of this present time are not worthy to be compared with the glory which shall be revealed in us" (Rom. 8:18; 1 Pet. 4:13). When we remain faithful to God and do not bring a charge against Him... regardless of whatever happens to us, when He returns, His reward is with Him (Isa. 40:10; Heb. 11:6).

He is the Potter – and we are the clay. Trust God. He is your Deliverer. Own this truth.

> "I beseech you therefore, brethren, by the mercies of God, that you present your bodies a living sacrifice, holy, acceptable to God, which is your reasonable *service* [*act of worship*; KJV]. ^{2} And do not be conformed to this world, but be transformed by the renewing of your mind, that you may prove what is that good and acceptable and perfect will of God Rom. 12:1, 2)

Worship is a form of imitation. When we worship God, we are choosing to deny many if not all aspects of who we are in order to enter into oneness with the Lord. We are sacrificing our individuality in order to be enjoined with the Lord and enter His Identity. How often do we feel this during worship? How often do we even sense His nearness? Awesome music and pious words will elevate our spirit, but the Lord is seeking souls who worship Him – in spirit and in truth (John 4:23, 24). The spirit within us was given to us by God (Eccl. 12:7; Ezek. 36:26; Dan. 6:3) to help us, as a living soul (Gen. 2:7), to enter into oneness with the Lord – and do all He commands.

> "For God has not given us a spirit of fear, but of power and of love and of a sound mind" (2 Tim. 1:7).

The good spirit God formed within us (Zech. 12:1)[102] assists our soul along the journey of life in a season called temporary so that our soul may continue to live eternally (Psa. 49:8, 9).

However, many have compromised this spirit with uncleanness and adopted other spirits to practice lawlessness, lewdness, lasciviousness and rebellion. When true conviction by the Spirit comes upon the heart of their soul, they will forsake these unlawful spirits and seek repentance from dead works, and then something truly remarkable happens: the soul is given a new heart and a new spirit. The remembrance by God of these former deeds – are completely erased – and even the former person himself – is rendered completely clean.

> "Then I will sprinkle clean water on you, and you shall be clean; I will cleanse you from all your filthiness and from all your idols. [26] I will give you a new heart and put a new spirit within you; I will take the heart of stone out of your flesh and give you a heart of flesh" (Ezek. 36:25, 26).

This new covenant with the Lord which involves the sacrifice of self upon the altar of repentance also includes a gift from God: the Holy Spirit.

> "I will put My Spirit within you and cause you to walk in My statutes, and you will keep My judgments and do them" (Ezek. 36:27).

In this moment, the repentant soul is restored to oneness with God and even the penalty has been removed – for His sake (Isa. 43:25; 1 John 2:12) – so that this new person (not new in time but new in character) is able to continue along the original path of life they started before they became sidetracked by sin and the desire to live according to sin.

---

[102] The Lord can place many spiritual attributes in our spirit to assist our soul. Read "Regensis" section titled: "The Spirit Of Man."

We are set free (from sin) through repentance and then we are set apart – to walk in holiness.

When we walk in holiness, the Spirit will enable our soul to be strengthened by our new spirit by His Spirit to continue along the path of grace and truth and live according to righteousness.

> "But seek first the kingdom of God and His righteousness, and all these things shall be added to you" (Matt. 6:33).

Oneness with the Lord enables us to perceive and experience the big picture of faith in Christ Jesus. These very words were only made possible by the Lord Himself. God loves us so much and His thoughts toward us are good always, yet we've all believed some dark lie and doubted His lovingkindness toward us… which caused us to create an alternate reality to reinforce some wound or offense that keeps us separated from the love of God.

> "Truly, this only I have found: that **God made man upright**, but **they have sought out many schemes**" Eccl. 7:29).

This is why Jesus came… to end the separation and remove the dividing wall of hostility between God and His beloved children. It was impossible for man to get right with God (which is called religion), so God sent Himself so man could be restored to Him by entering into a divine relationship – through faith in Jesus – and only Jesus! God desires man to be restored to his previous operating state of holiness – in heart, mind, soul and body – to operate in oneness with Him.

> "For I am persuaded that neither death nor life, nor angels nor principalities nor powers, nor things present nor things to come, [39] nor height nor depth, nor any other created thing, shall be able to separate us from the love of God which is in Christ Jesus our Lord" (Rom. 8:38, 39).

How can anyone refuse so great a love as this? Why – is perhaps – a better question?

Kingdom Built With Tithe

Many of us believe this: the truth will set you free. So let me ask: what did Jesus set you free from? What were you captive and in bondage to?

Many thoughts and ideas may be running through your mind right now, like: "What was I a captive of? Whose prisoner was I?" Let's answer those questions: you were taken captive of this world and held as a prisoner of Satan, who is the prince of darkness, and you were taught a worldly mindset that thinks and acts in rebellion against Jesus.

Through faith in Jesus, believers are set free, yet some still operate with a worldly mindset especially in regard to finances and the tithe. They think their stuff – is their stuff. Not so!

The interesting thing about worldly and spiritual kingdoms is – kingdoms have kings – and kings have the authority to expect things from you. Why? Because when a worldly king invades a territory and conquers a people, he now owns and controls everything and he will expect tribute. In a worldly sense, the trees in the forest and the gold in the soil belong to him (1 Kings 20:3). After the initial tribute come annual taxes to maintain your place in that kingdom. So, tribute and taxes must be paid to the king – or – one of two things happens: A) you are sold as a slave, or B) you are put in jail to die. Most people choose option #1: you agree to pay tribute and taxes.

If you don't pay taxes in any country, then what happens to you? Yup… you go to jail!

So I ask: is Jesus Lord of your life? If you say yes, that's fantastic! Since Jesus is Lord in you, then Jesus is also King over you. [pause and think about this for a moment]

Since King Jesus conquered your heart, then 100% of what you thought was yours actually belongs to Him. In fact, it already belonged to the King of the Universe before He conquered your heart, so don't reason around it. The earth belongs to Him. Everything on the earth belongs to Him. You are merely stewarding His things.

The wonderful thing about King Jesus is: He only demands 10% (the tithe). He lets you keep the 90 and expects you to be a good steward of His 90 that He has entrusted to you... and He expects you to create an increase with it. Your cars belong to Him, your house belongs to Him, and your children are His (Psa. 127:3)... and so forth. Everything belongs to Him. Even you body belongs to Him (1 Cor. 6:20). So what right, may I ask, do you have in withholding the tithe that rightly belongs to Him? What right? Are poor or rich people exempt? No, they are not!

I know someone who is living on 10% of their middle income salary – and they are still able to tithe. Tithing has nothing to do with ability or money management or how much you make – it has to do with your heart condition and whether Jesus truly is Lord in you and King over you.

We do not <u>give</u> a tithe. We <u>return</u> a portion of what rightfully belongs to Him. [103]

The word "holy" means: set aside, set apart from. Therefore, the tithe is holy. (Lev. 27:30)

Don't rob from God – what belongs to God!

> "Will a man rob God? Yet you have robbed Me! But you say, 'In what way have we robbed You?' In tithes and offerings. [9] You are cursed with a curse, For you have robbed Me, *even* this whole nation" (Mal. 3:8, 9)

---

[103] There are three types of tithe: free will (initially joyful response to salvation), obedience (the tithe) and sacrificial (offerings above the tithe). The tithe is an act of obedience; the sacrificial offering is an act of worship.

Let me challenge you with this thought: if you do not return the tithe to Him, then what are you spending the Kings money on? Deeply consider this predicament! What are you spending the King's money on? There are two kingdoms on this planet: the kingdom of God and the kingdom of darkness. *If you are not returning the tithe to King Jesus to establish the kingdom of heaven on earth, then you are robbing God of the tithe which is holy and belongs to Him.*

And furthermore, by not returning the tithe to King Jesus, you are – by default – spending that money to advance the kingdom of darkness. If you are using any portion of the tithe in this manner or for selfish personal pleasure, that is considered disobedience bordering on rebellion. Remember: King Jesus gave you two options: obedience to the King or slavery leading to death. Yes, Jesus will allow you to become a slave again to your own thoughts and imaginations leading to sin, but you are admonished to rule over this temptation – and make a firm determination to walk in obedience to what Jesus commands!

Which kingdom are you building with the 10% the Lord commanded to be tithed?

> Jesus said: "You are My friends if you do whatever I command you" (John 15:14).

Most people do not see King Jesus this way. They see Jesus as a kind, loving and merciful friend who forgives liberally... which is true. But He is also King and He has final authority on the Day of Judgment to judge your disobedience and cast both body and soul into hell's fire. Do you really think King Jesus will allow disobedient goats into Paradise with Him?

Absolutely not!

The tithe does not belong to you! The tithe belongs to King Jesus to establish the kingdom of heaven on earth. Whether you know it or not, your disobedience regarding the tithe is building the kingdom of His enemy. The money God entrusted to you – to tithe and steward the 90 on His behalf – must not be used against Him! Whose kingdom are you supporting with your 10%? Which kingdom are you sowing into? Do not rob God! Either you are for Jesus and you do His will – or – you are working against Him.

Tithing, then, employs two types of obedience: either obligatory because you have to (by law) – or as a free will offering (voluntary) because you want to! Align your will with the will of God – and be generously faithful and joyful with your giving to advance the kingdom of God.

Tithing is not a form of worship, as many churches erringly teach. Tithing is an act of obedience based upon a command. Offerings above the level of tithe are considered a voluntary sacrifice which is considered a form of worship. All acts of worship involve sacrifice (Gen. 22:5).

> "For if I do this willingly, I have a reward; but if against my will, I have been entrusted with a stewardship" (1 Cor. 9:17).

If you are faithful in the tithe, it is credited to you as obedience as someone entrusted with the stewardship of God's resources. However, everything you have belongs to Him and you were entrusted not only with the stewardship of God's resources (the tithe), you will also be held accountable for that which you were made a responsible partner of (the 90)… on God's behalf!

And another thing, you are not tithing to support the pastor's ministry or pay his salary. That perspective is worldly. In nearly every instance, pastors are brought to the Lord by a pastor who was brought to the Lord by another pastor and you are actually building upon and continuing the legacy of Apostles who were trained by the Lord Jesus Himself. You have a share in the Apostle's ministry and the Lord Himself when you honor Him with the tithe. In due time, this pastor will raise other pastors to continue the work of the gospel to build upon Christ's legacy!

The tithe is to be done... as unto the Lord Jesus Himself!!!

> "And whatever you do, do it heartily, as to the Lord and not to men" (Col. 3:23).

This spiritual truth will set you free from living in worldly captivity to disobedience. The person that sets you free, now – is you – from the tyranny of self in the kingdom of self!

Now, go and establish the kingdom of God... beginning with the tithe. Invest in the Kingdom!

> Jesus said: "Do not fear, little flock, for it is your Father's good pleasure to give you the kingdom" (Luke 12:32).

> "Then the King will say to those on His right hand, 'Come, you blessed of My Father, inherit the kingdom prepared for you from the foundation of the world" (Matt. 25:34).

The kingdom prepared for you – is your place in the New Earth – which is the inheritance for saints and faithful followers and servants of Jesus. This is the kingdom you've been sowing into the whole time, and it's the *'topos'* (topographic) place Jesus went to prepare for us (John 14:3).

True liberty in Christ is the freedom and willingness to do ALL that King Jesus says... and I close by saying this: ALL of His words are commands! "Return the tithe unto Me" says the Lord.

You will never be free unless Jesus is Lord *and* King over everything in your life.

I believe I hear the sound of chains breaking right now, in Jesus' name! Amen.

Tithing On Purpose

The Lord intended us to live as His faithful ones being generous in giving, and the tithe was instituted as "the minimum standard" of giving (or returning) that acknowledges "all" of it belongs to the Lord, so let me ask you this: is the tithe intended to put food in God's house for His consumption? What four things did the Lord specifically designate the tithe be used for?

> "I have brought the firstfruits of the land which you, O LORD, have given me.' "Then you shall set it before the LORD your God, and worship before the LORD your God. [11] So you shall rejoice in *every good thing which the LORD your God has given to you and your house, you and the Levite and the stranger who is among you*. [12] "When you have finished laying aside all the tithe of your increase in the third year—the year of tithing—*and have given it to [1] the Levite, [2] the stranger, [3] the fatherless, and [4] the widow, so that they may eat within your gates and be filled*, [13] then you shall say before the LORD your God: 'I have removed the holy tithe from my house, and also have given them to the Levite, the stranger, the fatherless, and the widow, according to all Your commandments which You have commanded me; I have not transgressed Your commandments, nor have I forgotten them. [14] I have not eaten any of it when in mourning, nor have I removed any of it for an unclean use, nor given any of it for the dead. I have obeyed the voice of the LORD my God, and have done according to all that You have commanded me. [15] Look down from Your holy habitation, from heaven, and bless Your people… " (Deut. 26:10-15).

The Old Covenant tithe was used mainly for three purposes: temple upkeep, supporting the Levites (the priestly line that ran the temple), and feeding the poor and strangers among them. This concept was carried forward into Christianity as New Covenant offerings intended to provide for: 1) ministers of the gospel, 2) orphans, 3) widows, and 4) strangers.

Can you see a problem in how we (the church) redirect the offering? How are we supposed to use it? Do we benefit the people that God intended us to help (even Abraham tithed to Melchizedek – a priest – before there was a Law), or do we use it based upon the dictates of deacons and elders? And yet the church (being apart from the Law) is still obligated to continue the principle of tithing because – if we didn't have some obligation to giving, the church would say: "My offering is dedicated to God" (Matt. 15:5) just like the Pharisees did, yet deny the greater requirements of the commandment: A) honor the Lord with the firstfruits – they are holy unto Him, and B) take care of one another... including the stranger in your land.

The minimum standard that God expects for the church in caring for PLOWS (the poor, lost, orphan, widow, stranger) – may be disregarded and then rendered as "unprofitable" by those with abundance and affluence in high estate... even within the church. The Lord put us alongside one another to take of one another! Does your church implement a one-third tithe?

Do we use the church offering for programs, utilities, insurance, the building fund and whatnot? Salaries for paid staff is permissible (i.e. do not muzzle the ox), but what about everything else? Do we implement a one-third budget as a dedicated offering toward these five people groups and then a two-third budget for whatever pleases us? The purpose of these questions is not to restrict our giving... but to influence church rules, laws and governance in keeping with God's original intent: assist those in need within the community, especially those "in the house" of God.

Consider what God told us we can do with the tithe if we are too far removed from the church:

> "But if the journey is too long for you, so that you are not able to carry the tithe, or if the place where the LORD your God chooses to put His name is too far from you, when the LORD your God has blessed you, ^{25} then you shall exchange it for money, take the money in your hand, and go to the place which the LORD your God chooses. ^{26} ***And you shall spend that money for whatever your heart desires***: for oxen or sheep, for wine or similar drink, for whatever your heart desires; you shall eat there before the LORD your God, and you shall rejoice, you and your household. ^{27} You shall not forsake the Levite who is within your gates, for he has no part nor inheritance with you" (Deut. 24:24-27).

Spend the money for whatever your heart desires… does not sound like any bible lesson or sermon I've ever heard preached. The desires of your heart (and mine) must include: rejoicing! If you tithe without rejoicing, then it has become a burdensome ordinance. The tithe must be used to advance the kingdom of heaven on earth as you: A) take care of your household and those whom He has entrusted to you; and B) take care of the Levite (i.e. any ministers that are under a commission to advance the kingdom of God) within your gates (community). The Lord wants to establish His kingdom – through you! The Lord wants happy followers that rejoice in doing well. Can you imagine what this world would be like if we spent our money joyfully on those things that matter most to God? Yes… it would be Paradise.

Consider the tithe as one way God connects our heart to His kingdom and His purpose on earth:

> "For where your treasure is, there your heart will be also" (Matt. 6:21).

> Meditate on that!

> "Do not lay up for yourselves treasures on earth, where moth and rust destroy and where thieves break in and steal; [20] but lay up for yourselves treasures in heaven, where neither moth nor rust destroys and where thieves do not break in and steal" (Matt. 6:19, 20).

Our heart is connected to our treasure; those things we value most are things we treasure most.

> Jesus said: "If you want to be perfect, go, sell what you have and give to the poor, and you will have treasure in heaven; and come, follow Me" (Matt. 19:21).

Kingdom of the Heavens

What you believe – creates the world you live in (both now and eternally).

> Jesus said: "Repent, for the kingdom of the heavens is at hand" (Matt. 4:17; literal Greek translation).

Which kingdom was Jesus referring to when He said this? The kingdom of heaven (on earth) is what Jesus proclaimed... so we should be expecting it and proclaiming it the same way He did.

Jesus came from Heaven as the Son of/from God to come against the kingdom of darkness on Earth and to teach us how to live as sons and daughters in God's kingdom of light.

> "No one has ascended to heaven but He who came down from heaven, *that is,* the Son of Man who is in heaven" (John 3:13)

"No one has ascended into heaven except Jesus" is a curious statement, but how can Jesus, who is the King of Heaven, be standing upon the earth and tell us that He is "in heaven"? Thus, I reveal a subtle yet enormous distinction between Heaven and heaven... which becomes one of the main keys to comprehending the scriptures. Heaven (small 'h') on earth is the presence of Jesus, and if Jesus abides in your heart through faith (Eph. 3:17), so does the presence of heaven.

> Jesus said: "The kingdom of God is within you" (Luke 17:21). [104]

---

[104] The term "kingdom of heaven" is found only in the gospel of Matthew. He was writing to Jewish people who regard the name of God with such religious zeal that they often substitute the word "heaven" for God. This subtle difference allows us to understand the kingdom of God better, especially in light of who Jesus is: Lord of heaven and earth! The kingdom of heaven and the kingdom of God represent the same reality of Christ's presence on earth.

When Jesus made these three statements, He made several very significant declarations: 1) I Am the King of Heaven; 2) I have authority to bring the tangible reality of heaven to earth; 3) the presence of God is in your midst; and 4) you must repent and turn away from the kingdom you are living in.

The reason Jesus could say this is because King Jesus is Lord of Heaven and Earth. Wherever King Jesus goes, He establishes His kingdom by His presence; and since Jesus abides within your earthen tabernacle according to faith, therefore – wherever you go, the Spirit of Jesus goes with you to do one very important thing: establish the kingdom of heaven through you wherever you go. So – let heaven out – and shift the atmosphere with love and grace wherever you go!

> "Heaven is My throne, and earth is My footstool.
> What house will you build for Me? says the Lord,
> or what is the place of My rest?" (Acts 7:49)

The kingdom Jesus wants us to build on earth – starts within us. Jesus gave His disciples authority with power to advance the kingdom of heaven on earth, which begins by building a heart-house for Him to permanently abide in your soul as you sojourn on earth. Whatever you do… is done through His abiding presence and Spirit within you. You are not doing it! You are allowing Jesus to be Lord in you – whereby the Lord is performing His works through you!

> "And I will give you the keys of the kingdom of heaven, and whatever you bind on earth will be bound in heaven, and whatever you loose on earth will be loosed in heaven" (Matt. 16:19).

As earthly representatives of Jesus, perhaps now you can apply this scripture as intended. "The kingdom of God is within you." The kingdom of God – includes heaven – and the church must thoroughly comprehend this: it's time to let heaven out! The atmosphere of Heaven will be manifested through obedient disciples of Jesus and they are given dominion authority (keys) to bind and loose things on earth – until Earth operates like Heaven.

The heavenly pattern for mankind is: imitate Jesus.
The earthly pattern for this world is: become like heaven.

The kingdom of heaven is a spiritual reality being established on earth – through the church – by disciples of Jesus Christ.

> "… and to make all see what is the fellowship of the mystery, which from the beginning of the ages has been hidden in God who created all things through Jesus Christ; [10] *to the intent that now the manifold wisdom of God might be made known by the church to the principalities and powers in the heavenly places*, [11] according to the eternal purpose which He accomplished in Christ Jesus our Lord" (Eph. 3:9-11).

Disciples who devote themselves to the Lord are entrusted to advance one of the three kingdoms (i.e. God's) while disregarding the kingdom of darkness (Satan's) and personal kingdoms which are insignificant and irrelevant to disciples because they know – the only kingdom that matters is God's kingdom, "the one which shall not be destroyed" (Dan. 7:14). However, before man could fulfill his mandate from Heaven to have dominion over the Earth (as the host of earth), Satan had to be vanquished by the Lamb of God… and rendered impotent.

> "If a kingdom is divided against itself, that kingdom cannot stand. [25] And if a house is divided against itself, that house cannot stand. [26] And if Satan has risen up against himself, and is divided, he cannot stand, but has an end. [27] *No one can enter a strong man's house and plunder his goods, unless he first binds the strong man. And then he will plunder his house*" (Mark 3:24-27).

Jesus bound Satan, the strong man, and now it's up to us to plunder his house (i.e. his demonic kingdom). How do we do this? We bind demonic authorities, powers and strongholds by using the same technique Jesus used when tempted by Satan: by rightly using the word of God as a weapon against Satan's lies and deception (Luke 4:1-13).

Jesus gave dominion authority to His disciples (which includes you) to plunder Satan's house:

> "Behold, I give you the authority to trample on serpents and scorpions, and over all the power of the enemy, and nothing shall by any means hurt you" (Luke 10:19).

Go therefore… and do likewise!

> "And these signs will follow those who believe: ***In My name they will cast out demons***; they will speak with new tongues" (Mark 16:17).

> "Heal the sick, cleanse the lepers, raise the dead, ***cast out demons***. Freely you have received, freely give" (Matt. 10:8).

The reason the church seems unable to do this… is because we really don't believe the truth!

Grant Them Dominion

But what exactly is dominion? ***Dominion – is the delegated authority with power given to a subordinate to act on behalf of a sovereign.***

Jesus told His disciples they were given authority with power to come against "all the power of the enemy." You were not given a just little power. The same Spirit that raised Jesus from the dead – with power – dwells in you! When Jesus abides in you, all the rights of His kingdom, His power and His dominion are resident within you.... as well as His Spirit! You are acting on behalf of the Sovereign One abiding in you – who is doing it through you.

> "But if the Spirit of Him who raised Jesus from the dead dwells in you, He who raised Christ from the dead will also give life to your mortal bodies through His Spirit who dwells in you" (Rom. 8:11).

Dominion, as best and as simply as it can be defined, is "the delegated right to act."

Dominion is often preached from man's perspective, but rarely understood from God's perspective. The best way to put man's dominion of earth into context is to see God's purpose for man's stewardship of earth – and how it was granted (then delivered) to him by God:

- "And Jesus came and spoke to them, saying, "All authority has been given to Me in heaven and on earth" (Matt. 28:18).
- Dominion of heaven and earth in God's kingdom belongs to the Lord Jesus Christ; "For by Him all things were created that are in heaven and that are on earth, visible and invisible, whether thrones or ***dominions*** or principalities or powers. *All things were created through Him and for Him*" (Col. 1:16). "Then to Him was given dominion and glory and a kingdom, that all peoples, nations, and languages should serve Him. His dominion is an everlasting dominion, which shall not pass away, *and His kingdom the one which shall not be destroyed*" (Dan. 7:14).
- The Lord God gave (granted) the dominion of earth to the host of earth; "Then God said, "Let Us make man in Our image, according to Our likeness; ***let them have dominion*** over the fish of the sea, over the birds of the air, and over the cattle, ***over all the earth*** and over every creeping thing that creeps on the earth." (Gen. 1:26). "So God created man

in His own image" (v.27) and our Creator's name is... Jesus Christ.
- Adam was put in the Garden of God with dominion in order to be a steward and caretaker for the earth, but Adam delivered man's dominion to Satan when he successfully tempted Adam in getting him to rebel against God. This is the same dominion that Satan tempted Jesus with: "Then the devil, taking Him [Jesus] up on a high mountain, showed Him all the kingdoms of the world in a moment of time. [6] And the devil said to Him, "***All this authority*** I will give You, and their glory; for this ***has been delivered to me***, and I give it to whomever I wish. [7] Therefore, if You will worship before me, all will be Yours." (Luke 4:5-7).
- Jesus accomplished perfectly the will of the Father and got this dominion and all authority back. "At that time Jesus answered and said, "I thank You, Father, Lord of heaven and earth, that You have hidden these things from the wise and prudent and have revealed them to babes. [26] Even so, Father, for so it seemed good in Your sight. [27] ***All things have been delivered to Me by My Father***, and no one knows the Son except the Father. Nor does anyone know the Father except the Son" (Matt. 11:25-27).
- And now Jesus has given it back to us; "***Behold, I give you the authority*** to trample on serpents and scorpions, and over all the power of the enemy, and nothing shall by any means hurt you" (Luke 10:19).
- And furthermore, Jesus said: "***And I will give you the keys of the kingdom of heaven***, and whatever you bind on earth will be bound in heaven, and whatever you loose on earth will be loosed in heaven" (Matt. 16:19).

Man was created for the earth – and earth was created for man. This should help explain the complexity of man's reason and purpose upon earth, as well as our positional relationship and subordinate dependence upon Jesus within a larger context. Our creeds and doctrines have correctly taught us "what" to believe, but they have not taught us the whole truth as to "why."

We were sent to earth to usher in a regime change – from darkness to light! We are world changers sent to manifest Christ's dominion, under His authority – with His power manifested through us.

We were sent to establish the kingdom of heaven – on earth!

> Jesus said, "As the Father has sent Me, I also send you." (John 20:21).

We have been entrusted with much… and we are able to accomplish much in the name of Jesus, who alone is worthy to receive all glory and honor and dominion! However, it's so easy to get off track on this planet because this ever-present darkness surrounding us seeks to confuse us and utterly destroy us, but there is a solution:

> "But seek first the kingdom of God and His righteousness, and all these things shall be added to you" (Matt. 6:33).

This is highly significant. Jesus wants us to seek the kingdom of God in order to escape the kingdom of darkness – and He wants us to seek *His Righteousness*! Jesus is "the Righteousness of God" i.e. *Jehovah Tsidkenu*: The Lord our Righteousness (Jer. 23:6; 33:16). Mankind has been offered two things – and it is a package deal! You cannot "enter" the kingdom of heaven unless you have also declared your sovereign allegiance to the King of Heaven: Jesus. And you cannot seek and find the kingdom of God apart from the guidance of the Spirit of God.

It's a package deal! Hosting the King of Heaven produces the kingdom of heaven in your midst.

"Have dominion" is God's first command to man. We were given His authority with power to act, but as so often is the case, man uses these God-given gifts to accomplish his own agenda, whereby the history of man on the earth has been a constant tug-of-

war between saints establishing God's dominion and unregenerate men exercising domination to build nations at the expense of many souls.

Not all who build "In the name of Jesus" are doing so with right motives.

Kingdom of Heaven People

> "Not everyone who says to Me, 'Lord, Lord,' shall enter the kingdom of heaven, but he who does the will of My Father in heaven. [22] Many will say to Me in that day, 'Lord, Lord, have we not prophesied in Your name, cast out demons in Your name, and done many wonders in Your name?' [23] And then I will declare to them, 'I never knew you; depart from Me, you who practice lawlessness!!" (Matt. 7:21-23)

Oftentimes we do things in God's name… but we do it with impure motives. Unless our agenda has been determined by the Lord, our agenda-driven life will amount to nothing in the end. Doing good things is irrelevant unless God gets the glory from those things. We should always be ready to ask this question: "If what I am about to do does not give glory to God, should I do it?" The answer is: no! If you can't give God glory for doing it, then simply put: don't do it!

The ability to give God glory by the work we do – is the litmus test to check the motivation of our heart before we do anything. Hearing His voice is the means we confirm the will of God is being done – before – we start building or doing anything.

> "My sheep hear My voice, and I know them, and they follow Me" (John 10:27).

Do you believe in a doctrine that says you have a personal relationship with Jesus – or do you "have" a personal relationship with Jesus by hearing His voice and obeying His message?

> "Pilate therefore said to Him, "Are You a king then?" Jesus answered, "You say rightly that I am a king. For this cause I was born, and for this cause [reason] I have come into the world, that I should bear witness to the truth. ***Everyone who is of the truth hears My voice***" (John 18:37).

If you claim Jesus dwells in you, how wonderful (He dwells temporarily in everyone because God is everywhere – without exception). Yet Jesus wants to permanently abide in you – and you in Him – because in Him we have life eternal by the Spirit He has given (John14:20; 15:5-8; 1 John 3:24; 4:13; 5:11, 12, 20). If His Spirit dwells within you, then your fervent desire must always be: hear His word, keep His word, obey His word, be His disciple and live according to righteousness and truth.

> "Now he who keeps His commandments abides in Him, and He in him. And by this we know that He abides in us, by the Spirit whom He has given us" (1 John 3:24).

Entering into the kingdom of heaven is not man's ascension in Heaven... but rather, man's conversion to live according to the truth within a personal relationship with Jesus Christ!

Kingdom-of-heaven people are disciples who do one thing really, really well: hear His voice, understand the message and obey Him. Yes, that is one thing! Disciples know what I mean. They understand maintaining a personal relationship with Him is not something done for fifty minutes on Sunday morning. Maintaining an intimate relationship with the Lord is what defines them every moment of every day. They are always listening and always ready to respond obediently to whatever the Lord requests... and all His requests are commands.

This is not just ordinary faith... this is saving faith in action!

Throughout my Christian life, I've prayed this prayer: "Lord, if you make your will perfectly clear to me, I will never disobey you." Disciples are always ready to obey – even when it doesn't go their way – even when it hurts! Disciples are under a commission to do what the Master says… in every circumstance and situation.

Debate – is not an option.

When the Lord tells us to do something, we may reason with God according to Christ's example (Luke 22:42), but this form of reasoning is not a worldly type of reasoning by which positions are debated resulting in compromise. When the Lord says, "Come, let us reason together" (Isa. 1:18), He is actually telling us – come to your senses and adopt His position on the matter!

> "What is man that You are mindful of him, and the son of man that You visit him" (Psa. 8:4).

God is mindful of man. God has thoughts and plans for us (Jer. 29:11-13), and God wants us to adopt His position on the matter. So it seems only logical… for us to become more mindful of God's thoughts, God's ways and God's things. This is His planet within His universe, and it's non-negotiable. You are free at any time to create your own world, which God allows, but in the end… it results in futility… it's a chasing after wind.

By faith, we will do what the Lord tells us – and through faith, the Lord regards us as friends. We cannot refer to Jesus as "friend" unless we hear His voice – and – obey His commands!

> "You are My friends ***IF*** you do whatever I command you" (John 15:14).

Heaven-hearted and Heaven-minded

Think about the kingdom of heaven, not as a physical place per se, but as an event happening in the heart and mind of your soul. We are kingdom builders who were sent to exercise God's authority to have dominion over the earth, and to invade and occupy earth with the atmosphere of heaven.

- Think about the food you eat – what goes into you becomes oneness with you; when the Spirit of grace is in you, the you begin to operate in oneness with the Spirit
- Think about the air you breathe – you cannot see it, but this breath sustains your life; when the Spirit dwells in you, the Spirit is life – both now and eternally

"Another parable He spoke to them: "The kingdom of heaven is like leaven, which a woman took and hid in three measures of meal till it was all leavened" (Matt. 13:33).

Saints were sent from Heaven to usher in a regime change on earth – partnered with the Spirit of God dwelling in them – which represents yet another way to interpret this scripture regarding leaven. Once heavenly truth by the Spirit becomes operational within us – much like leaven in bread – we will be changed and transformed to think heavenly thoughts whereby we are able to accomplish our primary objective: have dominion and establish the kingdom of heaven on earth.

The kingdom of heaven on earth is quite mysterious, which is why few find it because many cling to the kingdom they see... which is the one that will be destroyed.

God has always been seeking Noah's, Abraham's, Gideon's, Esther's, Moses', Sampson's, David's, Mary's, Isaiah's, Jeremiah's, Ruth's and Enoch's – to walk with Him and host His presence. God created us as the host of earth to host His presence whereby we yield our will in subordination to His will for this earth... which happens when we yield the sovereignty of our mind to the guidance of the Holy Spirit... and exalt Jesus upon the throne of our heart.

Being connected to the kingdom of God by the Spirit of God represents the kingdom of heaven (in man) on earth. Like a branch attached to a vine or a house protected from storms by a firm foundation and a strong '*oikodome*-3619' spiritual covering, the Lord spoke many timeless parables to teach us about the kingdom of heaven which has been ***established in us, by grace – and is manifested through us, through faith***. But Jesus also spoke a warning to us because the kingdom of "this world" is violently opposed to the kingdom of God… and His saints.

> "And from the days of John the Baptist until now the kingdom of heaven suffers violence, and the violent take it by force" (Matt. 11:12).

The kingdoms and powers and principalities and dominions of this world, which are demonic in nature, will do everything in their power to prevent the kingdom of Christ from being established – in you and through you. This world operates according to – the spirit of antichrist.

Two kingdoms are at war… and by faith… you've been placed on active duty military! Stand your ground! The enemy will seek you out and exploit your vulnerabilities. The enemy will attack you through doubt and many deceitful lies. The enemy will question your true identity in Christ and tempt you to deny His calling on your life. The enemy will make you feel insecure, insignificant and inferior every single chance it can – because if it can thwart the work of God through a disciple like you – then hundreds will fall by the wayside… or perhaps worse even… advance the kingdom of darkness.

Heaven On Earth

The title for this section seems a misnomer, but it isn't even though the darkness which surrounds us appears to be winning. Well, it isn't because Jesus already won the battle and claimed victory over the darkness! We were sent as heavens solution to this world's problems.

Jesus said: "I am the light of the world. He who follows Me shall not walk in darkness, but have the light of life" (John 8:12).

> Jesus said of us: "You are the light of the world" (Matt. 5:14).
>
> Jesus also said: "As the Father has sent Me, I also send you." (John 20:21).

Jesus was sent by the Father from Heaven to earth, and likewise... the Father sent you. You may not totally understand how this is possible, but it's really quite simple if you can imagine yourself as an eternal soul without the earth suit that was inserted into the fabric of time by the Holy Spirit when mommy and daddy came together in marital bliss. Your soul is eternal (Psa. 49:8, 9) both pre and post humanity. Your soul had a prior state of existence in the presence of your heavenly Father (which we have no remembrance of; Isa. 43:18; 65:17), and you were sent to earth by the Father as a representative of Heaven to do one thing:

Establish the kingdom of heaven on Earth!

What I am about to share with you is the ultimate big picture to understand life on earth.

1. God created us in His Own image according to His likeness (Gen. 1:26, 27) – to be His representational image and operate in the likeness of Jesus (which includes thinking and acting like Him).

2. God created man to have dominion over the earth – and do it according to His plan: through your spirit guided by God's Spirit (Gen. 1:26-28).

3. You are a member of an invading army called "the host of earth" (Gen. 2:1) with a specific mission to overthrow the kingdom of darkness that took earth captive to sin and death. Even the earth itself has been groaning in bondage

to this darkness waiting for the sons of God to be revealed and the restoration of earth (Rom. 8:19).

4. Elohim (capital 'E' God) – calls the sons of men: *elohims* (John 10:34, 35).[105]

5. Heaven is God's throne – and God sent us to advance the kingdom of heaven on earth.

God's Garden, the Paradise of God, is called: Eden – and God formed the first man of this invading army with the dust of His garden and then placed Adam in "his" own garden eastward of Eden (Gen. 28) called: eden (little 'e' change made by the author to illustrate a point).

Do you see the pattern: everything we do on this planet is subordinate to God and His kingdom: Heaven/heaven, Elohim/elohims; Eden/eden, Son of God/sons of God, Lord/lord, Spirit/spirit.

Jesus said: "The kingdom of the heavens is at hand" (Matt. 4:17; literal Greek translation).

What I am about to tell you is without question the most liberating truth you shall ever comprehend: God sent you here to establish the kingdom of the heavens (small h) – in His name.

To comprehend this you must understand – your soul has two parts: mind and heart. Your mind is the "thinker" and your heart is the "knower." The heaven you initiate with your mind – to establish a permanent abiding place for God to dwell in your heart-house – will become your *'mone'* eternal home. Therefore: ***your heart is a heavenly place.*** To the extent your mind is willing and able to establish a heart-home for God – is also your ability to establish nations and kingdoms on this planet for His sake in His name – which shall become your eternal inheritance.

---

[105] Elohim (little 'e') means: lacking little of God.

"He who overcomes shall inherit all things, and I will be his God and he shall be My son" (Rev. 21:7).

The kingdom of God is comprised of three permanent realms: Heaven, Earth and Hell. With this in mind, ponder deeply what Jesus said about man:

"The kingdom of God is within you" (Luke 17:21).

There are two kingdoms: one within you (Luke 17:21) and one around you.

The kingdom you are building in your heart is the kingdom God gives you as your inheritance in the New Earth. What you receive – ultimately depends upon you. The kingdom you inherit – is the world you are creating in your heart. What you believe – creates the world you live in – both now and eternally! Meditate on that!

"The kingdom of God within you operates according to the spirit to become manifest through you, but the kingdom of darkness that is around you operates according to sin to invade you and take you captive. I hope you can see this: two kingdoms are at work – one within you as an inner working to become manifest through your spirit, and the other around you that is trying to invade and control you through your flesh. Saints – we are being pulled apart in two directions!

"Inside out – or outside in – represent two spiritual kingdoms that are working life or death through you. You are a member of an invading army sent by God to usher in a regime change in this world, and our adversary is invading us through our flesh with sin to prevent us from accomplishing our mission to have dominion over him. We are at war... and the mind is the battlefield. The body is either an instrument of peace or lawlessness, yet this choice is yours!

"God gave you your body to be used as an instrument of

righteousness for His glory, but Satan is using your body as an instrument against you. He is using your own body as a weapon against you! How does he do this? He is speaking into your mind by tempting you with corrupt thoughts to act according to lawlessness. Literally, he is bombarding us with corrupt thoughts, songs, images, doctrines, attitudes, perceptions, feelings, and emotions – with things that are not aligned with the truth of God so we might act upon any of them and free-fall into bondage to lawlessness, sin, depression, despair and ultimately… disobedience leading to death. Please comprehend this one truth: your "temporary" body is being used by God to sanctify you **_and_** it is also being used by Satan to keep you captive to sin and death. How you allow God or Satan to influence your mind to use your body (your earthen vessel) is the mystery of man upon the earth. And yet, the spirit within us is the key to comprehending this mystery of Christ dwelling in us.

"You are in the world, but not of it!"[106]

> "I have given them Your word; and the world has hated them because they are not of the world, just as I am not of the world. [15] ***I do not pray that You should take them out of the world, but that You should keep them from the evil one***. [16] They are not of the world, just as I am not of the world. [17] Sanctify them by Your truth. Your word is truth. [18] As You sent Me into the world, I also have sent them into the world" (John 17:14-18).

The attributes of Earth were formed upon you, the attributes of God reside within your spirit (which is your divine nature; 2 Pet. 1:4), eternity was placed in your heart (Eccl. 3:11), and you were sent on a mission into the kingdom of darkness (i.e. this world) to come against the powers of Hell. This is why it seems you are being torn in half: two kingdoms are at war for your soul – and they are pulling you apart at the seams.

---

[106] Excerpts from "Commission" section titled "Two Kingdoms In Conflict."

The battle is being waged in your mind!

Your mind is the intersect between these kingdoms and you must decide which one you are going to focus on and submit your allegiance to. We are psychotic to think we can live peacefully in both kingdoms whereby many mental illnesses result, and thus, failing to spiritually comprehend what is happening to us is wreaking havoc in our minds. Craziness happens! This impossible journey seems utterly hopeless and crazy except for one thing: the Holy Spirit of God... who speaks to us all the time to guide our thoughts and help us deliberate our next steps.

There is a solution to this problem:

> "You must be born again" (John 3:7).

Believing in Jesus will initiate the faith journey to trust Jesus and go all in... whereby you must complete the transformation process that faith requires called: sanctification. You were saved (salvation) from death to life to walk in newness of life for one purpose: to imitate Jesus. You are being saved (sanctification) to be born anew and transformed (changed) by the Spirit in order to think like Jesus before you can act like Him.

> "Let this mind be in you which was also in Christ Jesus" (Phil. 2:5).

Church members who say they are saved through faith in Christ Jesus have been taught they have been born again, but this is a misnomer: salvation and transformation are two separate processes. ***Salvation brings conviction to your heart – transformation brings renewal to your mind.*** If you are saved but you still act like the world around you, then I hate to say this: you haven't been born again. You are still trapped in the operating system of sin. You can claim it but you cannot own it unless your thought process has been radically altered by the Holy Spirit.

Instead of asking this question – are you saved, perhaps we should ask: "Are you being sanctified and changed?" Disciples know what I'm talking about, but goats only get confused.

Jesus is Savior – and Jesus is Lord! Being born anew by the Spirit is a very significant spiritual transformational process which requires you to render yourself completely dead to the cares of this world (Gal. 2:20) as a living sacrifice and declare Jesus Lord of your life (which was His life to begin with; John 14:6). Your total allegiance to Jesus is the initial step in the transformational process – into newness – through truth, change and oneness. If you haven't been changed or are unwilling to be changed, then newness within your mind hasn't happened yet.

> "I beseech you therefore, brethren, by the mercies of God, that you present your bodies a living sacrifice, holy, acceptable to God, which is your reasonable service. ² And do not be conformed to this world, but ***be transformed by the renewing of your mind***, that you may prove what is that good and acceptable and perfect will of God" (Rom. 12:1, 2).

It is mission critical to comprehend this: you cannot accomplish what Jesus commands – if you cannot hear His voice. A hardened heart is one of the main reasons we cannot hear the Voice of Truth. If your heart is hardened, you need the conviction of the Holy Spirit to break through; if you are not operating in your right mind (sound mind) and are unable to understand the message of the gospel, then you must allow the Holy Spirit to renew your mind – with truth!

I will over-emphasize this point every chance I get because it is so vital to comprehend: you must be born anew!!!

> "You cannot *understand* (*oida*)[107] the kingdom of God unless you are born anew" (John 3:3).

---

[107] Most Bibles translate '*oida*' as "see" and also as "tell" in verse 8, but is better translated as perceive, understand.

You were sent here to establish the kingdom of heaven on earth. If you do not understand how the kingdom of God operates, this then is the litmus test that determines if you have been born anew – or not. You cannot establish it… unless you understand it and you've been trained in righteousness by the Holy Spirit to walk according to the truth – and live it.

When Jesus is Lord of your life, Jesus abides in you, heaven abides in you, His Spirit guides you… and now it's up to you to establish the kingdom of the heavens by yielding your will to do the will of the Father. The only way this is possible is by a renewed mind!

Angel Army On Earth

God has a plan for the earth and this plan includes the sons of men. We were created on purpose for this purpose: have dominion – and establish the kingdom of heaven here!

The main problem preventing us from understanding our mission and embracing our individual commission… is too much toxic theology coupled with small-minded thinking. So I ask: since God created us as the host (army) of earth to have dominion over the earth, don't you think our Commander would have given us all the tools we need to accomplish our mission? Indeed, He has! What, then, do we seem to be overlooking in our quest to understand? "What" is the answer! "What is man that you are mindful of him" (Psa. 8:4) is our quest to comprehend.

The Spirit tutored me on this subject regarding "what" man is for over five years and it seems the spirit He formed within us (Zech. 12:1) is the key to unraveling the mystery of man upon the earth. We are spiritual beings having a human experience! ***Jesus is God and He never stopped being God while walking on this planet***; however, He never operated out of His Divine Nature. All the miracles, signs and wonders Jesus performed were accomplished by operating out of His spirit (small 's') for one gigantic reason: in order to teach us how to do it. The Son of God came to teach us how to live like sons and daughters of God. "For such is the kingdom of heaven."

God (i.e. Jesus) did not need to be filled with the Holy Spirit (Luke 4:1, 14), yet it happened this way in order to teach us by example what we must do – in order to imitate His example.

The spirit that God gave us is no different in this regard. We are able to accomplish greater works – through our spirit – i.e. when we operate according to grace through faith… yet we are handicapped in these efforts while walking in sin. The spirit within us… is the key to operating as saints on earth to establish the kingdom of heaven – HERE – through faith!

The spirit, in this regard, is given by God to assist our soul and to attain and maintain our spiritual state of communion with Him – and to live in divine relationship and oneness with Him! God's commission for every believer is to become a disciple of Jesus Christ so as to continue the Lord's work – in us and through us – here, now and eternally.

> "In Him you also *trusted,* after you heard the word of truth, the gospel of your salvation; in whom also, having believed, you were sealed **with the Holy Spirit** of promise" (Eph. 1:13).

The Holy Spirit sealed you, not just for redemption and salvation and sanctification, but also as ambassadors of the Living God to operate in the similitude of Jesus according to His example. In order to accomplish this, we (our soul) is given a new heart and a new spirit… along with the indwelling Holy Spirit… to complete the spiritual transformation process by renewing our mind… to have a sound mind… so we think like Jesus.

In the new birth, we become a new creation and we're given the tools we need wherein the new spirit within us is the key to walking in dominion authority with "the keys of the kingdom" to establish the kingdom of heaven on earth. Consider this very important concept Jesus taught:

> "Take heed that you do not despise one of these little ones, for I say to you that ***in heaven their angels always see the face of My Father who is in heaven***" (Matt. 18:10).

This scripture seems to indicate we have an angel as part of our spiritual assignment on earth, but examine it closely. We are soul with spirit within a human body, so assemble these facts in your mind: you have an angel; your angel sees your heavenly Father's face; and your Father is in Heaven. So, now, there is only one condition whereby these facts may be unified: your spirit is your angel and the Father is in you! And so is heaven! And so is eternity (Eccl. 3:11)! ***Your angel is none other than your spirit that was given to you by God – to host His presence with your heart*** – whereby everywhere you go on planet earth – God goes with you!!!

Let the epiphany happen in your mind!

You may reject this idea initially, but it is fully supported by scripture including many teachings by Jesus on the subject, so read "The Last Chapter" in "Gateways" to learn more about this.

Men are gateways manifesting either heaven in the midst of chaos – or chaos in the midst of heavenly places on earth. ***Your heart is a heavenly place.*** You are a member of the host of earth who is either a kingdom builder for the kingdom of the heavens… or the kingdom of hell!

The original spirit God formed within us is angelic in nature and we were all born in a state of grace, but all of us entered into the paradigm of sin through free will… whereby the light within us began to get obscured until it seems… we lost the light. Sin acts like a veil of darkness that covers our spirit and prevents us from being what God created us to be: the host of earth. Consider what Jesus said about Judas – one of His disciples:

> Jesus answered them, "Did I not choose you, the twelve, and one of you is a devil?" (John 6:70).

Judas allowed his spirit to be corrupted through demonic influence, Jesus called him a devil, and shortly thereafter Satan entered Judas which led to the crucifixion of our Lord and King.

> "Now after the piece of bread, Satan entered him. Then Jesus said to him, "What you do, do quickly" (John 13:27).

What the soul thinks and does... affects the kingdom of our spirit... which has a direct effect upon our soul and our eternal destination. This concept is very important to grasp: our soul (by thoughts we think in our mind and plant in our heart) produces an act of our will. We decide to do it (our will) – and then we act on it. The thoughts we think will have an effect upon our heart and our spirit. Some of us have become like Judas: our heart has been hardened and our spirit has become darkened whereby... some are walking around as devils under the influence of demons and unclean spirits. A radical work of God's grace is the only thing that can save such a person.

> "But if your eye is bad, your whole body will be full of darkness. If therefore the light that is in you is darkness, how great is that darkness!" (Matt. 6:23).

The solution to man's predicament on earth is to be born anew by the Spirit of God.

In the new birth, we are given a new heart and a new spirit (Ezek. 36:26) plus the seal of the Spirit as a guarantee (v.27) to keep us under guard and guide us in the truth.

Jesus gave us insight into the solution to the problem: become like little children. Little children, in this regard, represent those very small children that do not know their left from their right – i.e. they do not have the knowledge of good and evil; they are under grace. The new birth enables us to become new again – just like little children – living under grace. We are born anew to walk in grace... under grace... just as we did while as little children before we knew sin.

> Jesus said, "Assuredly, I say to you, unless you are converted and become as little children, you will by no means enter the kingdom of heaven" (Matt. 18:3).

As little children – we are angelic, but sin corrupted our thought process and then we began to act unreasonable, illogical, disobedient, impenitent, rebellious, deranged and demonic. We were deceived to act independently of parents (and God) and enter into rebellion against God. Sin creates something (an environment) around us that is opposed to the things of God and the mind of Christ whereby our actions reflect the demonic powers influencing us – whereby little children throw tantrums... and eventually some became reprobate – meaning: failed the test!

> "And even as they did not like to retain God in their knowledge, God gave them over to a debased [reprobate] mind, to do those things which are not fitting" (Rom. 1:28).

But... the Good News of Jesus Christ is: God can redeem anything... including all the mistakes we've made while walking apart from Him in rebellion against Him.

We were created as image bearers to reflect the image placed within us... according to His Own likeness (Gen. 1:27), but we've all forgotten "what" we are and what we were created to do: host His presence as the host of earth. What do you see when you look in the mirror: do you see a child of God? Do you see someone on fire for Jesus? That, my friend, is the image you must behold in the mirror.

> "But we all, with unveiled face, beholding as in a mirror the glory of the Lord, are being transformed into the same image from glory to glory, just as by the Spirit of the Lord" (2 Cor. 3:18).

Are you beginning to see what has been happening to you during your sojourn? We partnered with deceitful lies to adopt the ways of this world and we fell out of grace into the paradigm of sin…. HOWEVER… the good news of Jesus Christ is this: through faith and repentance, we are adopted back into the family of God! We fell from grace into sin – yet through repentance we can reject sin and return to the paradigm (kingdom) of grace and good works. Amen!

The kingdom of grace and mercy requires us to reject sin and walk in the truth!

Through the new birth by the Spirit, we are becoming like little children again; we are being restored and returned to a prior operating system called "grace" when we reject the operating system of "this world" called – sin. In the new birth, we are given a new heart and a new spirit along with the indwelling Holy Spirit to accomplish our God-given commission. So I ask: how can we continue in sin if we've been born anew according to grace? This is illogical.

> "What shall we say then? Shall we continue in sin that grace may abound? [2] Certainly not! How shall we who died to sin live any longer in it?" (Rom. 6:1, 2)

Which kingdom do you want to dwell in eternally? Which kingdom are you building in your heart right now? That is what this book is about: kingdoms! What does your heart-kingdom look like? This shall be your eternal kingdom, so choose wisely.

When Jesus taught about the judgment and resurrection (Matt. 25:31-45)… "Inherit the kingdom prepared for you" has an interesting twist which (btw) is being prepared "by you" as you either host God's presence and Spirit while doing God's will here – or (negatively) demons and unclean spirits from the Pit of Hell (v.41). So, make the world a better place while you're here.[108] Therefore, I fervently challenge you: live like an angel... while you still have the light... and save others held captive in darkness.

Consider the significance of these two parables within the context of "heavens" on earth:

- "Again, the kingdom of heaven is like treasure hidden in a field, which a man found and hid; and for joy over it he goes and sells all that he has and buys that field" (Matt. 13:44)
- "Again, the kingdom of heaven is like a merchant seeking beautiful pearls, ^{46} who, when he had found one pearl of great price, went and sold all that he had and bought it" (Matt. 13:45. 46)

Some have asked: why would someone find treasure in one field, and then hide it another field and then buy that field? Why not just take the treasure from one field and go your own way? Well, it seems – that treasure only comes with that other field – it's a package deal. The King of Heaven and the field of heaven in your heart – are a package deal! The new field you purchase is the new heart you receive through repentance – and the Treasure (or Pearl) is the presence of Jesus who sits on the throne of your new spiritual heart.

The main point of both parables is: sell all and go ALL IN! Put all your effort and hope in eternal things to secure this eternal field and host the presence of Jesus in your heart.

"Inherit the kingdom prepared for you"... was prepared "by you" while doing God's will HERE... followed by the resurrection of life HERE. You get out of it what you put into it!

---

[108] It seems this idea was coded upon our soul since the beginning: "Leave this world better than you found it."

> "Do not be deceived, God is not mocked; for whatever a man sows, that he will also reap" (Gal. 6:7).

Either good or evil... physical or spiritual... angel or devil... we reap what we sow. How could it be otherwise! You are building the kingdom of your future self – in eternity – right now!

Whatever we sow in this life... we reap in the next.

Do you have any idea what you will be doing when you get to the other side? Or do you have any idea what you will be like? The reason this seems like such a great mystery is because our heaven-only doctrines teach us we will be in heaven, but they cannot teach us what we will be doing because... evidence for living this way is not found in the scriptures. So let me put this as simply as possible: the best (or worst) you are in this life is who you will continue to be in eternity. Your soul is who you really are... and your soul is eternal. When you wake up on the other side, you will still be who you truly are – with the same mind and heart of your soul that you are in this life.... but now... with life eternal. You reap what you sow. You sow it here – and you will reap it HERE! Therefore, I say... GO ALL IN! Live as a disciple of Jesus. Truly I say: it only gets better when you live this way for Jesus!

Seeds – represent those thoughts we produce in our mind and then plant in our heart.

> "Most assuredly, I say to you, unless a grain of wheat falls into the ground and dies, it remains alone; but if it dies, it produces much grain" (John 12:24).

> "But he who received seed on the good ground is he who hears the word and understands it, who indeed bears fruit and produces: some a hundredfold, some sixty, some thirty" (Matt. 13:23).

KINGDOMS

When we perceive our purpose on earth only from a spiritual perspective, we may have little regard for earthly things, but when we perceive our purpose from a kingdom perspective, we will see everything we accomplish on this earth from a spiritual perspective. We are all returning HERE to the New Earth... and we will inhabit homes and tend gardens for which we did not toil. This concept appears numerous times within many Old Covenant promises – which also applies to God's larger plan that includes the Promised Land (the New Earth) for man in the regeneration. We are building our own spiritual kingdom of heavens with homes, towns, cities and nations – and if glory is attached to it – these will be inhabited by saints in the regeneration.

> "For he who sows to his flesh will of the flesh reap corruption, but he who sows to the Spirit will of the Spirit reap everlasting life" (Gal. 6:8).

Put it all together: God created you as one member of the host of earth to operate under His authority to have dominion in His name to govern this planet. Every resurrected saint will inherit some place on this planet; the size is relative to the works you accomplished in this life to advance His kingdom HERE – in the name of Jesus.

> Jesus said: "I go to prepare a place for you" (John 14:3).

For nearly 1,600 years, we've been taught this place is a room *'mone'* within God's house in Heaven, however, the word "place" is *'topos*-5117' from which we get the word: topography. The place Jesus goes to prepare is a topographic piece of land in the New Earth place called:

PARADISE

There are many abodes (*mone* -3438-dwelling places) in the Father's *oikia* house; however, Jesus is going to prepare a *'topos'* (topography) place for us – a garden place in Paradise alongside

His '*oikos*' estate. God formed Adam of His garden (Gen. 2:7), then placed Adam in his own garden alongside His estate (Gen. 2:8) – **and then** God took Adam from his garden and put him in God's Eden to tend God's garden (Gen. 2:15). The principle of Sabbath by working six days **and then** resting one day to maintain intimacy with God to be strengthened in His presence – which Adam did before there was a Law – represents another big picture of what we will be doing in eternity: working, resting, worshipping and maintaining intimacy with the Lord.

> "And He said to them, "The Sabbath was made for man, and not man for the Sabbath" (Mark 2:27).

> "For as the new heavens and the new earth which I will make shall remain before Me," says the LORD, "**So shall your descendants and your name remain**. [23] And it shall come to pass that from one New Moon to another, and from one Sabbath to another, all flesh shall come to worship before Me," says the LORD" (ISA. 66:22, 23).

Jesus had a unique way of confronting religious doctrines by exposing the hypocrisy of work done on the Sabbath, as when a donkey needs water or falls into a ditch… by healing people (Luke 13:10-17; 14:1-5). Jewish Law said it was unlawful to touch a leper for fear of becoming sick, but when Jesus touched a leper, the leper got well. When manmade doctrines contradict what God intended for man on earth, then God will confront them so we may be restored right-side up. Jesus takes our brokenness, infirmity and messed up lives… and always makes us better; He never leaves us the way we are… if we were willing to be changed and transformed.

In His presence – we are changed! By His Spirit – we are transformed!

He redeemed us, and in His presence, He restores us to wholeness in truth and righteousness.

Jesus was a revolutionary within His own kingdom because others turned it into something He never intended... which includes our manmade doctrine of heaven as our eternal destination.

For example: Jesus used redeemed sinners of this world to reveal His greatest truths: Mary was a former prostitute who had seven demons cast out of her, yet she was the first person to see Jesus after He was raised from the dead to show her the Good News; and Jesus told the redeemed thief dying next to Him where we are all destined according to faith: Paradise.

> And Jesus said to him, "Assuredly, I say to you, ~~today~~ [now] you will be with Me in Paradise" (Luke 23:43).

Our heaven doctrines are totally upside down – which I perceive was promulgated by the spirit of religion to keep our eyes off focus and off mission, which is: have dominion – in the name of Jesus! Tricking us to focus on heaven rather than Jesus and diminishing our earthly relevance by seeking heaven rather than having dominion on earth – was intended by Satan for one purpose: to take our eyes off the prize: Earth! The New Earth is going to be our eternal homeland and Promised Land.

> "Blessed is he who shall eat bread in the kingdom of God!" (Luke 14:15).

The enemy knows what and who "the host of earth" are because we get our identity from the One who created us: Jesus. Mankind, however, has struggled to comprehend even a fraction of this despite 6,000 years of training by the Lord in righteousness and truth. Well... times have changed... but our mission hasn't... and it's time now to plunder the strong man's house.

Elohim (God) – *created us as elohims to be representational images of "His Own" image.*

The sad part about this awesome promise is very few people have entered into authentic faith to diligently seek and advance the kingdom of the heavens (small 'h'). Most people are utterly unaware of any of this. Worse even, they oftentimes create the kingdom of hell in their heart wherein they shall reap a whirlwind in the end.

> "Even as I have seen, those who plow iniquity and sow trouble reap the same" (Job 4:8).

The heaven (or hell) you find in eternity – is the reality you're building and establishing in your heart right now. And this is why Jesus gave us eleven examples of "the kingdom of heaven is like" to teach us how the kingdom of heaven operates so we can cultivate heaven in our heart – right now!

Our purpose on earth is not for us to get into heaven – but rather – to get the culture of heaven into us!!!

> "Do not fear, little flock, for it is your Father's good pleasure to give you the kingdom" (Luke 12:32).

The eternal kingdom you prefer – is ultimately the choice you're about to make right now.

Allow me to encourage you with one of the earliest scripture verses the Holy Spirit revealed and highlighted to me in order to guide my life and discover the path God established for me:

> "Sow for yourselves righteousness; reap in mercy; **break up your fallow ground**, for it is time to seek the Lord, till He comes and rains righteousness on you" (Hosea 10:12).

It's time to break up the fallow ground and destroy all the false images and idols we've created in the church and in our heart. All doctrines of man must bend to the gospel of Jesus Christ… or be broken. We need more subsoilers and disciples in the church to break up fallow ground.

Kingdom of Heaven Messages

The exact phrase "kingdom of heaven" occurs 31 times in the scriptures. The main point of studying the kingdom of heaven is: to implement these teachings here and now. These scriptures were not taught by Jesus to help us understand what will happen when we get to heaven (which is a false-heaven doctrine); ***these scriptures are to guide our daily affairs right now***.

Jewish Law and traditions never spoke of entering into heaven after a person died, so where did this idea come from? Excellent question! How did the church get so far off the path of righteousness by teaching "men go to heaven"? This is a mystery that historians may need to uncover… but only under the guidance, direction and anointing of the Holy Spirit – or else this answer may be used erringly. One scripture is likely linked to this wayside path:

> "For when they rise from the dead, they neither marry nor are given in marriage, but are like angels in heaven" (Mark 12:25).

Jesus said, in the resurrection, we will be like angels that are in Heaven, but He did not imply we would be in Heaven. We will be like angels (of Heaven), but we will be as angels – on Earth. This concept should reverberate in our mind until the epiphany happens: we will be like angels!

Why wait – when you can live like an angel now!

Jesus spoke of the resurrection while on earth and then continued to speak on this subject while in Glory to the Apostle John exiled on the island of Patmos. In Revelation, John detailed a holy city, the New Jerusalem, which comes down to earth '*ex*' – "from out of" Heaven. Even our new glorified body comes down to us '*ex*' – "from out of" Heaven (2 Cor. 5:2). Let me say this clearly: both our future body and the Holy City – come to us (*ex*) "from out of" Heaven.

Nonetheless, many "kingdom of heaven" verses are sufficiently able to guide New Earth doctrine both now, through the great tribulation, through the millennium... and beyond.

Here are "the kingdom of heaven is like" parables that Jesus said that describe how His kingdom operates:

1. (Matt. 13:24) "*The kingdom of heaven is like a man* who sowed good seed in his field"
2. (Matt. 13:31) "*The kingdom of heaven is like a mustard seed*, which a man took and sowed in his field"
3. (Matt. 13:33) "*The kingdom of heaven is like leaven*, which a woman took and hid in three measures of meal till it was all leavened."
4. (Matt. 13:44) "*The kingdom of heaven is like treasure hidden in a field*, which a man found and hid; and for joy over it he goes and sells all that he has and buys that field."
5. (Matt. 13:45, 46) "*The kingdom of heaven is like a merchant seeking beautiful pearls*, [46] who, when he had found one pearl of great price, went and sold all that he had and bought it"
6. (Matt. 13:47) "*The kingdom of heaven is like a dragnet* that was cast into the sea and gathered some of every kind"
7. (Matt. 18:23) "*The kingdom of heaven is like a certain king* who wanted to settle accounts with his servants."
8. (Matt. 20:1) "*The kingdom of heaven is like a landowner* who went out early in the morning to hire laborers for his vineyard.
9. (Matt. 22:2) "*The kingdom of heaven is like a certain king* who arranged a marriage for his son"
10. (Matt. 25:14) "*The kingdom of heaven is like a man traveling to a far country*, *who* called his own servants and delivered his goods to them." (Matt. 13:52)
11. (Matt. 13:52) "Therefore every scribe instructed concerning *the kingdom of heaven is like a householder* who brings out of his treasure *things* new and old."

KINGDOMS

12. (Matt. 25:1) *"**Then the kingdom of heaven shall be likened to ten virgins** who took their lamps and went out to meet the bridegroom."*

Is there anything we can glean from the *subject* of these parables? The kingdom of heaven is like: a man, a mustard seed, leaven, treasure in a field, a merchant seeking pearls, a certain king, a landowner, a certain king, a man, and a householder.

- Every *subject* in God's kingdom was created on purpose to produce something of value. Eleven *subjects* are co-identified by the *object* (things) they produce
- Another lesson to glean is: the investment/return principle. In parables 1-10, the *subject* invests something who has a right to expect a return on investment
- Another lesson is: the stewardship principle. Even parable #11 has a stewardship responsibility "like a householder" to manage resources (in this case: treasure)

Subjects in the kingdom will produce specific things according to Manufacturer's specifications.

Process – to – product! We are all under a commission to produce goodness for the kingdom.

We are purpose driven – under the guidance and direction of God's Spirit.

The twelfth parable is unique. Pay particular attention to the terminology change: "the kingdom of heaven is like" (present tense) changes to "the kingdom of heaven shall be like" (future tense). Eleven parables reveal how the kingdom of God operates, but the twelfth parable reveals the wild card within creation: mankind's free will. Ten virgins have a free-will choice: faithfully do what you're supposed to do – and produce the product for which you were commissioned: be a bride ready and prepared for the bridegroom. Only five responsible virgins were prepared.

375

We are stewards for God and co-partners with God to co-manage this planet under His dominion (authority with power) to produce goodness and glory that gives glory to God – and advances the kingdom of light in the shadow of darkness. We are the clean-up crew that God sent to usher in a regime change from darkness to light! We are in the world – but not of it!

- (Matt. 13:11) "He answered and said to them, *"Because it has been given to you to know the mysteries of the kingdom of heaven*, but to them it has not been given"
- (Matt. 16:19) *"And I will give you the keys of the kingdom of heaven*, and whatever you bind on earth will be bound in heaven, and whatever you loose on earth will be loosed in heaven"

We've been given a tremendous spiritual responsibility to understand how the kingdom of God operates and implement His kingdom – here and now. Jesus revealed the mystery of how it operates – and now we've been given keys with dominion authority and power to implement this regime change… in His name. How is it implemented: by the Spirit through faith.

What grace makes available – faith makes possible.

There are eleven major categories with similar themes to convey deep wisdom to guide New Earth doctrine (this is a synopsis from "Here" chapter 8 titled: "The Earthly (Kingdom of) Heaven"). Now, let's understand more about the kingdom of heaven, as Jesus taught us:

1. John the Baptist, the greatest prophet of the old covenant and forerunner for the King of heaven and earth, i.e. Jesus, came preaching and saying, "Repent, for the kingdom of heaven is at hand!" (Matt. 3:2) – indicating Jesus brought this new heavenly reality with Him to the earth
2. Jesus began to teach the multitudes that future residents of the kingdom will be invited to attend based upon the condition of their heart as it relates to the King and their

service to Him regardless of title, position, ordination or covenant belief under which you served
3. Jesus teaches us some requirements for entering the kingdom of heaven are restrictive
4. And Jesus tells His disciples the mysteries of the kingdom are revealed to those who earnestly seek kingdom truth and desire a personal relationship with Jesus
5. As a redeemed child of God, saved by grace and therefore a citizen of heaven, we have an obligation and responsibility as disciples to go into the world preaching the good news
6. And ultimately, Jesus explains through parables what the kingdom of heaven will be like "on earth as it is in heaven" when people hear, understand and comprehend this truth:
    - The quintessential timeless message about the kingdom of heaven that is both "upon the earth and in your heart" is found in the "The Parable of the Sower," for it describes the heavenly reality of living life from four different perspectives: the heart as the field of faith, how we accept or reject truth, how we listen, and how we understand kingdom truth… and we must nurture this truth in our garden to mature and produce an abundant harvest that continues from person to person, from generation to generation and from nation to nation (Mt. 13:1-23)
7. Jesus taught us another aspect regarding the kingdom of heaven that acts like an all-encompassing net to gather all things together so that they can be separated as good things apart from worthless, profane things; and things new (spiritually regenerate) from old things (unlawful, unregenerate)
8. These messages are principles for effective living and lifeway attitudes in the kingdom
9. Jesus goes on to describe Himself and the Father as "a certain" person in varying ways and manners to establish a concrete relationship between the Person and the place as operating inextricably in kingdom oneness

10. No one living upon the earth will be able to understand any of this, or comprehend what will happen next, apart from the new birth by the Spirit
11. Finally, there are three keys for effective Christian living according to Christ's kingdom on earth:
    - "The kingdom of God is within you" (Luke 17:21) – and since you are a representative of God, you are a citizen of heaven and therefore you are a representative of the kingdom of heaven that Jesus established upon the earth ... by grace through faith, but not everyone is living their life with the truth of this reality within their heart – it requires conversion by the Spirit and transformation according to the Spirit to live according to the kingdom of heaven that Christ established
    - "Where two or three are gathered together in My name, I am there in the midst of them" (Matt. 18:20)
    - "But seek first the kingdom of God and His righteousness, and all these things shall be added to you" (Matt. 6:23)

"... for the kingdom of God is not eating and drinking, but righteousness and peace and joy in the Holy Spirit" (Rom. 14:17).

Jesus commissioned every one of us to say and do what He said and did. The spirit within us – enables us by faith – through the Spirit – to imitate Christ's example and accomplish our mission: have dominion!

"And as you go, preach, saying, 'The kingdom of heaven is at hand'" (Matt. 10:7)

As you go, establish the kingdom of heaven on Earth!

Heaven Come Down

The church sings a beautiful song called: "Heaven Come Down." As much as I love this song as an anthem with military undertones to initiate divine revival on earth, it speaks the opposite of our true mission on earth: the kingdom of God is in you – now go – and let heaven out! Once the culture of heaven is within you – it is your mission to begin loosing the atmosphere of heaven onto earth. Waiting for heaven to come down – is faith in a false reality.

Heaven already came down. His name is Jesus!

Study the works of the Prophets and the acts of the Apostles – and you find something truly revelatory: they produced goodness on earth and established the kingdom of heaven wherever they went. The first two works of Elisha are an excellent example for us to imitate: A) he healed the land (he restored to perfect health a spring of water with salt), and B) he spoke against a faithless generation that was hostile to the works of God (2 Kings 2:19-24). If you are not imitating the apostles and prophets who sacrificed their lives to produce goodness in the earth – then what in the heck are you doing here anyway? Are you just treading water until King Jesus takes you home? King Jesus dwells in you. Going home to be with Jesus is the polar opposite of kingdom truth – home is where your heart is! Your eternal *oiketerion* home is already in you. Stop waiting for something miraculous to happen to you. The miraculous has already happened within you – now go with God's grace... and may signs and wonders follow you as you go. Elisha put salt into a demonically polluted well and the waters were healed; go and do likewise!

"You are the salt of the earth" (Matt. 5:13)!!! Jesus said: YOU – are the SALT of the earth! Flavor this earth with greater grace and greater works. Become the revival you've prayed to happen. Let heaven on earth begin with you.

Closure

You existed in His presence as sons and daughters of God, then you were sent to earth as the host of earth to come against a rebellious army that waged war against God in Heaven, and through faith – as you continue to endure and persevere – you will become again in the New Earth what you were to begin with: sons and daughters of God.

In the regeneration when God makes all things new again (not make all new things), saints will be rewarded for their faithful service to Jesus. And one more thing: the word **regeneration** '*palingenesia*-3824' (*palin*-again + genesis) literally means: **genesis again**!

Saints of God... we are all going back to the beginning... back to Paradise: the Garden of Eden.

The church must get back to this basic premise and guide people into "Jesus – only" faith!

> **It's all about Jesus – and God gets the glory!**

[page left blank for notes]

Read the entire Image Bearer series!

Book #1: "REGENESIS – A Sojourn To Remember Who We Are" - is being re-released as a second edition in 2019.
Book #9: "KINGDOMS" will be released in Spring/Summer 2019.
Book #10: "THE RENEWED MIND" will be released in 2019.

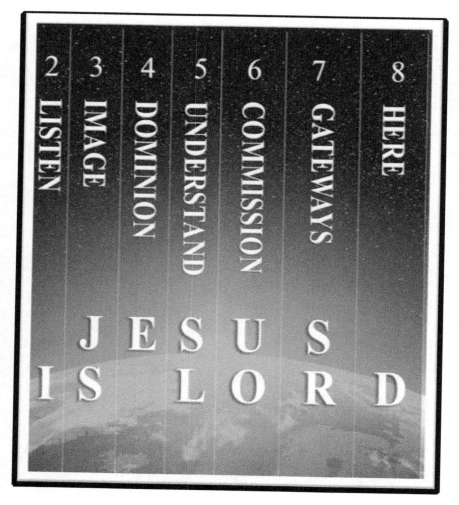

Grace and peace be yours in abundance, paul.